WHY WE NEED A CITIZEN'S BASIC INCOME

The desirability, feasibility and implementation of an unconditional income

Malcolm Torry

D1611074

First published in Great Britain in 2018 by

Policy Press
University of Bristol
1-9 Old Park Hill
Bristol
BS2 8BB
UK
t: +44 (0)117 954 5940
pp-info@bristol.ac.uk
www.policypress.co.uk

North America office:
Policy Press
c/o The University of Chicago Press
1427 East 60th Street
Chicago, IL 60637, USA
t: +1 773 702 7700
f: +1 773-702-9756
sales@press.uchicago.edu
www.press.uchicago.edu

British Library Cataloguing in Publication Data
A catalogue record for this book is available from the British Library

Library of Congress Cataloging-in-Publication Data
A catalog record for this book has been requested

ISBN 978-1-4473-4317-2 paperback
ISBN 978-1-4473-4315-8 hardcover
ISBN 978-1-4473-4318-9 ePub
ISBN 978-1-4473-4319-6 Mobi
ISBN 978-1-4473-4316-5 ePdf

Cover design by Andrew Corbett
Front cover image: www.alamy.com
Printed and bound in Great Britain by CPI Group (UK) Ltd, Croydon, CR0 4YY
Policy Press uses environmentally responsible print partners

This book is dedicated to past and present trustees of the Citizen's Basic Income Trust, and to everyone who gives time and energy to the debate on the desirability, feasibility and implementation of a Citizen's Basic Income

Contents

List of figures and tables

Figures

Tables

The structure of the book

Following some notes on terminology, Chapter 1 sets the scene by asking the reader to imagine some representative people trying to cope with our tax and benefits system, and then to imagine themselves creating a tax and benefits system in a country without one. Chapter 2 offers a historical sketch, and outlines the current state of the Citizen's Basic Income debate; Chapter 3 discusses the changing employment market, and finds a Citizen's Basic Income to be appropriate to any future scenario; and Chapter 4 undertakes the same task for changing family patterns. Further advantages of a Citizen's Basic Income are then discussed: administrative efficiency in Chapter 5, and poverty and inequality reduction in Chapter 6. Chapter 7 tackles the question of feasibility; Chapter 8 discusses implementation options; and Chapter 9 describes a number of pilot projects and other experiments. Chapter 10 responds to objections to Citizen's Basic Income; Chapter 11 discusses alternatives to a Citizen's Basic Income; and Chapter 12 offers a brief list of arguments for the advantages of a Citizen's Basic Income. An appendix contains recent microsimulation research results for an illustrative Citizen's Basic Income scheme and its gradual roll-out.

Terminology

'Unconditional' and 'universal'[1]

There are two kinds of conditionality: conditionality that we can affect and that requires enquiry if a benefits system is to know whether we fulfil the condition; and conditionality that we cannot affect and that requires no enquiry. Income and employment status would be examples of the first kind, and age an example of the second. By 'unconditional benefits' we mean social security benefits not subject to any conditions of the first type. Unconditional benefits can vary with someone's age because we cannot affect our age, and once the system knows our date of birth it never again needs to enquire about our age. When the word 'unconditional' is encountered in the literature, great care needs to be taken to ensure that it means genuine unconditionality: that is, that there are no conditionalities of the first type. This is not always the case.[2]

'Universal' means 'for everyone', and usually implies 'everyone within a particular jurisdiction': but in the social policy literature a variety of usages can be found, often within a few pages of each other.[3] Unconditional benefits, such as the UK's Child Benefit, are sometimes called 'universal benefits' because they are universal in relation to children. 'Universal benefit' can sometimes mean 'unconditional benefit', but care must be taken because it might not. The previous Labour government's Child Trust Fund was for all children, and so was universal, but it was means tested and therefore was not unconditional. So 'unconditional' implies 'universal', but 'universal' does not necessarily imply 'unconditional'.[4] The only benefit that would be both unconditional and properly universal would be a Citizen's Basic Income. However, for the purposes of this book, and in accordance with common usage, 'universal' will imply unconditionality: so Child Benefit will sometimes be termed a universal benefit.

'Citizen's Basic Income'[5]

A 'Citizen's Basic Income' – also known as a 'Basic Income', a 'Citizen's Income', or a 'Universal Basic Income' – is an unconditional and nonwithdrawable income paid to each individual by virtue of their citizenship or legal residence.[6] 'Nonwithdrawable' is often included in the definition to emphasise the fact that the Citizen's Basic Income would not be withdrawn as other income rose: but strictly speaking 'nonwithdrawable' is redundant because 'unconditional' implies that. As we shall recognise in Chapter 9, there is a difference between a varying annual payment and an unvarying weekly or monthly income. This book will understand a Citizen's Basic Income to be an income, of the same amount every week or every month, paid unconditionally to every legal resident of a country.

'Basic Income', like 'Basisinkommen', 'Grundeinkommen' and 'revenue de base', implies a foundational income: but the somewhat derogatory undertones of 'basic' in the English language ('basic' can imply that something is not very good) led to 'Citizen's Income' becoming common currency during the 1990s. More recently, the two have been combined into 'Citizen's Basic Income'.[7]

Some authors incorporate the word 'guarantee' into the name, as in 'Basic Income Guarantee'. I avoid 'guarantee' language because it can imply means testing.[8] For instance, the previous Labour government established a 'Minimum Income Guarantee', a means-tested payment to bring pensioners' household incomes up to a prescribed level.

Clarity about the definition of 'Citizen's Basic Income', 'Basic Income', 'Citizen's Income' and 'Universal Basic Income' is essential. Where clarity is lacking,[9] different contributors to discussion on the future of social security can mean different things, so rational debate cannot occur.

A Citizen's Basic Income is an unconditional, nonwithdrawable and unvarying weekly or monthly income paid to each individual by virtue of their citizenship or legal residence.

'Allowance'

'Child allowance', 'family allowance', or simply 'allowance', refer to payments made (in the case of child allowances, on behalf of the child to the main carer). 'Income Tax allowance' or 'tax allowance' refers to an amount of earned income on which tax is not levied, tax only being levied on income above the 'tax threshold'.

Tax Credits (real ones) and Negative Income Tax

A Tax Credit is an amount of money ascribed to an individual, usually weekly. It is paid in full if an individual has no other income, and it is withdrawn at a specified rate as earned income rises. As earned income continues to rise, the Tax Credit ceases to be paid and the worker starts to pay Income Tax. If the individual is employed then the employer manages the Tax Credit.

The 'Tax Credits' implemented by the UK's last Labour government are not Tax Credits: they are a means-tested benefit.[10] Until 2005, Working Tax Credits were paid through the employer-administered PAYE (Pay As You Earn) Income Tax system but were calculated separately from Income Tax. It could not have been otherwise because Income Tax is calculated on an individual basis whereas for 'Tax Credits' the household is the claimant unit. Since 2005, all 'Tax Credits' have been paid into people's bank accounts. They are not in any way integrated with the payment of wages or Income Tax, and are withdrawn if a spouse's earned income rises. Genuine Tax Credits are not withdrawn in this way. In order to distinguish between the two different uses of the same term I put quotation marks around 'Tax Credit' when the term is used with the meaning of 'means-tested benefit', and not when the term means a Tax Credit.

A Negative Income Tax (NIT) is the same as Tax Credits (genuine ones), but instead of specifying the amount of money that is paid out in the absence of earnings, it specifies the earnings threshold below which payment is made and above which income tax is paid, and the rates at which tax is paid above the threshold and payment is made to the employee below the threshold.

'Marginal deduction rate'

An important term employed throughout the book is 'marginal deduction rate' (also called 'marginal tax rate', 'marginal effective tax rate' or 'marginal withdrawal rate'; and sometimes the marginal deduction rates experienced by individuals initially in employment and those not are distinguished from each other, with the former termed 'marginal effective tax rate' and the latter 'participation tax rate'). If someone earns an extra £1 then usually they are not better off by £1. First of all, Income Tax and National Insurance Contributions will be deducted. If the household is on Housing Benefit then that will be reduced if earnings rise, and if they are on 'Tax Credits' then those will be reduced. Let us suppose that after all of these deductions the worker finds themselves 30p better off. This means that 70p has been deducted: a marginal deduction rate of 70%.

It is a 'marginal' deduction rate because it relates to *additional* earnings. The marginal deduction rate is important because it affects incentives to earn additional income. If the marginal deduction rate is low – that is, if not much of one's additional earnings is lost through the tax and benefits systems – then it is more worthwhile to earn additional income than if the marginal deduction rate is high.

Contributory benefits

Contributory benefits are paid to individuals on the basis of records of contributions deducted by employers and paid to HM Revenue and Customs (HMRC) along with Income Tax payments, or paid directly to HMRC by the self-employed. While the contributions record determines the amounts of benefits paid, there is no direct link between the amount of benefit paid and the contributions made.

Means-tested benefits

A means-tested benefit is one calculated on the basis of means available, that is, as other income rises, the amount of the benefit payment falls. Means-tested benefits are often 'tested' in other ways too. They might only be paid if someone is employed or is available for employment and looking for it. They might also be subject to relationship tests. If two people on means-tested benefits who are both living alone decide to live in the same household, then, because the government assumes that it is cheaper for them to live together than for them to live apart, the benefits they receive will be less in total than they were receiving before they moved in together.

'Universal Credit'

In-work and out-of-work means-tested benefits (for instance, Jobseeker's Allowance, Income Support and 'Tax Credits') are being combined into 'Universal Credit'. Unfortunately, 'Universal Credit' will not be universal. It will be withdrawn as earned income rises: so for every set of household circumstances there will be an earnings level above which Universal Credit will not be received. I shall therefore treat the term in the same way as I treat the term 'Tax Credit'. Where 'Universal Credit' means the government's new means-tested benefit, I shall add quotation marks. A Universal Credit without quotation marks would, of course, be a Citizen's Basic Income, but we already have a perfectly good name for that.

Capitalisation

This book will follow the convention that the names of particular taxes or benefits will be capitalised, but names for types of benefits or taxes will not be. So 'income tax' denotes any tax on income, whereas 'Income Tax' means the income tax charged on income in the UK along with its regulations, rates and thresholds. By analogy, 'Welfare State' is the UK's welfare state, and 'welfare state' would refer to any Welfare State. 'Basic Income', 'Citizen's Income', 'Citizen's Basic Income', 'Universal Basic Income', 'Negative Income Tax', 'Participation Income' and other particular proposals will also be capitalised.

Notes

[1] Torry, 2017a.
[2] For instance, in Honorati, Gentilini and Yemtsov, 2015: 28, it becomes clear that the World Bank does not mean 'nonwithdrawable' when it uses the word 'unconditional', which means that it can include means-tested benefits in its 'Unconditional Cash Transfers' category. This is unfortunate.
[3] For instance, Béland and Petersen, 2014: 222–63.
[4] Kuitto, 2016: 176.
[5] Torry, 2017b.
[6] See Chapter 10 on who should receive a Citizen's Basic Income.
[7] As in the Scottish organisation 'Citizen's Basic Income Network Scotland', and, at the request of its publisher, in Torry, 2016b.
[8] Meade, 1978: 269–79.
[9] For instance, in Murray and Pateman, 2012: 2, 252; Bregman, 2017.
[10] Godwin and Lawson, 2009: 12.

About the author

Dr Malcolm Torry is the Director of the Citizen's Basic Income Trust and a Visiting Senior Fellow at the London School of Economics.

Acknowledgements

During my university holidays my Uncle Norman arranged for me to work in Bexleyheath's Department of Health and Social Security (DHSS) office, filing the cards on which employers stuck stamps to the value of their employers' and employees' National Insurance Contributions; and after university I worked on the public counter in Brixton's Supplementary Benefit office for two years. I am grateful to the DHSS and its staff for educating me in the UK's benefits system.

Sir Geoffrey Otton, the DHSS's Permanent Secretary, invited me to a departmental summer school when I was a curate at the Elephant and Castle, where the department's headquarters were located. At the summer school I met Hermione (Mimi) Parker, who invited me to join the group that became the Basic Income Research Group and which later became the Citizen's Income Trust and now the Citizen's Basic Income Trust. It has been a pleasure to have served the Trust as its honorary Director for most of its existence, and I am grateful to its trustees for making that possible and to successive Bishops of Woolwich for permission to do it.

I am grateful to Professor David Piachaud for supervising my London School of Economics (LSE) Master's Degree dissertation on a Citizen's Basic Income's likely effects on the employment market and family structure; to the LSE's Social Policy Department for appointing me a Visiting Senior Fellow; to Professor Hartley Dean for supervising my recent work at the LSE; to Professor Holly Sutherland and her colleagues at the Institute for Social and Economic Research for introducing me to the microsimulation programmes POLIMOD and then EUROMOD, and for publishing my work in EUROMOD working papers; to Alari Paulus, of the Institute for Social and Economic Research, for significant assistance with the working paper[1] on which the appendix of this book is based; to participants of the various conferences at which some of the ideas in this book have been tested; and to the trustees of the Citizen's Basic Income Trust for permission to quote from material previously published by the Trust.

In relation to this book I am grateful to all of those who contributed time and energy to the first edition, and particularly to Dr Alex Cobham and Professors Hartley Dean, Jay Ginn and Bill Jordan. In relation to this edition, I am most grateful for the diligence with which Mark Wadsworth has read and commented on a draft of the text. In relation to the first edition, and to this second edition, any remaining mistakes and infelicities are of course entirely my responsibility. I am most grateful to Emily Watt, Laura Vickers, and their colleagues at Policy Press for their help and encouragement, and to Policy Press's referees, whose suggestions I have found most helpful.

All royalties from this book will be donated to the Citizen's Basic Income Trust.

Note

1   Torry, 2017c.

Foreword

Guy Standing

When Malcolm Torry published *Money for Everyone* in 2013, I welcomed it with enthusiasm. I welcome *Why we need a Citizen's Basic Income* with even greater enthusiasm.

Whether this book is a second edition of *Money for Everyone* or a new book is a significant question: significant, because the fact that so much of the book has had to be newly written shows just how far the Basic Income debate has moved on in just five years. *Money for Everyone* was mainly arguments for the desirability of Basic Income, with the occasional mention of feasibility and implementation. Now public and policymaker debate is far more about both the feasibility of Basic Income and options for its implementation, so it has been essential to include substantial chapters on those subjects, and also a fully evaluated illustrative Basic Income scheme – lacking in *Money for Everyone*. The new book also contains a chapter on objections to Basic Income: an essential addition that I also included in my own book on the subject seen from an international perspective.

But however different parts of it might be, this is still in many ways the original book. It is written by someone with a sense of compassion, by a 'man of the cloth', as British people used to say with a sense of respect. One does not need to be a Christian or to belong to any religion to recognise the value and appeal of real compassion. And we should remember the difference between compassion and pity, just as we should that between rights and charity. Compassion derives from treating people as equals; pity derives from treating people as inferior, as fallen. Social policy should be about strengthening compassion and rights, leaving pity and charity to individual consciences.

Compassion emphasises our commonality, our human similarity, recognition that while today we may need help and may be in a position to help others, tomorrow it might be the other way round. Pity, by contrast, as David Hume taught us, is akin to contempt. At best it is paternalistic and patronising. Worse, it easily leads lazy minds to think they are superior and are being magnanimous in giving a little to help the 'deserving poor'. That is not a worthy sentiment, because it does not exercise our will to do something to change the situation that produces wretchedness among affluence. It is compassion that reinforces our sense of social solidarity, so that we see ourselves in each other.

This book is about an idea that has a long heritage. Some of the greatest minds through history have supported it. Today, there are reasons to believe that its time is coming. Across the world, suddenly we find numerous thoughtful people responding to the call for a Basic Income with a 'Why not?' retort, when only a few years ago we heard 'What utopian folly!'

The international network we established in 1986, named BIEN (Basic Income Earth Network), has drawn thousands of members from across the world, so that there are now national networks in countries as different as Germany, Italy, Japan, South Korea, Brazil, Argentina, the US and the Netherlands. The UK has its network member in the Citizens' Basic Income Trust, which has been ably led by Malcolm Torry. I urge readers to join BIEN and the Citizen's Basic Income Trust. The BIEN Congress is held every year, when dozens of papers are presented and discussed avidly, as they were in the Lisbon Congress in September 2017. The 2018 Congress will be held in Tampere, Finland, and the 2019 Congress will be held in New Delhi.

The growing interest in an unconditional Basic Income as a right for all stems from many ethical and social rationales. It is also a pragmatic reaction to the reality that during three decades of economic growth inequalities have grown remorselessly, while millions of people in the UK have wallowed in impoverishment. Governments have tinkered, but have found all sorts of excuses for leaving inequality to grow to historically unprecedented levels. We have had a steady drift to political utilitarianism that does nobody any credit. Make the 'middle class' happy. That is where the votes are! Give the deserving poor conditional benefits, in pity. Give all those undeserving 'scroungers' some harsh medicine, to be kind to them in the longer term. How smug and prejudiced.

Those who claim there are numerous 'scroungers' across the country – some alien breed who are 'not like You and Me' – and that swathes of people are 'dependent' should be confronted by a simple question: how do you know? And are we not all dependent on others, just as some are dependent on us? Anecdotal evidence of a few people makes for prejudicial and moralistic policy, which is invariably bad policy.

Recently, a much-cited opinion poll found that a majority of British people agreed with the proposition that benefits should be cut. This has been the claim made by newspapers and mainstream politicians, none of them relying on benefits for subsistence. Now, suppose those polled had been asked first, 'What is the weekly amount an unemployed person receives? What is the average amount someone with disability receives?' How many of them would have known the correct answers, or the conditions in which the vast majority seeking benefits have to live? And yet those who responded to the poll had been persuaded that the level should be cut. It is a mentality that stems from decades of moving away from solidaristic systems based on principles of compassion to one based on targeting, probing and stigmatising, through means tests and behaviour tests.

There is something else happening that may turn the tide in favour of a Basic Income. Today, millions of people, in Britain and globally, are entering the precariat, which I have depicted in my books as the new dangerous class because they see their need for basic security wilfully ignored by the mainstream political parties described as 'centre right' and 'centre left'. Most of those in the precariat are just trying to create a meaningful life for themselves. And yet so far they have been factored out of political calculations. It would be dishonest of politicians to pretend that a combination of means tests and behaviour tests could overcome the poverty traps – whereby the precariat often pay a marginal tax rate of over 80 per cent, twice what the 'middle class' is expected to pay – let alone what I have called the precarity traps, which make it the fact that many end up paying more than 100 per cent 'tax' on income gained in some precarious short-term job.

Those in the precariat know that, and are beginning to growl about the inequity and inequality in which they have to live. Their anger is justifiable, and it will not go away. The anger and hurt will grow much worse if Universal Credit is rolled out across the country. It is a mean-spirited policy coloured by arbitrary sanctions and stigmatisation.

Malcolm Torry is a voice of reasonableness. He can see that providing every one of us – sinners as well as saints – with a Basic Income is affordable and would actually help make people more productive, not lazier, and make more people more likely to be responsible citizens, with a greater sense of altruism and tolerance.

Like most of us who support moving towards a Basic Income – and it is the direction that counts – he is realistic enough to know that it will only come about when those who believe in it have the courage and energy to struggle for its realisation.

Malcolm Torry's is one of our best voices: rational and persuasive, and persuasive because rational. His book makes an important contribution to a debate that is becoming livelier by the day.

Preface

A Citizen's Basic Income is an unconditional and nonwithdrawable income paid to every individual: that is, the same amount of money, every week or every month, for each person (with higher amounts paid to older people, and smaller amounts for children). It is a remarkably simple idea, with the potential to make our economy and our employment market more efficient, make work pay, encourage training and enterprise, make our society more cohesive, reduce poverty and inequality, and set people free from bureaucratic intrusion.

Discussion of the desirability, feasibility and implementation of Citizen's Basic Income will often be context specific because it is in relation to a particular tax and benefits system that many of the arguments will have to be formulated. The context envisaged in this book is the UK's tax and benefits system, and readers in other countries will need to ask how those arguments might need to be adapted for their own situations.

This book is a second edition of *Money for Everyone*, published in 2013. The reasons for publishing *Money for Everyone* were that it was then more than 10 years since the previous general treatment in English of arguments for a Citizen's Basic Income;[1] following the urban unrest of August 2011 there was considerable concern about growing inequality, and, although the suggestion was often made that a Citizen's Basic Income might be able to help, little detailed exploration of the idea had been offered;[2] whatever solutions to the problems facing our benefits system were tried, the problems only seemed to get worse; and a Citizen's Basic Income was being actively debated and occasionally piloted in other parts of the world.[3] *Money for Everyone* filled a gap, and might have been one of the reasons for the increasing level of debate on Citizen's Basic Income in the UK from 2013 onwards.[4]

We had expected *Money for Everyone* to serve as a general introduction to the topic for a number of years, and we placed details of illustrative Citizen's Basic Income schemes on the Citizen's Income Trust's website because we believed that the figures would go out of date more quickly than the book. In fact, the Citizen's Basic Income debate has evolved so quickly during the past five years that it is now the book that is seriously out of date: hence this new edition – or rather, this new book. So much of *Money for Everyone* has had to be rewritten and reorganized that the publisher has decided that a new title and a new cover would be appropriate.

There is now a vast literature on Citizen's Basic Income. When I wrote *Money for Everyone* I could legitimately claim to have kept up to date with all of the relevant literature in English, and with some of it in other languages. I can no longer make that claim, and neither can anyone else. There are now several introductory books and reports on the market, each from its own point of view, along with a plethora of books, reports and articles tackling aspects of the debate.[5] *Money for Everyone* aimed to provide a carefully evidenced general introduction to Citizen's Basic Income, and its approach might best be described as 'social administration'. In this it remains distinctive. During the past five years political and public interest in Citizen's Basic Income has increased considerably, and important symptoms of the seriousness with which the issue is now taken are the abuse and purposeful selection of evidence.[6] It is therefore even more important that an up-to-date and thoroughly evidenced introduction to the desirability, feasibility and implementation of Citizen's Basic Income should be available. This new edition intends to provide that.

A reader who has read *Money for Everyone* will notice some significant differences between the two editions. *Money for Everyone* was largely about why it would be a good idea to implement a Citizen's Basic Income. *Why We Need a Citizen's Basic Income* is still about that, as the title suggests: but there is now more emphasis on feasibility and implementation, as those are the issues in which the public debate is increasingly interested. The increasing attention being paid to Citizen's Basic Income has of course generated vigorous objections to the proposal, so this new edition pays careful attention to several of those. So that new material could be included, the reader will find less attention being paid to the history of the benefits system, and to such broad issues as citizenship and social justice: in the case of citizenship, because readers can refer to *Money for Everyone* for such a discussion; and, in relation to social justice, because there are already excellent recent treatments of social justice arguments for Citizen's Basic Income.[7]

One thing that has not changed since *Money for Everyone* was published in 2013 is the fact of social and economic change. The world continues to change, and to suppose that our benefits system can simply go on as before, with the occasional tinkering at the edges, will be to consign our society, our economy and our employment market to entirely unnecessary rigidities. We can do better than that. There was a time when the UK's Welfare State led the world, as did much else about this country. We are still capable of innovation. Now is the time to show how to create a tax and benefits system fit for this still new millennium. If the UK does not do it then someone else will, and the UK will again be playing catch-up.

In 2013, Citizen's Basic Income was a minority interest, whereas now it is not. I hope that this new book will be as useful a resource for those involved in the current debate as *Money for Everyone* was for those involved in it five years ago.

Notes

1   Parker, 1989; Walter, 1989; Fitzpatrick, 1999.
2   Wilkinson and Pickett, 2009; Dorling, 2010.
3   Werner and Goehler, 2010. See Chapter 10 of this book for material on pilot projects.
4   This suggestion was made by Professor David Piachaud at a seminar at the London School of Economics on 9 November 2016.
5   Painter and Thoung, 2015; Torry, 2015b; Reed and Lansley, 2016; Standing, 2017; Van Parijs and Vanderborght, 2017; Walker, 2016; Miller, forthcoming; Martinelli, 2017a, 2017b. Examples of literature on the debate in particular countries are Mays, Marston and Tomlinson, 2016; Vanderborght and Yamamori, 2014; Walker, 2016.
6   http://citizensincome.org/news/members-of-parliament-debate-citizens-income/; http://citizensincome.org/news/new-royal-society-of-arts-podcast-and-a-report-from-the-work-and-pensions-committee/, 02/11/2017.
7   Van Parijs and Vanderborght, 2017; Standing, 2017: 25–45; Widerquist, Noguera, Vanderborght and De Wispelaere, 2013: 39–77.

ONE

Imagine ...

Imagine this ...

Wages have continued to stagnate, so people are either spending and getting into debt, or they are not spending. But inflation is still low, so the government decides to print some extra money and to give equal amounts to every citizen. Some of it gets spent on goods and services, creating employment; and some of it is saved and contributes to investment. As the economy picks up, inflation starts to rise, so the government decides that it can no longer print money: but we have got used to receiving an unconditional income, so the government reduces the Income Tax Personal Allowance and continues to pay equal amounts of money to everyone. Disposable incomes are now back where they were before the government printed extra money, but things are now different. People who had been on means-tested Jobseeker's Allowance are now on lower amounts of it, so lots of them decide that they have had enough of bureaucratic interference in their lives and they come off benefits and look for paid work. Often a part-time job, or part-time work and a bit of self-employment, will be enough to top up their Citizen's Basic Income. Starting a business looks more attractive than it once did: after all, nobody is going to take away their Citizen's Basic Incomes, so they will always have that to rely on. And someone on 'Tax Credits' or 'Universal Credit' now receives a Citizen's Basic Income, which is not taken away as their earnings rise, so they look for a better job, or they do a training course so that they can look for a better job, and their partner also looks for paid work or starts a small business – it was not worth their doing that before because so much of the household's 'Tax Credits' or 'Universal Credit' would have been taken away if they had.

Families now feel more secure, they are in control, they can make choices that they could not make before, and for many families there are no forms to fill in, no more interviews, no more questions about who is living with whom, no more signing on, and no more investigations into how much they are earning. That does not mean that nobody is looking for a job. Everyone is looking for a job, because it is now so much more worthwhile to work for a living: and if people cannot find jobs then they create their own.

It still feels a bit odd that stupendously wealthy bankers receive the Citizen's Basic Income too: but they are paying far more in Income Tax than they receive in Citizen's Basic Income, so it really doesn't matter that they receive the unconditional income. It is the simplicity of the Citizen's Basic Income that matters. If it were withdrawn from the wealthy then everyone would be back to form filling and intrusion. Now we really are all in it together, and we know that we are in it together because we all receive a Citizen's Basic Income.

Then a Chancellor of the Exchequer suggests means-testing the Citizen's Basic Income.[1] What she had not realised was that even if the general public is not always keen on unconditional benefits before they happen, once they are established we value them. The Citizen's Basic Income's unconditionality and universality had become as important as those of the National Health Service (NHS). The Chancellor's political advisers tell her that if the party is to be re-elected then she had better quietly drop the idea of means-testing the Citizen's Basic Income; and economists tell her that as so many countries have now followed the British example, Britain's financial position would suffer if marginal deduction rates were to rise and people became less likely to seek employment, to seek training, or to start their own businesses. She raises Income Tax rates, and leaves the Citizen's Basic Income alone. At the General Election she declares that 'the Citizen's Basic Income is safe with us', and the other parties have to say the same.

Now back to the present.

Imagine these people ...

Imagine a woman. Her child is born, she registers the birth, and she completes the simple Child Benefit claim form.[2] If the child continues to live with her then she will continue to receive Child Benefit until the child is 16 years old, or for longer if the child remains in full-time education or training. She will need to notify any change of address, and she will receive additional Child Benefit for each additional child. If she earns nothing, she will receive Child Benefit. If she takes a part-time job, or a full-time job, then her Child Benefit will not change. If one week she earns nothing, the next week £500, and the week after that £50, then her Child Benefit will not change.

The woman we have imagined was in paid employment before her child was born, but the shop she worked in has closed. She claims 'Universal Credit'.[3] The questions about her partner and his pay are a bit complicated because he is a builder and sometimes he lives with her and sometimes he does not, and sometimes he earns a good wage and sometimes he earns little or nothing. She does not know whether they are together or whether they are separated. She phones up the department, and she asks her friends, and everyone is very helpful. She fills in the form and the payments begin. Her friend finds her a part-time job in another shop. It is mornings only, which is just right, as her mother can look after the child. She tells the department about the earnings. The money stops. There is some problem about the shop not reporting her earnings. The money stays stopped, and she gets into rent arrears; and then the money starts again, at a lower rate. She is offered lunchtime work in the café next to the shop. After a couple of weeks she tells the department. Nothing happens for a while, and then her money stops again. There's a problem because she has two employers. After a couple of months the café no longer needs her: but she is still working mornings at the shop, and her 'Universal Credit' payments have resumed. She's asked if she might be able to work Wednesday afternoons as well. She says no.

Imagine a man with a young family. His wife has a part-time job. The firm he works for closes down, and because he isn't in a 'Universal Credit' area he claims Jobseeker's Allowance.[4] It takes about an hour at his computer to fill in the form, but he gets there in the end, though his wife's missing payslips make a bit of guesswork necessary as she earns different amounts each week. He cannot find a full-time job, but his friend's boss offers him labouring work on Saturdays. He accepts. He goes to the Jobcentre and they make a note. His money stops. He phones them up. They say they will look into it. His money starts again, but at a lower rate. The Saturday work becomes more intermittent. He tells them that the Saturday work has stopped. After four weeks his money goes back up again. The next time he is offered weekend work, he tells them nothing.

He gets a job. He earns lower wages than he is used to, and he claims 'Tax Credits', Housing Benefit and Council Tax Reduction. But the family does not seem to be much better off. It is still a struggle to pay the bills. He is offered overtime, and he takes it, as he will be able to pay for a holiday and buy bikes for the children. A year later, he gets a letter telling him to pay back £500 of 'Tax Credits', but he no longer has the money. The next week he is made redundant, and he claims Jobseeker's Allowance. Next time he is offered an interview he goes, because he has to, but he is not trying to get the job. He gets depressed, he hits his wife, and she tells him to leave. She claims 'Tax Credits', and then Housing Benefit and Council Tax Reduction. Her employer, knowing that she could do with the money, asks her if she wants to increase her hours. She declines.

Following the publication of the first edition of this book a suggestion was made that I might have included a case study on someone sick and on Employment and Support Allowance. I would have done so in this edition if Ken Loach had not made his film *I, Daniel Blake*: but he has, and, if you haven't seen it, you should.

The stories that I have told are based on people I have known. They might fit people you have known, and one of the stories might fit you. None of them are lazy people. They all want to support themselves and their families and to contribute to society. But the only income that they can rely on is Child Benefit. For neither of these households did Child Benefit ever stop coming, and the amount that they received for their children only ever altered if they had a new child or a child reached 16 or reached the end of their education or training. Everything other than Child Benefit is at risk, and people want to avoid risk, because risk can mean deeper poverty: so they choose not to seek employment, or they refuse employment, and when they do that they are doing it for the best of reasons. If someone is receiving 'Tax Credits', then for every additional £1 of earnings above the Income Tax Personal Allowance, disposable income rises by just 27p;[5] and if they are receiving 'Universal Credit' then any £1 increase beyond a small work allowance translates into additional disposable income of just 25p.[6] They are suffering marginal deduction rates of 73% and 75% respectively, which hardly seems fair when anyone earning £50,000 p.a. experiences a marginal deduction rate of 42%. As well as so little additional income turning into additional disposable income, to increase the number of hours worked, to add casual earnings or another employment, or for one's partner to change how much they earn, can mean gaps in benefits payments, or overpayments that need to be paid back. If a new job only lasts a few weeks, then again there might be gaps in income, and administrative problems to cope with. Disincentive in the employment market is not just about the marginal deduction rate: it's about a broad combination of consequences of any change in someone's relationship with the employment market.

None of what I have said is a criticism of the people who work for HMRC, the Department for Work and Pensions, or local authorities. They are as frustrated as claimants are that the current system is such a mess. I used to work for the Department of Health and Social Security, the Department for Work and Pensions' forerunner, and my experience of the benefits system that we administered in Brixton's Supplementary Benefits office led me to the conclusion that the best way to tackle poverty is an income that everyone would receive all the time, always the same amount, and entirely without conditions. Like Child Benefit, it would never change, however much we earned, whoever we were living with, and however many hours we worked: and it would be as simple to administer as Child Benefit, which means administrative costs per claim of about one tenth the cost for means-tested benefits.[7]

But would it not be a problem that the rich would get it too? No, it would not. It would be no more of a problem than that the rich are treated on the NHS, or that they receive Child Benefit – for, after all, the rich pay more in tax than they cost the NHS, and far more in tax than they receive in Child Benefit. It is far more efficient for the NHS to treat everyone for free, and then to tax the rich, than it is to ask people to pay for their healthcare if they can afford it. Why create all of that administrative hassle when it is entirely unnecessary?[28] And why take people's benefits away from them when their earnings rise if it is more efficient to give everyone the same Citizen's Basic Income and then tax people in relation to their income? Nobody need be worse off or better off. The important change would be that everyone would be able to rely on their Citizen's Basic Incomes, just as families with children can now rely on Child Benefit. That sense of security, and the knowledge that we could take whatever decisions seemed sensible and that our Citizen's Basic Income would never change, would make a massive difference to every individual, every family and every household in the country. We would be able to change our hours of work from week to week, and our Citizen's Basic Income would not change. We would be able to earn more one week, less another, and our Citizen's Basic Income would not change. We would be able to accept a weekend of labouring, and our Citizen's Basic Income would not change. A child's father could move in, and neither the mother's nor the father's Citizen's Basic Incomes would change. The rent might go up, or the family might move into cheaper accommodation, and their Citizen's Basic Incomes would not change. And overpayments and underpayments would be impossible, so there would never be money that needed to be paid back.

As we shall discover later in this book, in the first instance it might be necessary to retain the means-tested benefits structure in order to ensure that no household would be worse off at the point of implementation of a Citizen's Basic Income scheme: but even if that did have to happen, a lot of households would find that their Citizen's Basic Incomes took them off means-tested benefits; and many others would be so close to coming off them that a few hours a week of additional employment would soon take them off.

Imagine the difference that a Citizen's Basic Income would make to the households that we have imagined in this chapter. These households are not untypical. We lead complex lives. Things change. In the future, things will change even faster than they do now. Our households, relationships, wages, hours of employment, kinds of employment – they will all change, and sometimes every week something will change. Our Citizen's Basic Income would be the one thing that would never change and would give us the security that we need if we are to plan for changes in our lives and to welcome them.

Imagine a country ...

Imagine that you live in a country in which everyone belongs to a household earning enough money to provide a good standard of living; and let us assume that in every household everything is shared so that everyone has everything that they need. This imagined country does not need a benefits system. It will need taxes to provide for other things, but not to provide an income for anyone.

But now suppose that in this country there are people who do *not* have enough to live on: elderly people without children to support them; households in which no one receives a wage because their members are too disabled or ill, or because the companies that they worked for have closed down; and households in which earned incomes are too low to provide a decent standard of living. The country's government might decide to give money to those who need it, which would mean setting up a tax and benefits system to collect in and pay out money. But how should the money be collected and how should it be paid out?

We would need a tax system, but we shall come to that later. What interests us now is how we should *distribute* the money. There are choices to be made: do we give money to everyone, or only to particular groups of people? And should we give everyone the same, or should we give them different amounts?

If we choose to give everyone the same, then we have only one further decision to make: how much? But if we decide to give different amounts to different people, or to give money to some and not to others, then we have rather more decisions to take: we shall have to decide how much different kinds of households need to live on, how fast the income allocated should fall as earnings rise, who is living with whom, and how much people earn.

It is all beginning to look rather complicated. So now let us ask another question: how are we going to collect the money that we are going to give out? What is the fairest way to do that? Presumably by doing what we do now: we shall ask those who have more to pay more.

The decision we were trying to make about how to organise an ideal benefits system is now starting to look a bit different.

If we give everyone the same to start with – a Citizen's Basic Income – and we then take more from the rich than we take from the poor, then we shall be taking from the rich more than they receive in Citizen's Basic Income: so it won't matter that they are receiving money that they do not strictly need. But if we give more to those who earn less, and less to those who earn more, then we shall be doing the same job twice: first working out who can afford to pay more tax, and then working out who should receive less benefit – and they will often be the same people. So let us not do that.

In our imagined country with no benefits system, the decision is an easy one: we should give to every individual a Citizen's Basic Income – unconditional, nonwithdrawable, and paid to individuals – and we should take more tax from those who earn more, and less tax from those who earn less. Easy.

Creating the ideal benefits system

If we were inventing a benefits system for a country that did not have one, then we would give to everyone the same amount of money, and we would take more tax from those with higher incomes and less tax from those with lower incomes. This would be both fair and efficient. But in the UK we already have a complex benefits system, because for 400 years we have kept benefits separate from taxes, we have never thought about them together,[9] and we have never asked whether just one of them could do the work, leaving the other without any work to do. It is particularly strange that governments that tell us that they are keen to save money do not seem to have noticed the waste involved in studying people's incomes and other circumstances twice over.

There are two ways in which the discussion can legitimately proceed:[10] by asking what we would do if we had a blank sheet (the thought experiment already described) and comparing with that the mess that we've got into; or by asking how we can solve the problems that the current system has given to us.

To undertake the first method we shall need a list of desirable characteristics for a benefits system, so here is a tentative list based on previous suggestions:[11] Our tax and benefits structure should

- reflect the employment market of today, and should remain serviceable as the employment market changes in the future;
- reflect today's family and household patterns, and remain serviceable as household and family patterns continue to change;
- be coherent (different parts should fit together), be simple to administer, and avoid error and fraud; and
- reduce poverty and inequality.

It is legitimate to mix the two methods, of course, because we can argue that a Citizen's Basic Income conforms to these requirements whereas the current system does not. In this book I shall usually concentrate on arguing for a Citizen's Basic Income on the basis that it provides the kind of system that we need: but there will also be times when it will be appropriate to compare it with the current system.

This approach can feel problematic because when we are presented with new ideas we often compare them with what we do now, as if somehow what we do now is normal and right and every new idea should pass the tests that the current system passes. This is irrational, because the tests that the current system passes might be irrational, irrelevant, or both. Take, for instance, a test that the current benefits system passes: are we only giving money to people who need it most? A Citizen's Basic Income does not pass that test: but, as we have seen, it is not a sensible test in the first place. As the tax system takes from those with higher incomes more than they would receive in Citizen's Basic Income, it is irrelevant that those who do not need to receive a Citizen's Basic Income will receive one along with everyone else. Perhaps instead we should try a test that Citizen's Basic Income would pass: do the rich end up paying more to the government than they receive from the government? This is in fact the same question, but differently phrased: and, worded like this, both a Citizen's Basic Income and the current system pass the test.

Take another test: is it as simple as possible to administer? A Citizen's Basic Income passes that test, but the current system does not. And another: does the system encourage risk taking in household employment patterns? A Citizen's Basic Income will pass that test more convincingly than the current system ever could. If the new idea generates the questions, and the new idea passes the tests and the current system does not, then it really is time that we started to look afresh at the way that we do things now, at the new proposal, and at their relative merits. We might find that a Citizen's Basic Income beats the current system in relation to every test; and, as we have seen, when the old system's tests are reworded a little, a Citizen's Basic Income passes those as well.

Similarly, if we replace one system with another, then there might be winners and losers. Some people could end up with more money, and some with less. We tend to assume that that means that there is a problem with the new system. It could equally well mean that there is a problem with the present system, and that the new system would give us a fairer distribution than we have now. Where there might be gainers and losers, we need to ask three questions: 1. Is the new system fairer than the old one? 2. Can every individual and every household end up in a better position in the end? 3. Can we ensure that no low-income household suffers a loss, and that no household suffers a significant loss?

We shall be studying the redistribution that a Citizen's Basic Income scheme might deliver later on, but it is worth saying here that if we find that the incomes of the wealthiest reduce by 4%, and the incomes of the poorest rise by 20%, then we might regard the new distribution as fairer than the current one. It might also be worth saying that increasing income equality would have a variety of beneficial effects both on our society and on our economy.

As for the second question: take two individuals. A has an annual income of £16,000, but for every extra £1 she earns she loses 75p in Income Tax and reduced benefits. B has an annual income of £15,000, but for every extra £1 he earns he loses just 32p because he receives a nonwithdrawable Citizen's Basic Income and not the means-tested benefits under which A is suffering. Which of them is better off? In the short term, the answer has to be A. In the longer term, the answer could easily be B, by a long way, because he will have more incentive to seek additional earnings and the training that would make that possible: and, if he obtains higher earnings, then he will keep more of them. A will have less of an incentive to earn more, less incentive to train or retrain, will keep less of any additional earnings, and, crucially in this age of austerity, will be less able to make up for cuts in benefits levels by seeking additional hours of employment.[12] So, in the longer term, B is likely to be better off than A.

In answer to the third question: a Citizen's Basic Income scheme that abolished means-tested benefits would cause significant losses for some low-income households at the point of implementation:[13] but if means-tested benefits were to be retained, and recalculated on the basis of each household's Citizen's Basic Incomes and changed net earnings, then the only losses would relate to any increased Income Tax and National Insurance Contribution rates required to pay for the scheme. This would mean that low-income households would not suffer losses, and that no household would suffer unsustainable losses. This kind of scheme is sometimes called a 'hybrid' or 'modified' Citizen's Basic Income scheme.[14] This is misleading. There would of course be many different ways of reorganising the existing benefits system if a Citizen's Basic Income were to be implemented, but the Citizen's Basic Income would still be what it always is: an unconditional and nonwithdrawable income for every individual. It would be neither hybridised nor modified. If for any reason a distinction needs to be made between a Citizen's Basic Income implemented in the context of continuing means-tested benefits, and one that abolishes means-tested benefits and provides a subsistence income, then the former could legitimately be called a 'Supplemental' or 'Partial' Citizen's Basic Income and the latter a 'Full Citizen's Basic Income'.[15] They would both be genuine Citizen's Basic Incomes.

When considering any change in policy, a question that we really ought to ask is this: if we were running the new system, would we be better off if we changed to what we are doing now?[16] If everyone received a Citizen's Basic Income, then would we vote for a government that planned to abolish it in favour of means-tested benefits? The answer to that question is: possibly, yes. However good the arguments for unconditional benefits, however beneficial their effects, and however efficient they are for the government, for individuals and for households, there will always be people who will want to means-test. To means-test is irrational, but there does seem to be some innate desire to do it, even though it is entirely unnecessary, it is expensive, it is inefficient and it has a variety of unfortunate social and economic effects. The debate about Citizen's Basic Income will never be over, so there will always be a need for books like this one.

You might already believe that a Citizen's Basic Income would be a good idea, perhaps because it coheres with your political ideology, or because you believe that it would promote a 'good life' defined in terms of 'the ability to frame and execute a plan of life reflective of one's tastes, temperament and conception of the good'.[17] If you do already think that a Citizen's Basic Income would be a good idea, then I hope that this book will confirm you in your belief. If you think that a Citizen's Basic Income would be a bad idea, or if you are not sure, then I hope that I have already persuaded you to keep an open mind as to the best way to reduce poverty and inequality, to ensure that everyone receives the income that they need, to create social cohesion and to incentivise employment, self-employment, and training:[18] and that by the end of the book you will have sufficient information to enable you to come to an informed view.

Notes

1 Eyal, 2010.
2 www.gov.uk/child-benefit, 24/04/2017.
3 www.gov.uk/universal-credit, 24/04/2017.
4 www.gov.uk/jobseekers-allowance, 24/04/2017.
5 'Tax Credits' are withdrawn at 41% of gross earnings: so for additional earnings above the £11,200 p.a. 2017/18 Income Tax Personal Allowance, and the National Insurance Contributions Primary Earnings Threshold of £157 p.w. (£8,164 p.a.), Income Tax is withdrawn at 20%, National Insurance Contributions at 12%, and Working Tax Credits at 41%, adding up to a total withdrawal rate of 73%. So for every additional £1 of earnings, disposable income rises by just 27p: www.gov.uk/government/publications/rates-and-allowances-tax-credits-child-benefit-and-guardians-allowance/tax-credits-child-benefit-and-guardians-allowance, 24/04/2017.
6 'Universal Credit' is withdrawn at 63% of net earnings: so for earned income beyond a small work allowance, every additional £1 above the Income Tax Personal Allowance suffers Income Tax and National Insurance Contributions withdrawal of 32%, leaving 68p; then 63% of this is withdrawn, leaving 25p of additional disposable income. www.gov.uk/government/publications/universal-credit-different-earning-patterns-and-your-payments/universal-credit-different-earning-patterns-and-your-payments-payment-cycles, 24/04/2017.
7 See Chapter 5 on the cost of administering Child Benefit.
8 Spicker, 2011: 117; Torry, 2018.
9 The Institute for Fiscal Studies Mirrlees review of taxation in the UK treated income taxation as if it was the only government instrument that relates to a household's net income: Adam et al, 2010; Adam et al, 2011; Albi and Martinez-Vazquez, 2011; Alm, 2011; and Institute for Fiscal Studies, 2011: all of which study the tax system largely in isolation from the benefits system.
10 Torry, 2014b.
11 Beveridge, 1942; Torry, 1992; Meade, 1978: 269.
12 Hirsch and Valadez, 2014: 3.
13 Torry, 2012b; 2014a; 2015a.
14 Reed and Lansley, 2016: 8.
15 Piachaud, 2016; Miller, 2016: 167.
16 Birnbaum, 2012: 59.
17 Skidelsky and Skidelsky, 2012: 160.
18 Walker, 2011: 149–50.

TWO

How did we get to where we are now?[1]

A means-tested past and a means-tested future?

We have got to where we are now by evolutionary change rather than by radical reform, and by the swing of a pendulum, moving back and forth between universality and selectivity, between providing for everybody and providing for people who fit into particular categories. The pendulum has rarely reached either of the extreme ends of the spectrum. It has more often been near to the selectivity end, but has taken an occasional lunge towards universality, only to be dragged swiftly back again.

The 1601 Poor Law set up local administrations to provide for people unable to provide for themselves, and to provide 'houses of correction' for able-bodied men who could not find work. By the end of the eighteenth century, unemployment was increasing and wages were not keeping up with living costs. The administration of the Poor Law being local, experiment was inevitable, and in 1795 at Speenhamland the Poor Law Guardians began to subsidise low wages as a means of relieving poverty. Amid (somewhat unjustified[2]) fears that this policy would lead to a general reduction in wages, and a belief that a man who cannot provide for his family loses his dignity, a review was held. The ensuing debate led to the Poor Law Amendment Act 1834, which enshrined the idea of 'less eligibility': that is, that the unemployed man or woman should not be paid as much as they would get if they were employed. Before 1834, 'out relief' had provided food for families that could not afford to feed themselves. After 1834, those who could not support themselves were admitted to the workhouse and isolated from the rest of society: a system meant to deter people from voluntary poverty.[3]

By the beginning of the twentieth century, the poverty in which many elderly people found themselves was causing concern, and the government implemented a flat-rate non-contributory pension for elderly people who had not received Poor Relief and whose incomes were below £31 per annum. Central government administered the pension, and since then there has been a constant movement away from the local management of benefits payments and towards centralised administration.[4] The next development was contributory Unemployment Benefit in certain industries in 1911, paid for out of employee and employer contributions, and payable for 26 weeks.[5] In Germany, Bismarck had instigated a social insurance scheme in 1883 to give workers a financial stake in the government's stability, and similar motives no doubt contributed to developments in the UK; but there was also a genuine concern to tackle poverty and to increase social cohesion: hence the gradual replacement of means-tested benefits by contributory schemes.[6]

The 1920s brought high unemployment, and National Insurance benefits were extended beyond the period for which they could be funded by contributions. By 1930, the financial cost could no longer be sustained, so assistance when Unemployment Benefit had expired was given via a rather draconian household means test.[7]

During the Second World War, the government extended its influence into many areas of people's lives, and the scene was set for substantial government intervention in healthcare, education and income maintenance. In the midst of the war, a population looking forward to a better life welcomed William Beveridge's 1942 report, which proposed a comprehensive system of National Insurance benefits, and centrally administered National Assistance to maintain the incomes of people without sufficient resources.[8] Acts of Parliament led to Family Allowances (the forerunner of Child Benefit) in 1945; National Insurance (contributory) Retirement Pensions, Unemployment Benefit and Sickness Benefit in 1946; and means-tested National Assistance in 1948. Beveridge intended contributory benefits to be the heart of the system, and National Assistance to be a safety net for the few: but because National Assistance covered housing costs, and the levels at which contributory benefits were set were never sufficient to cover the cost of housing, far more people than Beveridge had intended ended up on means-tested benefits.[9] This compromised his original intention of improving social cohesion by creating a social insurance system sufficient for every citizen's needs.[10]

One group of people not well served by National Insurance was people with disabilities because they and their carers were less likely to have paid the required contributions: so between 1970 and 1975 the government implemented a number of non-contributory benefits, both for people with disabilities and for their carers.[11] Provision has continued to evolve, and people with disabilities now have available to them a 'patchwork quilt of provision',[12] some of which is contributory and some not, and some of which is means tested and some not, with the different parts of the now complex system based on a variety of different principles.[13] As we shall see in Chapter 10, the complexities of disability mean that provision will always exhibit some level of complexity.

In 1971, in order to supplement low wages, the government implemented the means-tested Family Income Supplement, which became Family Credit, then Working Family Tax Credits, then Working Tax Credits and Child Tax Credits, and now Universal Credit, [14] the roll-out of which has experienced major administrative problems, and the employment incentive characteristics of which have been severely compromised.[15] Alongside the continuing means testing of in-work and out-of-work benefits, we have seen the development of 'passported' benefits, such as free school meals and free prescriptions, which can be claimed by households already on means-tested benefits. Passporting has the advantage of avoiding additional means tests, but also the disadvantage that a household coming off means-tested benefits can find itself having to pay for school meals and prescriptions at the same time as losing their in-work or out-of-work means-tested benefits.

Apart from renaming benefits, tinkering with regulations, and imposing increasingly punitive conditionalities,[16] not much has changed since 1948. We are still living with Beveridge's structure: National Insurance (contributory) benefits, means-tested benefits for people who do not have enough to live on, and universal Child Benefit.[17] And we are still living with the presuppositions that benefits should be paid to households (whereas Income Tax has been individualised for 30 years);[18] that households are stable, and constituted by permanent relationships; and that permanent employment is the norm, and diverse employment patterns therefore an aberration. The reason for the lack of structural reform is that 'the UK social security system is a large, complex juggernaut that has grown in a largely incremental way over at least the last century', and ministers' relative inexperience in this complex field means that it is easier to tinker than to create coordinated change across the system as a whole.[19] This is unfortunate given the massive changes that we have seen in our society, the economy and the employment market since 1945.[20] Far from developing beyond the Poor Law and the Beveridge Report into a new third stage, our benefits system is increasingly characterised by means tests which 'play a strong and exceptional role by international standards',[21] by sanctions that disproportionately target the already vulnerable,[22] by stigma, and by tinkering (which includes 'Universal Credit'). The result is a system that is simply 'baffling … there is a limit to how clear it is possible to make things – the structure of benefits does not make sense:'[23] and it certainly does not make sense in relation to the way our society, economy and employment market work today. It is time for a change; [24] and the history of universal benefits provides a direction in which relevant change might be possible.

Universal[25] benefits in the UK: a brief history[26]

The UK already has a variety of universal benefits. The three most important are the NHS (in which consultations with a GP and treatment in hospital have been free at the point of use for 70 years), education up to the age of 18, and Child Benefit (paid for every child until they are 16, or for longer if they remain in full-time education or training): but there are others, including the Winter Fuel Allowance for every pensioner, free dental care for the under 19s, free prescriptions for children and pensioners (free to all in Scotland), free television licences for the over 75s, and public libraries.

Family Allowance

Before the First World War, Seebohm Rowntree, on the basis of his survey of poverty in York, had called for wages sufficient for families with three children, and allowances from the state for the fourth and further children; and during that war the families of soldiers received an addition to their income for each child. After the war, Eleanor Rathbone argued that a worker's wage could never be expected to support a large family, so mothers needed an income from the state to enable them to care for their children.[27] In 1924, she wrote *The Disinherited Family*, making the same point.[28] William Beveridge suffered 'instant and total conversion',[29] and instigated unconditional child allowances for staff at the London School of Economics, of which he was Director; and when he was asked to chair a committee on the future of social insurance and found that child allowances were not on the agenda, he simply wrote them into the presuppositions at the beginning of his report. The reason for this recommendation was that child allowances were already being paid with Unemployment Benefit, but when unemployed men with large families found paid employment they could find that the wage on offer, unsupplemented by child allowances, could be lower than the benefits that they had been receiving; and the reason given for their unconditionality was that 'little money can be saved by any reasonable income test'. Another of the presuppositions on which Beveridge based his report was the NHS.[30]

In order to achieve the level of child allowance that he wanted, Beveridge had had to compromise and agree not to pay an allowance for the first child; and the Treasury achieved another victory: 'Family Allowance' rather than 'Child Allowance': but in 1945 the Family Allowance Act was passed with all-party support, and the first Family Allowances were paid in 1946.

Among the reasons for Rathbone's and Beveridge's success were 1. the argument that wages would never provide sufficient income for large families; 2. that by the time of the Second World War more women were members of trades unions (women were more likely to support child allowances, men more likely to support Child Tax Allowances); 3. the employment market disincentives that had so disturbed Beveridge; 4. the unhealthy state of young adults; 5. fear of inflation (Family Allowances would reduce the pressure for higher wages[31]); and, for a few, 6. the enhanced status for women that child allowances would promote. Above all, the war had raised expectations of a better Britain, and no political party wanted to vote against the popular new child allowances because they might have lost votes if they had. Different arguments weighed more heavily with different parties, so during the parliamentary debate the arguments for and against were little discussed. The cautious nature of the debate in Parliament was another reason for the measure's success.[32]

Family Allowances happened because of Eleanor Rathbone's consistent campaigning, because of her book, because different interests converged on a single policy option, and because of a crucial conversion. Rathbone campaigned as she did because she believed that child allowances would enhance the status of women and reduce their families' poverty: but it was on entirely other grounds that she and Beveridge persuaded those they needed to vote for it.[33]

Family Allowance becomes Child Benefit

Just for once, a name change was not just that. Child Benefit really was an improvement on Family Allowance.

By the mid-1960s, Family Allowance was suffering neglect. The rate at which it was paid had hardly risen at all, yet means-tested benefits were paying age-related additions for every child in the family, and not just for the second and subsequent children. Of families with someone in full-time employment, and with six children or more, 14% were living below National Assistance levels.[34] Child Tax Allowances were still being paid, and because these reduced the amount of pay subject to Income Tax, higher rate taxpayers benefited more than anyone else; and for families near to the tax threshold, and who therefore paid little or no Income Tax, the tax allowances had little or no value.[35] In 1965, the Child Poverty Action Group showed that high-earning families obtained three times the benefit from Child Tax Allowances than low-earning ones;[36] research showed that one in five families were on incomes below half the average;[37] and in 1966 the television play *Cathy Come Home*, which recounted a family's slide from unemployment into homelessness and disintegration, brought home the realities of poverty to a broad spectrum of the population. The new Child Poverty Action Group argued for higher Family Allowances, for Family Allowances to be paid for every child, including the first,[38] and for the abolition of Child Tax Allowances; and by 1968 the idea of paying 'Child Benefit' for every child[39] had gained substantial support in the Cabinet, largely because it would increase employment market incentives.[40] The Labour Party returned to government in 1974, and a Bill was passed to establish Child Benefit, but no start date was set. In 1976, Frank Field, Director of the Child Poverty Action Group, published in *New Society* some leaked Cabinet minutes that revealed government concern that to abolish Child Tax Allowances would reduce net incomes for men, and would therefore cause higher wage demands and higher inflation; and also that it would look as if public expenditure had increased, whereas in fact Child Benefit would have been paid for by increased tax revenue caused by the reduction in tax allowances.[41] The Child Poverty Action Group's 'Child Benefit Now' campaign resulted in Child Benefit being established, for every child, and at a level higher than the previous Family Allowance.[42]

Child Benefit came about because of such individuals as Margaret Herbison MP (a former Minister of Social Security), Barbara Castle MP, Frank Field, and the Cabinet mole;[43] because trades unions now contained more women members, and arguments against equality for women were beginning to crumble,[44] so a benefit for children payable to their mothers was coherent with social change; and because of 20 years' positive experience of Family Allowance. Family Allowance was simple to claim and administer, very little went unclaimed, and it attracted no stigma. It was popular with women because they received it; and it reduced child poverty because mothers were more likely to spend the Family Allowance on their children than fathers were to spend the value of their Child Tax Allowances on them. Above all, Family Allowance did not change with the family's circumstances and so did not discourage household members from seeking additional earnings, as means–tested benefits did.[45]

Child Benefit's birth was not easy, it has often failed to thrive,[46] and there has been little understanding that Child Benefit is a more efficient way of supporting a family's income than means-tested Family Income Supplement and its successors.[47] Campaigns to increase the value of Child Benefit[48] have been met with new proposals for Child Tax Allowances, which research has shown would redistribute from poor to rich, whereas Child Benefit redistributes from rich to poor.[49] And then in 2010 the Chancellor of the Exchequer announced that he intended to withdraw Child Benefit from every household containing at least one high earner. This is not what has happened, presumably because to match up Child Benefit recipients with individuals paying higher rate Income Tax would require the kind of intrusive examination of relationships that currently applies only to those poor enough to require means-tested benefits. What has happened is an additional tax charge applied to everyone earning over £50,000 p.a. who declares that someone in their household is in receipt of Child Benefit.[50] This has of course created some major anomalies. A household in which two adults each earn just below £50,000 p.a. does not pay the tax charge, whereas a household in which just one adult is earning £60,000 p.a. will pay additional tax equal to the value of their household's Child Benefit. High earners living with partners with children from other relationships can resent the charge, causing children's carers to withdraw their Child Benefit claims. The tax charge generated £475m of additional government revenue in 2015/16, but government accounts do not report separately on the cost of administering it.[51]

Paying Child Benefit for every child, however wealthy their family, is efficient for everyone. It is efficient for the government because Child Benefit's administrative costs are one tenth of the cost of administering means-tested benefits.[52] And it is efficient for families with children. After the initial few minutes of form filling when the child is born, no time has to be spent claiming Child Benefit – unlike most other benefits, for which hours can be spent visiting and phoning offices, and filling in forms online.[53] It is also efficient in the sense that it does not interfere with decisions about how much employment to take, how much to earn, the number of hours each partner should work, and so on. This means that it is efficient for people's employers, too. In the economist's language: Child Benefit does not compromise the efficiency of the employment market or the efficiency of the household's economy. Above all: there is no reason not to give Child Benefit to every family with children, and there is no reason for an extra tax charge, because the rich will in any case be paying more in tax than they receive in Child Benefit.

The UK is now in the bizarre position of paying a still unconditional Child Benefit, and of taxing children – the very opposite of a Child Tax Allowance. But as we shall see, the civil service will be in full support of the tax charge;[54] and, as television interviews revealed at the 2010 Conservative Party conference at which the plan to means-test Child Benefit was announced, a lot of people believe the tax charge to be right because 'the rich don't need Child Benefit'– which suggests that the only factor preventing the means testing of Child Benefit is the difficulty of doing so. What those interviewees do not realise is that the poor need the rich to receive Child Benefit.

As Paul Spicker puts it:

> The argument for universality is the argument against selective approaches: the process of selection is inefficient, inequitable, difficult to administer, and it fails to reach people. By contrast, universal social provision can reach everyone, on the same terms. The degree of uniformity simplifies administration … . But there are also positive reasons for universality. One is the view that everyone has basic needs, and those needs can often be supplied more simply and effectively through general provision to everyone. … Second, universality has been seen as a way of establishing a different kind of society – one in which every citizen has a right to basic services, and the basic texture and pattern of social life is one in which people do not suffer unjustifiable disadvantages.[55]

Proposals that failed

Child Benefit happened, and it is still with us: but other attempts at major reform of the tax and benefits systems have not reached the statute book. Why not?

Tax Credits [56]

It is a particular difficulty that the UK's 'Tax Credits' are in fact a means-tested benefit, because in the early 1970s a Conservative government proposed a genuine Tax Credit scheme. These Tax Credits would have replaced Income Tax Personal Allowances, would have been paid in full if an individual had no other income, and would have been withdrawn at a specified rate as earned income rose. As earned income continued to rise, the Tax Credits would have ceased to be paid and the worker would have started to pay Income Tax.[57] Tax Credits were to be withdrawn at 30% as earned income rose: that is, for every extra £1 of earnings below the tax threshold, the employer would have deducted 30p of the Tax Credit, meaning that the individual would have been 70p better off; and for every £1 of extra earnings above the threshold, tax would have been deducted at 30%, again meaning an additional 70p of net income. The scheme would have redistributed resources because tax allowances are worth more to higher earners than they are to those on lower incomes,[58] whereas Tax Credits are not.[59] Because the lowest earners would have been excluded, married men would have received a larger Tax Credit than single men, and administration would have shuttled between employers and the government as workers moved in and out of employment, the scheme would have been complicated to administer; and research showed that some households would have suffered losses at the point of implementation:[60] but the select committee that studied the proposal recommended acceptance of the Tax Credits scheme because it appeared 'to offer the possibility of improving the amount of income retained from increased earnings', [61] and also recommended that the Child Tax Credits should be paid to the mother as cash payments at the Post Office, thus effectively increasing Child Benefit rather than being part of the Tax Credits system. This was an interesting recognition of the efficiency and effectiveness of Child Benefit, and of universal unconditional benefits generally.[62]

The General Elections of 1974 delivered a Labour administration, which preferred means-tested Family Income Supplement to Tax Credits.

Why did Tax Credits not happen?[63] There was enough enthusiasm, particularly from Sir Arthur Cockfield, who formulated the scheme. Members of Parliament had plenty of reasons to support it: Tax Credits would have reduced poverty among working families, would have offered greater incentives to seek additional earnings, and would have promoted the 'free functioning of the market'.[64] Unfortunately, the particular scheme planned would have been very difficult to administer:[65] but even so, if the Conservative Party had won the General Election in 1974, then we might by now have had nearly 40 years' experience of real Tax Credits. We would also have learnt that revenue foregone in the form of tax allowances, and revenue paid out in the form of benefits, have the same effect on the Public Sector Borrowing Requirement: an obvious fact, although not obvious enough to encourage the government to include revenue foregone in the public expenditure figures.

Attempts at a Citizen's Basic Income [66]

In 1796, Thomas Paine published his *Agrarian Justice*:

> [T]he earth, in its natural, uncultivated state was, and ever
> would have continued to be, the common property of the
> human race, … every proprietor … of cultivated lands owes
> to the community a ground-rent … for the land which he
> holds; and it is from this ground-rent that … there shall be
> paid to every person, when arrived at the age of twenty-one
> years, the sum of fifteen pounds sterling, as a compensation,
> in part, for the loss of his or her natural inheritance, by the
> introduction of the system of landed property. And also, the
> sum of ten pounds per annum, during life, to every person
> now living, of the age of fifty years, and to all others as they
> shall arrive at that age … to every person, rich or poor, …
> because it is in lieu of the natural inheritance, which, as a
> right, belongs to every man, over and above the property
> he may have created, or inherited from that who did. [67]

A year later, Thomas Spence proposed a locally administered income
dividend paid 'fairly and equally among all the living souls in the parish,
whether male or female; married or single; legitimate or illegitimate;
from a day old to the extremest age; making no distinction between
the families of rich farmers and merchants … and the families of poor
labourers and mechanics'. [68]

By the early twentieth century, the adverse consequences of means
testing were hard to ignore, and Mabel and Dennis Milner and Bertram
Pickard, all Quakers, established the State Bonus League to campaign
for a Citizen's Basic Income, or 'state bonus'. [69] In 1921, the Labour
Party Executive Committee discussed the idea, and rejected it.

Not everyone agreed with the conclusions of William Beveridge's
1942 report *Social Insurance and Allied Services*. Lady Juliet Rhys
Williams, Secretary of the Women's Liberal Federation, [70] issued a
minority report, which she then expanded and published as *Something
to Look Forward To*. [71] Her objection was that the combination of
time-limited National Insurance benefits and means-tested National
Assistance benefits would mean that many families would receive too
little of any additional earnings, and that there would therefore be
too little incentive to seek paid employment. This would mean that
to get people to accept employment would require coercion, which
was anathema to Liberal politicians.

> The hope of gain is infinitely preferable to the fear of
> punishment and the fear of want as a motive for human
> labour ... The real objection to the Beveridge scheme does
> not lie in its shortcomings in respect of the abolition of
> want, which could be made good, but in its serious attack
> upon the will to work.[72]

Rhys Williams wanted to see every worker receiving 'the whole benefit
of wages (less taxation)',[73] but there was also a principle involved:

> The State owes precisely the same benefits to all of its
> citizens, and should in no circumstances pay more to one
> than to another of the same sex and age, except in return
> for services rendered ... Therefore the same benefits [should
> be paid] to the employed and healthy as to the idle and
> sick. ... The prevention of want must be regarded as being
> the duty of the State to all its citizens and not merely to a
> favoured few.[74]

Rhys Williams' scheme was conditional and was not for a Citizen's
Basic Income, as she would have required workers to visit the Labour
Exchange and to accept any employment offered:[75] but it would have
been close, and would have resulted in greater administrative simplicity,
less means testing, increased possibilities for useful activity during
periods of unemployment, an improvement in married women's status,
lower marginal deduction rates,[76] and therefore raised employment
incentives. Under the National Insurance Act, a man, wife and child
could earn £3 per week and be only 5/- [25p] better off. Under
Rhys Williams' scheme they would have been £1/16/- [£1.80] better
off.[77] The problem was that Beveridge, the trades unions, government
ministers, the Treasury and civil servants, were committed to the
contributory principle, to a means-tested safety net, and to keeping
taxation and social security benefits separate from each other, which
made it difficult to appreciate the logic and the advantages of Juliet
Rhys Williams' ideas.[78]

Juliet Rhys Williams was a Liberal MP. Her son, Sir Brandon Rhys
Williams, was a Conservative MP, but that did not stop him from
sharing his mother's enthusiasm for reforming the tax and benefits
systems. In March 1973 he was a witness during the parliamentary select
committee hearings on Sir Arthur Cockfield's Tax Credits proposal;[79]
and in 1982 he recommended a 'Basic Income Guarantee' – a Citizen's
Basic Income – to another select committee.[80] As Hermione Parker's

synopsis of the scheme explained: 'Every citizen would be entitled to a personal basic income or PBI. These guaranteed basic incomes would replace virtually all existing benefits and allowances.'[81] The committee recommended that more work should be done, and that 'the Government should put such work in hand. ... Meanwhile, it is desirable that changes to the present system should be compatible with an eventual move to an integrated structure of tax and social security.'[82] There is no evidence that the government did put work in hand, and no evidence of changes to tax and benefits being evaluated for their coherence with a future move to a Citizen's Basic Income.

However, one implemented reform does fulfil this condition. The UK is now rolling out a Single Tier State Pension that might one day look remarkably like a Citizen's Pension: an unconditional income for everyone over state pension age,[83] of the kind now being paid in New Zealand, the Netherlands, Bolivia and elsewhere.[84] The pension will be paid at a higher rate than the current Basic State Pension, it will take no account of earnings or savings, and it will remove a lot of pensioners from the current means-tested Pension Credit. It will not be entirely unconditional because the full pension will require a full 35-year National Insurance Contribution record.[85] This will mean that many pensioners with incomplete National Insurance Contribution records will still need means-tested Pension Credit:[86] but it will ensure that civil service jobs are not lost – the relevance of which will become clear.[87] A genuine Citizen's Pension would make the kind of employment market behaviour that results in low incomes in later life less optimal,[88] it would reduce pensioner inequality, and it would go a long way towards equalising pension provision for men and women.[89] The Single Tier State Pension will have similar consequences, but not to the same extent.[90]

Steven Webb, the Minister of State for Pensions responsible for establishing the Single Tier State Pension, is no newcomer to Citizen's Basic Income. In 1990 he published a book on the subject with Samuel Brittan.[91] Webb's proposal was not for a Citizen's Basic Income because it was for a household-based payment, which would have skewed employment market decisions, and would have required the government to inquire into every adult's intimate relationships: but it would only have taken a minor change to turn the book's proposal into a genuine Citizen's Basic Income, with all of the advantages that its simplicity would offer; and, in a similar way, it would only require the Single Tier State Pension's National Insurance Contribution record conditionality to be replaced by a residence requirement for the UK to experience a genuine Citizen's Pension.

What conclusions can we draw from this history?

We shall return to questions of feasibility in Chapter 7, and to questions of implementation in Chapter 8, but here we shall ask why a number of reform proposals were and have been implemented: the Poor Law, National Insurance Benefits, National Assistance, Family Allowance, Child Benefit, 'Universal Credit', and a Single Tier State Pension, and why no proposal for a Citizen's Basic Income has yet been implemented.

It is possible to identify four patterns here:

1. *The proposals that have been implemented have been for identifiable groups of people, whereas the proposals that have not been implemented have been for everyone (Citizen's Basic Income) or for working-age adults (the Heath Government's Tax Credits).*

It might be thought that William Beveridge's 1942 proposals were for everyone and so constitute a counter-argument: but they do not, because different demographic groups were served by different aspects of the plan. We can therefore still draw the tentative conclusion that only those proposals that relate to definable groups of people are likely to be implemented.

2. *The proposals that have been implemented have benefited from long-standing and widespread debate, and a reasonable level of public understanding of what was intended.*

Do we conclude that only publicly debated and understood proposals are likely to be implemented? Given the level of public ignorance of the tax and benefits systems,[92] and the fact that ubiquity of means testing[93] means that means testing is experienced as a fact of life rather than one option among others, this would be a high bar to jump. The level of public debate in Switzerland,[94] Finland[95] and Denmark has been far higher than in the UK, and there have been periods when debate in the Netherlands[96] and Ireland[97] has been lively. Perhaps the size of a country's population is a factor in the level of debate that we can expect: so an independent Scotland might implement a Citizen's Basic Income before the rest of the UK achieves that.[98] The Scottish National Party has already committed itself to such a possibility.[99]

A possible counter-example is this: when Gordon Brown was Chancellor of the Exchequer, he replaced the means-tested Family Credit, run by the Department for Work and Pensions, with the means-tested 'Tax Credits', run by his own department. There was no meaningful public debate. 'Universal Credit' and Single Tier State Pension are both being rolled out, even though there has been little public understanding or debate about either of them. So while public understanding and debate might once have been a prerequisite for success, it would appear not to be so now: at least, not in relation to the benefits system.

3. *Those proposals that have been implemented are those that have not reduced the number of civil servants, and those that have not been implemented would have done.*

Family Allowance was a new benefit and so added to the total number of civil servants. Child Benefit displaced Child Tax Allowances, but overall there would have been little change in the number of tax inspectors. The 1970s Tax Credits proposal might or might not have reduced the number of civil servants, so it might have happened; and Steven Webb's Single Tier State Pension retains contribution records and so is unlikely to reduce the number of public servants by very many, if at all. The tax charge now related to Child Benefit will have increased the number of public servants.

As Harris has suggested: 'Like most schemes for abolishing bureaucrats, Lady Juliet's proposals met with an official wall of silence'.[100] Juliet Rhys Williams' and Brandon Rhys Williams' proposals would have reduced the number of civil servants administering existing benefits. In the UK, Permanent Secretaries have an interest in maintaining the size and functions of their government departments, and it is Permanent Secretaries who brief ministers. A scheme that would reduce the size and functions of a department would therefore be unlikely to be implemented unless the Secretary of State were to be so convinced of its advantages that they could achieve sufficient institutional momentum, in the Cabinet, in Parliament and in their own department, to propel it onto the statute book.

A Citizen's Basic Income scheme that abolished means-tested benefits would reduce the number of civil servants considerably; a Citizen's Basic Income scheme that left means-tested benefits in place would require additional civil servants to administer the Citizen's Basic Income and would reduce the number of civil servants required to administer the reducing number of means-tested benefits claims. The net effect on civil service numbers might be close to zero.

4. *Benefits systems evolve by addition rather than by replacement.*

First came means-tested social assistance schemes, and then social assistance: but far from replacing social assistance, social insurance enabled it to escape from collapse and to fulfil a gap-filling role.[101] Such universal benefits as the UK's Family Allowance have fulfilled a similar function. The result is a diverse benefits system characterised by 'universal benefit schemes, social insurance schemes, social assistance schemes, ...'.[102] We might see the same process repeat itself if a developed country were to implement a Citizen's Basic Income scheme. Continuing means-tested benefits would enable the scheme to be implemented without imposing losses on low-income households; continuing social insurance benefits would continue to fulfil their contribution-based, short-term wage replacement role; and unconditional benefits would take the pressure off both of them, and enable them to survive. The question to ask is not just 'What should we abolish?' but also 'How should we rebalance the mix?'[103]

We shall return to this set of conclusions in Chapter 7.

The National Health Service

This book is about the tax and benefits system, but no history of unconditional benefits would be complete without at least mentioning the milk that used to be provided free to every schoolchild,[104] the free school meals for every child that are slowly returning in some local authorities, and particularly the UK's highly successful provision of universal, unconditional and nonwithdrawable healthcare, which offers free visits to a GP and free inpatient and outpatient treatment in hospital, to every legal resident of the UK.[105] By paying for healthcare out of income taxation,[106] and by ensuring that GPs function as gatekeepers and thus as an essential rationing mechanism, the NHS has achieved higher efficiency ratings than any other Organisation for Economic Co-operation and Development (OECD) healthcare system.[107] The NHS exhibits an unconditionality different from that of Child Benefit – it is an unconditionality of provision free at the point of use, rather than a constant free provision (which is why a Citizen's Basic Income could never replace the NHS's universal healthcare[108]). But the principle is the same: an unconditional and nonwithdrawable provision for every individual legally resident; and, like unconditional incomes, universal tax-funded healthcare experiences none of the failures of alternative schemes, and it cannot be beaten on efficiency.[109]

In Dingeldey and Rothgang's *Governance of Welfare State Reform*,[110] a five-page discussion of the Netherlands' pension system[111] gives four lines to the residence-based flat-rate Citizen's Pension and five pages to the funded industry-based sector, in spite of the fact that it is the residence-based state system that contributes so much to income maintenance and poverty reduction;[112] the internal governance of Britain's NHS is discussed, but not its universal provision or its funding, which is what really ought to have been compared with insurance-based healthcare systems; and the UK's Child Benefit does not get a mention, even where it would have been highly relevant.[113]

The editors and authors clearly regard unconditional provision as not worth discussing, yet it has been a highly successful welfare system in its own right, particularly in relation to its low administrative costs and its capacity to reduce poverty and provide income and healthcare security.[114] So here is a hypothesis: universal provision is so successful when implemented that it creates no problems. It is problems, not successes, that demand the attention of policy makers and academics. Therefore universal provision drops off the policy agenda. This means that universal provision is not considered as an option when welfare reform options are discussed. This is a pity. The NHS is universal, unconditional and nonwithdrawable, and it is both efficient and effective. It should be the model for healthcare everywhere.

A global debate

In 1984, a group of individuals interested in Citizen's Basic Income founded the Basic Income Research Group (BIRG) (renamed the 'Citizen's Income Trust' in 1994, and now the 'Citizen's Basic Income Trust'), and for 34 years it has organised meetings, maintained a library and website, responded to requests for information, and published a regular newsletter (originally the *BIRG Bulletin*, now the *Citizen's Income Newsletter*) and other publications. Occasional flurries of activity have punctuated that period, such as the 1994 Labour Party Commission on Social Justice report, *Social Justice: Strategies for National Renewal*:

> It would be unwise ... to rule out a move towards Citizen's Basic Income in future: if it turns out to be the case that earnings simply cannot provide a stable income for a growing proportion of people, then the notion of some guaranteed income, outside the employment market, could become increasingly attractive.[115]

But when *Money for Everyone*, the first edition of this book, was published in 2013, the extent of the debate on Citizen's Basic Income in the UK was much as it had been for the previous 34 years. Although I do not credit my books with the influence with which Professor David Piachaud has credited them,[116] soon after the publication of *Money for Everyone* the first full-length article about Citizen's Basic Income appeared in a serious British newspaper,[117] and further articles quickly followed. Finland's proposal for an experiment, which has removed the conditionalities from the unemployment benefits paid to a sample group of unemployed individuals for a period of two years, was initially misunderstood as a proposal for a Citizen's Basic Income for the whole population, which generated further articles and television and radio programmes and interviews, during which it had to be explained that the proposed experiment, while interesting, was of a somewhat limited nature. Proposals for pilot projects, often with little detail attached to them, continue to raise interest.[118]

An important element of the infrastructure of the debate during the past 30 years has been publications (first in printed form, and now by email and on websites) from national organisations, such as the Citizen's Basic Income Trust, and also from the global umbrella group BIEN, founded in 1986 by the representatives of the BIRG and a number of other individuals from a variety of European countries. Another important element has been the biennial BIEN congress, each one organised by a different national group.[119]

Political interest, once thin on the ground, is now accelerating. In the UK, the Green Party has reiterated its support;[120] in a context of a gradual devolution of control over tax and benefits systems to Scotland, the Scottish National Party has voted to consider a Citizen's Basic Income when planning a benefits system for Scotland;[121] and the leadership of the Labour Party want debate and research to occur.[122] In other countries, political parties with varying degrees of influence are studying the possibility of implementing a Citizen's Basic Income, and the issue is now a battleground during elections.[123]

There is nothing new about articles on Citizen's Basic Income in academic journals, and there is nothing new about books on the subject: but what is new is the volume of literature now being published, and the seriousness with which the issue is being treated in academic, media and political circles.

Where the global debate will go now is difficult to say. The extent and depth of the debate – which is now as much about feasibility and implementation as it is about the desirability of Citizen's Basic Income – mean that it is unlikely to disappear in the way that it often has during its 300-year history. An early indication of where the debate might move next was provided by a seminar at the London School of Economics. Following a presentation in which Professor David Piachaud suggested that a 'full' Citizen's Basic Income would be both unfair and unaffordable, and that a small Citizen's Basic Income that required the retention of some or all existing benefits would not deliver simplicity (which it would, of course, for those households enabled to escape from a variety of means-tested benefits[124]), both Polly Toynbee of *The Guardian* and Donald Hirsch, Director of the Centre for Research in Social Policy at the University of Loughborough, suggested that while Citizen's Basic Income might not be an idea whose time had come, it is an idea whose time might well come as increasing automation continues to change the employment market: the argument being that if employment no longer provides the normal route to a subsistence income, then another route will have to be found.[125] It might be that we see the debate now taking a step beyond desirability, feasibility and implementation, and towards the timing of implementation. We are now asking 'Should we … ?', 'Can we …?' and 'How …?' We shall increasingly be asking 'When …?'

Notes

[1] Torry, 1996; Barr, 1987; Hill, 1990. For a longer account of this history, see Torry, 2013: 17–48.
[2] Block and Somers, 2003.
[3] In rural areas 'out relief' continued because there wasn't enough space in workhouses (Hill, 1990: 16).
[4] Housing Benefit is administered locally, but the scheme is a national one. What was Council Tax Benefit and is now Council Tax Reduction is now regulated and administered locally.
[5] Barr, 1987: 19; Thane, 2011: 211–19.
[6] Thane, 2011: 218.
[7] Lynes, 2011, 221–33.
[8] Beveridge, 1942.
[9] Atkinson, 1969: 24.
[10] Thane, 2011: 218.
[11] Köhler and Zacher, 1982: 200; Spicker, 2011: 163–73.
[12] Spicker, 2011: 168.
[13] Spicker, 2011: 172.
[14] Banting, 1979: 89; Department of Health and Social Security, 1985; Dean, 2012a, 2012b.
[15] National Audit Office, 2013; Thompson, 2013; House of Commons Work and Pensions Committee, 2014; Millar and Bennett, 2017; Finch, Corlett and Alakeson, 2014: 35; Judge, 2014; Field and Forsey, 2016: 122–3.
[16] Deacon and Bradshaw, 1983: 196.
[17] 'Universal' is used here in the sense described in the note on terminology at the beginning of this book. Later in this chapter the new tax charge relating to Child Benefit is described. Child Benefit itself remains unconditional and is not itself means tested.
[18] www.gov.uk/government/publications/universal-credit-and-couples-an-introduction, 25/04/2017.
[19] McKay and Rowlingson, 2008, 53.
[20] Bauman, 2000.
[21] Bahle, Hubl and Pfeifer, 2011: 152; Deacon and Bradshaw, 1983: 204; Adler, Bell, Clasen and Sinfield, 1991: 208.
[22] Reeves and Loopstra, 2017.
[23] Spicker, 2011: ix–x.

[24] Huws, 2016.

[25] 'Universal' is used here in the sense described in the note on terminology at the beginning of this book.

[26] Torry, 2012a.

[27] Macnicol, 1980: 5–10, 20–23; Thane, 1996: 202.

[28] Rathbone, 1986: 139, 167, 353.

[29] William Beveridge, in Rathbone, 1949: 270.

[30] Beveridge, 1942: 154, 157, 163, 177.

[31] Harris, 1981: 249.

[32] Macnicol, 1980: 93, 172, 176, 191–3, 202; Thane, 1996: 63–4, 226; Land, 1975: 169, 173–9, 195–6, 205, 221.

[33] Land, 1975: 227; Creedy and Disney, 1985: 41.

[34] Atkinson, 1969: 24.

[35] Banting, 1979: 95. The problem had to some extent been ameliorated by Family Allowance being taxed as earned income and by a 'clawback' mechanism that reduced the Child Tax Allowance by an amount for each child for whom Family Allowance was in payment. In 1974–5, a Child Tax Allowance of £240 was reduced by £52 for each child for whom Family Allowance was paid (Barr and Coulter, 1991: 279–80). The significance of this seemingly insignificant piece of history is that it marked the first direct relationship between the tax and benefits systems (Banting, 1979: 66).

[36] Townsend, 1979: 151.

[37] Abel-Smith and Townsend, 1965; Titmuss, 1962.

[38] Hill, 1990: 41.

[39] Walker, Sinfield and Walker, 2011: 83.

[40] Atkinson, 1969: 141.

[41] Spicker, 2011: 118.

[42] Walley, 1986: 8–11.

[43] Malcolm Wicks MP's posthumously published memoirs revealed that he was the junior civil servant who had leaked the cabinet papers: www.bbc.co.uk/news/uk-politics-25807245, 26/04/2017.

[44] Barr and Coulter, 1991: 291. See also the film, *Made in Dagenham*, 2010, on the campaign for equal pay for equal work.

[45] Spicker, 2011: 119; Barr and Coulter, 1991: 279–80.

[46] Barr and Coulter, 1991: 297; Hill, 1990: 57.

[47] Brown, 1988: 63. As Brown points out, Child Benefit's 'target' is families with children, and it hits the target.

[48] Walsh and Lister, 1985: 42; Brown, 1988: xiii, 15.

[49] Parker and Sutherland, no date: 133.

[50] www.gov.uk/child-benefit-tax-charge/overview, 26/04/2017.

[51] Her Majesty's Revenue and Customs, 2016: 193.

[52] See Chapter 5 on the cost of administering Child Benefit.

[53] Bennett, Brewer and Shaw, 2009.

[54] Harris, 1981.

[55] Spicker, 2014: 218–19.

[56] For a longer account of the Tax Credits proposal, see Torry, 2013: 29–32.

[57] Her Majesty's Government, 1972.

[58] Because a tax allowances reduces taxable pay: so for higher earners the allowance reduces the amount of earnings taxed at the higher rate.

[59] House of Commons Select Committee on Tax-Credit, 1973: 3, 28.

[60] Atkinson and Sutherland, 1984: 10.
[61] House of Commons Select Committee on Tax-Credit, 1973: 7.
[62] House of Commons Select Committee on Tax-Credit, 1973: 5, 20–4.
[63] On other Tax Credits proposals, see Vince, 1986: 5; Parker, 1989: 168–89; Philip Vince, correspondence to the author, dated 6 April 2011; Creedy and Disney, 1985: 38–46, 198.
[64] Page, 2015: 69.
[65] Page, 2015: 69.
[66] For histories of the Citizen's Basic Income debate, see Van Parijs and Vanderborght, 2017: 51–98, and Van Trier, 1995.
[67] Paine, 1796/2004: 4–7.
[68] Spence, 1797/2004: 87.
[69] Milner and Milner, 1918/2004; Pickard, 1919/2004: 134–40; Macnicol, 1980: 9; Van Trier, 1995: 31–142.
[70] Harris, 1981: 258.
[71] Rhys Williams, 1943; Cunliffe and Erreygers, 2004: 161–9.
[72] Rhys Williams, 1943: 13, 45, 141.
[73] Rhys Williams, 1943: 147.
[74] Rhys Williams, 1943: 139, 145.
[75] Rhys Williams, 1943: 167.
[76] Rhys Williams, 1953: 138.
[77] Booker, 1946: 232; Meade, 1978: 44, 45.
[78] Sloman, 2016.
[79] House of Commons Select Committee on Tax-Credit, 1973: 341-I.
[80] 'Guarantee' here means that the citizen is guaranteed to receive an unconditional income. This was before the use of 'guarantee' for a guaranteed net income level, so its use did not cause any confusion.
[81] House of Commons Treasury and Civil Service Committee Sub-Committee, 1982: 423, 425, 459; Rhys Williams, 1989; Parker, 1989: 224–53; Parker, 1995.
[82] House of Commons Treasury and Civil Service Committee, 1983: §13.35, quoted in Parker, 1989: 100.
[83] Basic Income Research Group, 1986; Salter, 1990; O'Connell, 2004a, 2004b; James and Curry, 2010; Spicker, 2011: 121; Parker, 1989: 298–302 (all of the reform schemes that Parker studies contain a Citizen's Pension, apart from Patrick Minford's); Citizen's Income Trust, 2011.
[84] Hippe, 2009: 52–7; O'Connell, 2004b; Ginn, 2016; www.worldbank.org/en/news/feature/2014/03/13/better-pensions-latin-america?cid=ISG_E_WBWeeklyUpdate_NL, 07/06/2017.
[85] www.gov.uk/government/uploads/system/uploads/attachment_data/file/607128/your-state-pension-explained-apr-2017.pdf, 17/06/2017.
[86] Ginn, 2015.
[87] Department for Work and Pensions, 2011: 10, 29–35; Salter, Bryans, Redman and Hewitt, 2009: 178; Salter, 1997: 9–11.
[88] Creedy, 1998.
[89] Ginn, 1996: 10–12.
[90] Crawford, Keynes and Tetlow, 2014: 47–9; Ginn, 2015.
[91] Brittan and Webb, 1990.
[92] D.V.L. Smith and Associates, 1991: 5, 29.
[93] Evans and Williams, 2009: 140; Evans and Eyre, 2004.
[94] Citizen's Income Trust, 2016.

95 Kansaneläkelaitos Kela, 2016; Andersson, 2001.
96 Van der Veen, 1997: 11–13.
97 Callender, 1989: 10–13; O'Malley, MEP, 1989: 13–16; Clark, 2002; Miller, 2003: 1–5; Baker, 1995: 10–11; McManus, 1997; FitzGerald, 1997: 4–6; Lee, 1997: 7–8.
98 McKay and Sullivan, 2014.
99 http://citizensincome.org/news/snp-conference-votes-for-citizens-income/, 09/06/2017.
100 Harris, 1981: 258.
101 Van Parijs and Vanderborght, 2017: 62–7; lecture by Philippe Van Parijs at the Foundation for International Social Security Studies conference at Sigtuna, Sweden, 6/06/2017.
102 International Labour Office, 2013: 6, 36.
103 Citizen's Income Trust, 2017c.
104 Creedy and Disney, 1985: 41.
105 www.nhs.uk/chq/Pages/888.aspx?CategoryID=68&, 28/04/2017. Prescriptions and dental care are subsidised.
106 The National Insurance Fund pays for National Insurance benefits and part of the cost of the National Health Service. Additional funding from general taxation is always required. National Insurance Contributions probably ought to be termed an 'earnings tax': www.publications.parliament.uk/pa/cm201314/cmhansrd/cm140225/debtext/140225-0001.htm, 07/06/2017.
107 Davis, Stremikis, Squires, and Schoen, 2014: 7.
108 Clarke, 2017.
109 For a detailed discussion of the economic and other efficiencies of the NHS, see Torry, 2018.
110 Gerlinger, 2009.
111 Hippe, 2009: 52–7.
112 Hinrichs and Jessoula, 2012: 244.
113 Dingeldey, 2009: 75–7.
114 Citizen's Income Trust, 2010.
115 Commission on Social Justice, 1994: 264–5.
116 This suggestion was made by Professor David Piachaud at a seminar at the London School of Economics on 9 November 2016.
117 Elliott, 2014a.
118 See Chapter 9 on pilot projects.
119 www.citizensincome.org; www.basicincome.org. BIEN first stood for 'Basic Income European Network', and when non-European organisations affiliated to it changed its name to 'Basic Income Earth Network' in order to retain the BIEN acronym.
120 http://citizensincome.org/news/the-green-party-reaffirms-its-commitment-to-a-citizens-income/, 28/04/2017.
121 http://citizensincome.org/news/citizens-income-news-may-2016/, 28/04/2017.
122 http://citizensincome.org/news/jeremy-corbyn-on-citizens-income-in-a-huffington-post-interview/, 28/04/2017.
123 http://basicincome.org/news/2017/01/france-hamon-becomes-socialist-party-presidential-candidate-following-basic-income-focused-campaign/, 28/04/2017.
124 See the appendix for a scheme that achieves this.
125 Citizen's Income Trust, 2017b: 1.

THREE

The economy, work and employment

An efficient economy

The financial crisis that began in 2008 has revealed that there is something not quite right about the way that we run our economy: reckless bank loans; debt being sold as a commodity; governments supporting the banks and reducing public expenditure; an increasing proportion of the proceeds of production going to capital, and a decreasing proportion to labour,[1] reducing demand and increasing personal debt.[2] As Galbraith puts the solution: '*Sufficient* equality in the distribution of income, within a country, is a proper goal of efficient economic policy, and is part of a strategy for shared prosperity and full employment; it is both effect and cause.'[3]

Trades unions used to extract from the proceeds of production a sufficient return to labour to enable households to consume the products of capitalism and thus maintain it in existence. This process is now in a state of collapse,[4] so we need to find a new way of redistributing income that ensures that we can increase rather than decrease economic efficiency.[5] Economic theory recognises that an original distribution of incomes is not necessarily the distribution required to achieve the most efficient allocation of resources. We shall need taxation that does not interfere with the preferences of those being taxed, so we shall need a tax that cannot be affected by the payee's behaviour. This is called a 'lump sum' tax.[6] A Citizen's Basic Income would be a negative lump sum tax, and so might be more efficient than benefits that can be affected by our behaviour.[7]

But how large should a Citizen's Basic Income be in order to maximise efficiency? Presumably quantity of supply needs to match quantity demanded.[8] This condition will be met if the level of the Citizen's Basic Income is equal to a subsistence income. However, the revenue required to pay such a Citizen's Basic Income needs to be collected in such a way as not to compromise economic efficiency, and it is difficult to see how lump sum taxes could achieve that. We shall therefore need to balance the efficiency offered by a Citizen's Basic Income with the inefficiency created by income tax and other taxation. Wherever we strike that balance, to move from a system of means-tested benefits to a system based on a Citizen's Basic Income cannot fail to improve economic efficiency, and we can conclude that a Citizen's Basic Income would provide a basis for reducing inequality at the same time as improving the efficiency of the economy:[9] a rare achievement.

However, in the context of existing market failure, an economy without taxes or benefits might in fact be less efficient than one with an appropriate tax and benefits system, particularly if public provision enhances human capital available to the economy,[10] and constitutes 'corporate welfare' that enhances business success.[11] As Atkinson suggests: 'When we allow for real-world phenomena like incomplete information and the absence of markets, it is conceivable that the payment of basic incomes, and the levying of the associated tax, may improve the allocation of resources.'[12]

Even if a Citizen's Basic Income scheme did not redistribute income on the first day of its implementation, by lowering marginal deduction rates for low earners it would enable them to increase their disposable incomes more easily, and it would therefore increase the spending power of workers in the lower earnings deciles. A Citizen's Basic Income would therefore be likely to share the output of the economy more evenly between the less well-off and the better-off, and, because poorer people spend a higher proportion of their incomes on goods and services in the national economy,[13] a Citizen's Basic Income would increase the consumption of goods and services, and would create a more efficient economy in which the real economy both produces what we need and provides us with the means for obtaining it. Eleanor Rathbone thought it an important argument for her proposed child allowances that there would be 'an increased demand for cotton frocks and woollen jerseys, for boots and coal'.[14] A Citizen's Basic Income could have the same effect.

To pre-empt an argument in the following section: a Citizen's Basic Income would facilitate a more flexible employment market at the same time as protecting individuals in the midst of such flexibility. A more flexible employment market would enable industries of all kinds to allocate labour more efficiently, thus making the economy more efficient.[15]

When these different factors work together and reinforce each other, we could be surprised at the increased economic efficiency that might be the result.

A changing employment market[16]

I grew up in Dartford, on the edge of London, and for most of my life I have lived close to the south bank of the Thames: a microcosm of our changing economy and changing employment market during the past 70 years.

By the 1930s, the whole of the South Bank, from Battersea to Erith, was dominated by manufacturing: heavy and electrical engineering, food processing, brewing, ship repairers and printing; and the south bank at Dartford and beyond by paper making, cement manufacture and Littlebrook Power Station.[17] During the Second World War, many of these companies turned to arms manufacture: but after the war they failed to update their machinery; the large labour forces gave trades union leaders considerable power in relation to managers, enabling workforces to resist change; and managers were either authoritarian or unrealistically benevolent, and showed little interest in innovation or in the competition building up around the world.[18] Industries began to close. From 1961 to 1966 there was a decline of 20% in the number of people employed in manufacturing in South London, and during the late 1960s warehouses and factories closed and remained empty. A particularly traumatic event was the loss of 5,000 jobs at AEI (Associated Electrical Industries) in 1968. By the end of the 1970s, heavy engineering had almost completely disappeared from South London, and, with it, vast numbers of full-time, semi-skilled male jobs. Office developments mushroomed during the 1960s and 1970s, and offices, homes and empty land now stand where major industrial premises once stood.[19]

My grandfather worked for Vickers Armstrong, a major engineering company on the South Bank, for his entire working life, first as a toolmaker and then in more senior roles. My father worked in public sector administration for his entire working life, occasionally moving from one local authority to another. Our three children, who are now in their late 20s and early 30s, represent a more contemporary pattern. One has already worked in engineering and software for several companies in the renewable energy industry, and is now working for companies on a contract basis; another has undertaken a variety of short-term and agency employments and now has full-time permanent employment in the charity sector; and the other has had a variety of employments and self-employments, sometimes being employed and self-employed at the same time, and is now a nurse working for an organisation contracted by the NHS.

No longer are there workforces of 5,000 on a single site, all in full-time employment. Increasing numbers of jobs are 'flexible', either geographically or organisationally; and an increasing number of individuals in a significant number of occupations now operate in the 'gig' economy, accessing very short-term employment on online platforms such as 'Uber'.[20]

For men, employment rates peaked in 1971 at 92% and have now decreased to 79.4%, and during the same period the employment rate for women has risen from 53% to 69.9%. The increasing presence of women in the employment market might help to explain another slight trend. Between 1995 and 2011, the average number of hours worked per week fell from 33.5 to 31.5, but that has now risen again to 32.4.[21]

Individual workforces are now smaller, institutional arrangements are diverse, no sector is immune from change, and the hardest hit workers have been the semi-skilled and those with skills related to particular industries.[22] Perhaps the most significant recent change has been towards zero-hour contracts: that is, contracts that do not guarantee a stated number of hours of employment per week. During the fourth quarter of 2016, 905,000 employed individuals (2.8% of people employed) were on such contracts: an increase of 101,000 on the same period just one year earlier.[23]

There are multiple reasons for these changes. One is technological change. The twentieth century saw colossal change: first of all the assembly line,[24] and then communication and information technology, enabled the principle of the assembly line to be applied to such industries as call centres.[25] Automation and computerisation are displacing low-paid and relatively low-skilled workers;[26] and because smaller numbers of workers can now control large-scale manufacturing processes, there are now few larger workforces, and the ability of trades unions to negotiate terms and conditions has declined. Low-skilled workers are still employed if their wages are low enough to compete with the costs of automation, so manufacturing has moved to countries where wage expectations and actual wages are low; and as we now live in a globalising economy, in which goods and services required in one place can easily be created in another, wage levels will continue to harmonise around the planet, and wages for low-skilled workers in the UK will eventually fall to the level of low-skilled workers in Shanghai.[27] Highly skilled workers will still be needed for complex design, cultural, technological, policy and management tasks that cannot be automated (yet): so the outcome is job polarisation, particularly in countries like the UK that have put too little effort into maintaining innovative manufacturing capability and upgrading their skills.[28] The result is an increasing division between individuals with permanent, secure, fulfilling and well-paid employment, within which they can progress in 'careers', and those with less secure, less well-paid and generally less fulfilling, employment:[29] that is, into 'insiders' and 'outsiders'.[30] Employment is now characterised by 'flexibility' and 'security': both somewhat ambiguous terms. 'Flexibility' can be a positive experience[31] if it means 'autonomy, creativity, freedom of manoeuvre, responsiveness, convenience, adaptability': but it can also mean 'precariousness, insecurity, contingency, marginalisation and instability'.[32]

Guy Standing lists the many different levels of security available under pre-1980s 'industrial citizenship' and compares them with the insecurities experienced by the 'precariat': a new pattern of existence that has now infected most occupational groups, for all of which 'labour is instrumental (to live), opportunistic (taking what comes) and precarious (insecure)'.[33] The phenomenon is global;[34] it leads to 'fluid and repeated movements between low-paid employment and benefits receipt'[35] and to labour being regarded as a commodity that is rewarded only financially.[36] Anxiety, alienation and information overload are some of the results; and now any of us can find ourselves in the precariat, doing 'work for labour':[37] that is, job-search and personal financial management.

The future trajectory is uncertain. The extent to which the employment market has in fact changed is debatable;[38] we cannot generalise about the employment market changes that we shall now see;[39] and a particularly significant area of uncertainty is the extent to which previously highly-paid and sought-after activities will be automated. We are now in the 'second machine age',[40] in which machines are now replacing human brain-power as well as human muscle-power. As higher education courses increasingly employ new information and communication technology, lecturers are finding themselves on short-term variable-hours contracts:[41] that is, in the precariat. We might find that few occupations are immune from this process, and that the 'middle classes' are as much in need of a Citizen's Basic Income as anyone else.[42]

Given all of these problems, should we not be resisting their causes, and particularly globalisation and technological change? No. First of all, these trends, if carefully handled, have much to offer;[43] secondly, any country that resists might find itself down a social and economic cul de sac and might continue to experience rapid economic and social change without the benefits of globalisation and technological change; and thirdly, economic renaissance might require rapid technological change, and might need the state to facilitate it.[44] What will be important will be enabling people to feel secure and to adapt to change: and particularly important will be income security, which can no longer be purely a function of the employment market. 'Upheaval in the market for jobs'[45] is now a significant cause of poverty; and the insecurity that so many suffer is now '"insecurity cubed" … job insecurity, insecurity caused by the welfare state, and that caused by technological change'.[46] How, in this situation, can we provide the financial security and the accompanying sense of security necessary for constructive functioning in employment markets that will be, and will need to be, increasingly flexible?[47] One requirement is clearly a 'welfare system that promises social security not greater insecurity';[48] and Standing's and Lansley and Mack's well-argued response is a Citizen's Basic Income,[49] because in an era of employment market and income insecurity we need a firm base on which to stand if we are going to be able to take the risks that we shall need to take if we are to thrive as individuals and as a society.[50] As Standing recognises, a more precarious lifestyle is not necessarily worse than one founded on a secure full-time job, and might offer possibilities which that did not, provided a certain level of security can protect us through the inevitable changes. After all, what we need is an income, and we need a job in order to provide to provide us with income:[51] so for the state to provide a secure income, even a small one, would mean that we could afford to be more flexible over paid employment. The UK's NHS has provided precisely the kind of secure healthcare foundation that we all need in a period of change and uncertainty. A secure income to match secure healthcare would go a long way towards making a more flexible employment market a creative reality for a lot more people.

What is not clear is the extent to which a Citizen's Basic Income ought to be allowed to 'price workers into many more jobs which at present do not pay enough for people to live on',[52] and to what extent a National Minimum Wage would still be required,[53] particularly if a Citizen's Basic Income's lowering of marginal deduction rates resulted in a significant increase in demand for jobs at the lower end of the earnings range.[54] The safest approach would be an empirical one. Following the implementation of a Citizen's Basic Income, a close watch would need to be kept on both wage levels and disposable incomes.

For a stable employment market of mainly full-time permanent employment, wage labour along with social insurance and means-tested safety nets can provide a secure disposable income: but no longer are full-time jobs and full-time workers the only norm. As researchers at the McKinsey Global Institute suggest, a more highly automated economy that results 'in a significant reduction in employment and/or greater pressure on wages, some ideas such as universal basic income, conditional transfers, and adapted social safety nets may need to be considered and tested'.[55] The problem is that we do not know what the employment effects of future rounds of automation and computerisation will be, as many tasks cannot be automated,[56] and new jobs will be created.[57] A diverse and unpredictable employment market requires a tax and benefits system that would suit *any* future employment market configuration, which suggests that a Citizen's Basic Income would be a good candidate if its effects on employment are likely to be advantageous.

A Citizen's Basic Income's effects on employment

The current benefits system imposes significant traps, whereas a Citizen's Basic Income would release us from them.

The precarity trap

The UK's benefits system can make employment market transitions extremely difficult, and can exacerbate the damage that a more flexible employment market can impose.[58] If someone on 'Tax Credits' loses their job then they will need to apply for Jobseeker's Allowance, or possibly for 'Universal Credit'. Either way, they will experience a significant administrative burden and might face a period without benefits payments. Someone already on 'Universal Credit' can experience similar problems as their employer will cease to provide information on their earnings, leading to miscalculated payments or a period without payment. And whatever someone is on, they will suddenly find themselves subject to work tests and an increasingly onerous sanctions regime,[59] as will someone not previously on in-work benefits. When someone finds a job, miscalculated and delayed payments are again a risk, and the administrative burden can be significant for both the worker and for Jobcentre staff. A string of short-term employments interspersed with periods of unemployment can be particularly difficult to handle; and just as difficult can be a series of zero-hour and part-time contracts, particularly if some of them are concurrent. By combining in-work and out-of-work means-tested benefits, 'Universal Credit' was designed to ease transitions between employment and unemployment, but it is little better than the previous benefits structure at coping with increasingly complex employment patterns, and its administrative methods are imposing a variety of new problems on claimants.[60]

Whether a household is on 'Tax Credits' or 'Universal Credit', the administrative complexity, and the uncertainty of outcomes, can become an unsustainable burden on the individual and their family,[61] and life becomes a matter of 'getting by' via a series of 'coping strategies'.[62] As McLaughlin has found: 'OECD comparisons of unemployment insurance and assistance systems concluded that it is the rules and administration of systems (e.g., seeking work tests) rather than the level of benefit paid which most affects the rate of unemployment.'[63]

It is entirely rational to wish to avoid unpredictable changes in household disposable income,[64] and the understandable consequence is either an increasing unwillingness to experience changes in employment status, or attempts to conceal such changes.

A Citizen's Basic Income would make a considerable difference. Most importantly, it would never stop, so the household's disposable income would have a secure base constructed out of household members' Citizen's Basic Incomes, whatever else was going on. For households in which their Citizen's Basic Incomes had taken them off means-tested benefits, there would no longer be administrative complexities to cope with, no longer would there be work tests to manage, and no longer would sanctions be feared. Depending on the details of the Citizen's Basic Income scheme, all or most households still receiving means-tested benefits would be on less of them, and the solid base that their Citizen's Basic Incomes provided would give them the option of deciding not to apply for means-tested benefits, but instead to build an income strategy based on a variety of kinds of employment and self-employment. In areas of high housing costs, a means-tested Housing Benefit would still be required,[65] but for a household that had previously been on 'Tax Credits' and Housing Benefit, or on 'Universal Credit' with its housing element, other means-tested benefits will have reduced or disappeared, providing more of an option to escape from Housing Benefit via a variety of employment options: options that would not previously have resulted in escape from means-tested benefits.

Marginal deduction rates

Because means-tested benefits are withdrawn as earned income rises, a household can suffer significant marginal deduction rates on additional earned income.[66] If a working-age adult has no paid employment and they face high marginal deduction rates if they find a job, then they are in the 'unemployment trap'.[67] If they are already in employment, and increasing their earned income would provide them with little additional disposable income, then they are in the 'poverty trap'. The extent to which marginal deduction rates are a disincentive is debatable, and it would appear that full-time employment is relatively inelastic in relation to marginal deduction rates (that is, as the rate of withdrawal of additional earnings increases, employment participation does not go down very much): but there can be an effect,[68] particularly in relation to part-time employment and the employment of someone whose spouse loses their job.[69] Often the individual will not be aware of the depth of the unemployment or poverty trap that they face when they make an employment market decision: but it only takes a couple of wage rises, or a couple of employment market transitions, for someone to discover how little additional disposable income is generated, and for realisation to dawn: that however much additional earned income they manage to put together, their household's disposable income will rise by very little. The disincentive effect will be cumulative over time. This is as much a concern to governments as it is to individuals in the traps, because in the context of means-tested benefits the desire to assist households with low incomes collides with the desire to incentivise employment.[70]

A Citizen's Basic Income would take a lot of households off means-tested benefits, and households still on them would be on them for narrower earnings ranges, providing far more possibility of escaping into an earnings range at which high marginal deduction rates would no longer apply. If Income Tax rates were raised in order to fund the Citizen's Basic Income, then households not in receipt of means-tested benefits would experience a small rise in their marginal deduction rate, suggesting a minor disincentive effect: but the change in low-income households' ability to increase their disposable incomes could be dramatic, providing immediate enhanced employment market incentives.[71]

All of this assumes that it is the overall marginal deduction rate that a household suffers that matters, whereas in fact the component relating to loss of benefits might be more psychologically significant than the component relating to increased income tax payments:[72] so to prevent benefit loss could have more of a positive effect on work effort than preventing tax increases. A complementary conclusion can be drawn from Thaler's finding that the certainty of not losing is preferable to uncertain gain or loss,[73] suggesting that a Citizen's Basic Income will always be preferable to a system containing only taxes and benefits that vary with uncertain earned income. Motivation is complex, but it would appear that a variety of effects of a Citizen's Basic Income would all tend to motivate work effort.

Part-time employment

At the moment, part-time employment in particular can add very little if anything to disposable income,[74] especially if a second earner in a household that receives 'Tax Credits' or 'Universal Credit' starts a low-paid part-time job.[75] A Citizen's Basic Income would enable a lot of households to escape from this trap, and would bring every household closer to escaping from it: and once off means-tested benefits, any number of hours of employment would add considerably and predictably to disposable income, so a wider variety of household employment patterns would become productive for the household. A full-time employee might choose to reduce their employment hours, or might take part-time employment and start their own business, making their life more flexible; or a non-earner might take part-time employment because it would enable their partner in full-time employment to avoid overtime.

Increasing choice in employment patterns

All of this shows that the current system restricts choice in the employment market, but a Citizen's Basic Income would enhance it. The current system imposes few problems on higher-paid individuals: but for low-paid individuals, there are few viable options. Full-time permanent employment is always a viable option for either earner in a couple: but part-time employment can impose high marginal deduction rates, and under 'Universal Credit' workers can find themselves subject to a sanctions regime that continues into paid employment.[76] Taking on a varying mixture of employments and self-employments can be particularly problematic: but it is precisely this option that might serve the needs of a low-skilled or medium-skilled household, and which might also serve the industries in which they are working.

By releasing individuals and households from a variety of traps, or bringing them within striking distance of such release, a Citizen's Basic Income would provide households with a larger number of viable employment options, leading to something closer to a classical free market in labour, and thus greater efficiency;[77] to families more able to balance employment with caring and community responsibilities;[78] to an increased ability to shorten the working week, with the benefits that that might bring;[79] and to a variety of individual freedoms in relation to employment: a greater ability to choose desired employment; a greater ability to leave a job and find a new one; and an enhanced ability for one's voice to be heard in the workplace[80] – although whether a threat to leave if one's voice is not heard would be credible would depend on a variety of factors.[81] Unemployment would be less feared, and wages would more nearly reflect the economic value of people's work, thus creating the conditions for rational industrial planning, for the modernisation of both manufacturing and service industries, and for genuine wage bargaining based on the value of the worker's labour.[82]

Education and training

If Britain is to compete in the global economy then it needs a highly skilled and highly educated adult population:[83] but what we have now is a school system still posited on the assumption that academic ability is what is required; a higher education system that attracts students by offering degrees too easy to pass (this is particularly true of postgraduate degrees in many of our universities); a student loans system that saddles young adults with a mountain of debt, and therefore discourages young people from entering higher education;[84] and spasmodic and unconvincing attempts to reinvent apprenticeships. This is not the place to discuss how best to create an education and training system suitable for a modern global economy, but the morass of funding systems, and their accompanying prohibitions, really do not help. A simple unconditional income for 16 to 21 year olds, alongside high-quality training and education, would be a colossal incentive to people to educate and train themselves for the kind of economy that we shall need.

But just as important is encouraging people to retrain and to undertake continuing training. At the moment there is little incentive to do so. Why spend time and money on training in order to retain employment, or to move into new and growing industries, when most of any increase in pay will be taken away? If an increase in earnings were to translate into an increase in net income then there would be rather more incentive to train or retrain. In the same way that Beveridge made Family Allowances a presupposition of his contributory benefits system,[85] we ought now to make a Citizen's Basic Income a presupposition of both income maintenance and education and training policies.

A benefits system appropriate to any future employment market

Is Citizen's Basic Income 'a partial admission of a failure in the organisation of social and economic affairs [because] such schemes implicitly concede that a significant section of the population will be excluded from full economic and social participation'?[86] No, it is not. As we have seen, Citizen's Basic Income would facilitate the efficient functioning of an employment market and would incentivise employment of various kinds at the same time as protecting incomes as the employment market changes.

In the next chapter we shall be studying how a Citizen's Basic Income would provide a level of autonomy and therefore make it easier to enter a new personal relationship. In much the same way, a Citizen's Basic Income, by providing every individual with a level of economic autonomy, would make it easier to enter a new employment relationship.[87] If you know that you will receive your Citizen's Basic Income before, during and after this new relationship, then the risks attached to entering the relationship will be reduced.

The question, both in relation to personal relationships, and in relation to employment relationships, is this: should social policy create change in society, or should it adapt to change? If we want to create change, then we shall need to work out what changes we want to impose on the employment market and then design tax and benefits systems accordingly. If we want to adapt to trends rather than to cause them, then we shall need to refashion our tax and benefits systems to match changes occurring in society, the economy and the employment market. Leaving the current tax and benefits systems as they are is not an option. They might fit previous employment patterns, but they will no longer fit the way that employment is now, nor how it might look in the future. Only if society, the economy and the employment market are now as we might wish them to be, if they will never change, and if the current tax and benefits systems fit the way they are, should we leave things alone. This is rather unlikely, which means that the tax and benefits systems, as currently organised, will need to change, and to change constantly.

Unfortunately, change is expensive and disruptive, and it also tends to be inefficient.[88] This raises an interesting question: if we do not wish to have to change the system too often, then what kind of system should we seek? That is: what kind of system will serve the greatest possible variety of social and economic configurations? The answer is simple: the simplest possible system.

We simply do not know how the employment market will evolve in the future. We can predict that income redistribution of some kind will continue to be required, that redistribution of the proceeds of production from capital to labour might become more of a necessity,[89] and that it will remain desirable to distribute paid employment as widely as possible:[90] but predicting the shape of employment patterns will not be easy. A Citizen's Basic Income's ability to redistribute paid work at the same time as redistributing buying power, and its suitability to a wide variety of employment market patterns makes it an excellent candidate for the foundation of any future economy. Far from a distraction from seeking to meet the goal of full employment,[91] a Citizen's Basic Income could make the goal more achievable. A major requirement for individuals and households in a context of unpredictable change is a secure income floor that incentivises economic activity and provides as many choices as possible; and a major requirement for businesses in a context of economic and social change is an employment market that is as efficient as possible.[92] Only a Citizen's Basic Income can provide all of that.[93]

'Work'

A useful aim of any tax and benefits system is that it should not disincentivise productive labour or household formation. A rather different question is this: should our benefits system positively promote certain public goods?

To take an example: it is generally a good thing for children, older people and people with disabilities to be cared for by family members. It is therefore important that our benefits system should not discriminate against carers. Part-time rather than full-time employment is more likely to fit in with caring responsibilities, whereas our current system, based as it is on the assumption of full-time employment, disincentivises unpaid care work. A Citizen's Basic Income, by making part-time employment more beneficial, would impose fewer disincentives.

But should our benefits system positively *value* unpaid care work, as the UK's Carer's Allowance does to some extent?[94] A Citizen's Basic Income would make it easier for people to spend time on care work, but because the Citizen's Basic Income would be paid to everyone, whether or not they were caring for family members, it would not ascribe a value to care work and would not be perceived to do so. It is for this reason that Ruth Lister is ambivalent towards a Citizen's Basic Income. Only a benefit restricted to people undertaking care work within the family would positively ascribe a value to such work. However, Lister does recognise that a Citizen's Basic Income would help to share employment more evenly across the working-age population and that it would break the income/work relationship, thus both economically and psychologically freeing carers, and particularly women carers, to pursue more varied work–life patterns if they should wish to do so.[95]

The word 'work' can encompass a wide range of activity, both paid and unpaid, both individual and corporate, and a Citizen's Basic Income, by disconnecting work and income, would ascribe value to all kinds of work[96] and would create a level playing field between paid employment, care work and voluntary activity in and for the community.[97] A Citizen's Basic Income would promote a more gender-inclusive citizenship 'without reinforcing the existing gendered distribution of labour or the primacy of the public sphere';[98] it would 'increase the amount of work done both paid and unpaid, ... people would *willingly* be in the employment market, or *willingly* out of it; this surely cannot but help job satisfaction, productivity, and human welfare'.[99] A Citizen's Basic Income would give to people greater control over their use of time, and would therefore increase a country's level of equality;[100] and because a Citizen's Basic Income would be income received on the basis of one's citizenship or legal residence, it would recognise every aspect of our engagement with society.

Participation in society, through caring work among family members and neighbours, and through community activity, is essential to our society and to our economy; and alongside paid employment it constitutes the reciprocity that in the public mind has to underlie any provision of an income,[101] including incomes provided with the intention of enhancing our freedom:[102] which does *not* mean that a participation test should be applied to Citizen's Basic Incomes.[103] A Citizen's Basic Income could enable us to participate in a wider variety of ways, giving us lives more characterised by 'variety and stability, freedom and security ... true human flourishing consists in varied and integrated lives, overcoming the division of labour and the one-sided humans it produces, encouraging all to engage in many types of activity as far as possible'.[104]

Who is contributing more to society – the man employed in a full-time post designing a machine to make cigarettes, or the unpaid volunteer taking older and disabled people to their hospital appointments?[105] For many people, the options are too limited. A Citizen's Basic Income could help to broaden them.

Conclusion

We have seen that a Citizen's Basic Income would serve today's changing employment market, but that that is far less relevant than whether it would serve the employment market as it continues to change. A system designed for the ways in which our society, economy and employment market worked 70 years ago is unlikely to be useful today or tomorrow. Similarly, systems designed with today's employment market and economy in mind will be unlikely to be useful in 10 years' time. It is time to stop discussing the detail of today's welfare state and to start discussing the income maintenance system that we shall need in a *changing* future. The only way to approach a world of change is to design systems that will be robust in the face of rapid and unpredictable change. The more system variables there are that might or might not suit a future social and economic configuration, the less likely it is that the system will serve our future needs. We therefore need to remove the variables. An individual-based, nonwithdrawable and unconditional benefit is the only one to fit this condition. As Robert Goodin puts it:

> the best response to the destandardisation of life would be to abandon conditionality … . Let's give up trying to second-guess how people are going to lead their lives and crafting [category-based] responses to the problems they might encounter. Instead, simply give them the money and let them get on with it.[106]

Only national governments can pursue this agenda: so it is time for the UK's government to promote a well-informed and wide-ranging debate, and the research necessary to make that debate intelligent.

As with other innovations, it is the first movers who will reap the benefits of innovation. For the UK to replace the employment age social compact[107] with a postmodern one[108] before others get there first would enable our economy, our employment market and our social structures to adapt to new global conditions more quickly than would be possible for other countries. This would provide the UK with both economic and social advantages: and post-Brexit we are going to be sorely in need of those. And because the Citizen's Basic Income would cohere with any future changes in the employment market, first-mover benefits would continue to operate until other countries established their own Citizen's Basic Incomes.

49

Notes

[1] Piketty, 2014: 199–234, original emphasis.
[2] Lansley, 2011a: 12, 14; Lansley, 2011b.
[3] Galbraith, 2002: 224.
[4] Mason, 2015.
[5] Spicker, 2000: 169.
[6] Hindriks and Myles, 2006: 38–9, 373–5.
[7] Mason, 2015: 284–6.
[8] Spicker, 2000: 169.
[9] Zelleke, 2005.
[10] Costabile, 2008: 225–31.
[11] Farnsworth, 2012: 42.
[12] Atkinson, 1989a: 13.
[13] Ehrenfreund, 2015; Hobijn and Nussbacher, 2015.
[14] Eleanor Rathbone, quoted in Levitas, 2012: 451.
[15] Van Parijs, 1990b: 19–21.
[16] Torry, 1996.
[17] Avery, 1963: 148.
[18] Sedwick, 1974: 127.
[19] Keeble, 1978; Martin and Seaman, 1974.
[20] www.feps-europe.eu/assets/a82bcd12-fb97-43a6-9346-24242695a183/crowd-working-surveypdf.pdf, 10/06/2017.
[21] Spence, 2011: 2, 9, 10; Office for National Statistics, 2017a.
[22] Evans and Williams, 2009: 306.
[23] Office for National Statistics, 2017b.
[24] Braverman, 1974; Blauner, 1964.
[25] Taylor and Bain, 1999; Ritzer, 2000: 13–14; Ritzer, 2010: 77.
[26] Lawrence, 2017; Arntz, Gregory and Zierahn, 2016.
[27] Hawkins, 2011: 15–16.
[28] Goos and Manning, 2007; Elliott, 2017.
[29] Padfield, 2011; Shildrick, MacDonald, Webster and Garthwaite, 2012.
[30] Jordan, 1998: 65.
[31] Maitland and Thomson, 2014: 48, 206.
[32] Huws, 1997: 13, 21, 37, 39.
[33] Standing, 2011b: 14.
[34] On Canada's experience, see Swift, Balmer and Dineen, 2010: 25.
[35] Patrick, 2017b: 197.
[36] Standing, 2009.
[37] Standing, 2011b: 117, 120.
[38] Doogan, 2009: 1–21; Coats, 2012; Booth, 2017.
[39] Eichhorst and Marx, 2015.
[40] Brynjolfsson and McAfee, 2014; Floridi, 2014.
[41] University and College Union, 2016.
[42] Barnes, 2014.
[43] Mason, 2015; Bregman, 2017; Srnicek and Williams, 2015.
[44] Mullan, 2017.
[45] Lansley and Mack, 2015: 89.
[46] Painter, 2016a: 93.
[47] Mowshowitz, 1994: 287.

48 Shildrick, MacDonald, Webster and Garthwaite, 2012: 223.
49 Standing, 2011b: 41, 171–3; Standing, 2014: 316–38; Lansley and Mack, 2015: 237.
50 Wong, 2012.
51 Lemieux, 2014: 15, 28.
52 Gamble, 2016: 109.
53 Gray, 2014.
54 Gray, 2017.
55 Manyika, 2017.
56 Arntz, Gregory and Zierahn, 2016.
57 Manyika, 2017.
58 Dean, 2012a; Dean, 2012b.
59 Edmiston, Patrick and Garthwaite, 2017.
60 Keohane and Shorthouse, 2012; www.bbc.co.uk/news/uk-politics-41433019, 02/11/2017.
61 Standing, 2011b.
62 Edmiston, 2017: 266.
63 McLaughlin, 1994: 2; cf Atkinson, 1985: 9; Atkinson, 1995: 130–53.
64 Jordan, James, Kay and Redley, 1992; Smithies, 2007.
65 See Chapter 11 on this problem.
66 See the note on terminology at the beginning of the book for an explanation of marginal deduction rates.
67 Parker, 1995: 27.
68 Emmerson, Johnson and Miller, 2014: 161.
69 Atkinson and Mogensen, 1993: 191.
70 Adam, Brewer and Shephard, 2006: 1.
71 Martinelli, 2017b: abstract.
72 Avram, 2015.
73 Thaler, 2015: 33–4.
74 Torry, 2008.
75 Cory, 2013.
76 See Chapter 10 on psychological aspects of this problem.
77 Roberts, 1982: 13.
78 Purdy, 1988: 234.
79 Coote, Franklin and Simms, 2010.
80 Casassas, 2016; Herzog, 2016.
81 Birnbaum and De Wispelaere, 2016.
82 Walter, 1989: 101, 113.
83 Mayhew, 1995: 13–15.
84 Berg, 2010.
85 Beveridge, 1942: 154, 157, 163.
86 Auerbach, 2016: 369.
87 Offe, 2008: 23.
88 Because only government department insiders know the minimum resource requirements for efficient delivery of a public service, because ministers do not know, and because insiders inevitably maximise resource requirements in order to maximise the size of their departments and to provide a cushion against future hard times, the only way for ministers to control budgets is to reduce the budget until the public service is seen to suffer. However, this only works if the service delivery structure stays the same. (NHS reforms have been highly inefficient because

ministers have attempted to make savings at the same time as they changed the structure.) By constantly tinkering with the tax and benefits systems, successive governments have suffered additional unpredictable administrative costs. A Citizen's Basic Income would be modelled on a known system, Child Benefit, so costs can be confidently predicted.

[89] Esping-Andersen, 1994: 182–3.

[90] Piachaud, 2016: 17.

[91] Piachaud, 2016: 17.

[92] www.europeanceo.com/business-and-management/is-unconditional-basic-income-the-reform-europe-needs/, 07/06/2017; Van Parijs, 1990b.

[93] Piven, 1994: 189.

[94] www.gov.uk/carers-allowance/overview, 25/06/2017.

[95] Lister, 1997: 189–90.

[96] McKay, 2005: 182–224; Robertson, 1988: 23–5.

[97] Jordan, 2008: 250.

[98] Zelleke, 2011: 38.

[99] Walter, 1989: 56.

[100] Haagh, 2011.

[101] White, 2003: 168.

[102] Van Parijs, 1995: 2, 89, 96, 133; Widerquist, 2013: 15; Srnicek and Williams, 2015: 126–7.

[103] See Chapter 11 on the proposal for a Participation Income.

[104] Hughes, 2007: 232.

[105] Pasma, 2010: 7.

[106] Goodin, 2001: 93.

[107] Ashdown, 1990; Ashdown, 1992; Silva, Ponti, Balzarotti and Dore, 1995.

[108] Robertson, 1996.

FOUR

Individuals and their families

The message of this chapter is similar to that of the last one: our tax and benefits structure should reflect today's family and household patterns, and should remain serviceable as household and family patterns continue to change.

So we shall begin with a discussion of the ways in which households and the family have changed during the past half century; and then ask what kind of benefits system today's families require, and how that compares with the benefits system constructed in an era with rather different social structures. Finally we shall ask what kind of benefits system will most benefit women and enhance individual dignity.

The changing family[1]

Whereas a generation ago someone might have lived with their parents until they married and moved in with a partner, or moved in with a partner and then married, today the only generalisation that we can make is that the situation is diverse. A young adult might share a house or a flat with people they know, or with people they don't. If they have a partner, whether of the same gender or of a different gender, then they might live apart, they might live together, or they might rotate regularly through a variety of household patterns. A mother and her child might live with the child's father, might leave him and move in with the child's grandmother (on either side), and might then form a household with a friend and her child. Are we discussing families or households here? The fact that we can use the two terms almost interchangeably, and that precise definitions of either of them are difficult to construct, is symptomatic of the fluid nature of today's social structures.

We have known some of the basic trends for some time, but research undertaken for the Centre for the Modern Family shows just how diverse families in the UK now are, and how diverse people's attitudes to the family are too. In 1961, 38% of families consisted of a married couple with two or more children, but by 2011 'just 16% of the UK population believe that they fit the "traditional model". In short, there has been a meltdown in the traditional nuclear family.'[2]

The number of households containing six or more people rose 25% between 2001 and 2011; and London had the highest proportion (3.9%) of households with six or more people, and saw the largest proportional increase between 2001 and 2011 at almost 50%.[3] At the same time, average household size decreased from 3.1 persons in 1961 to 2.4 persons in 2011. A smaller proportion of households in Great Britain had children living in them in 2010 than in 1961, and the average household with children had fewer children than before. The most common type of family in the UK in 2010 contained one child (46.3% of all families in 2010). The number of people living alone increased from 7 million to 7.5 million between 2001 and 2010; and more couples have delayed having children or have remained childless: another reason for smaller families. A woman in a reasonably well-paid job, and particularly a woman in a career in which progress relies on staying involved, will now think twice about having children. Having children carries an opportunity cost: a loss of income and status if the mother looks after the children herself, or the cost of the tensions that she will face if she hires childcare. A woman might think the cost worth it, but she might not; and having decided not to have children, or not to have children yet, she might eventually decide to have them when she can no longer put it off, and might therefore have fewer children and face a greater risk of not being able to have children at all. In 1971, nearly four out of five births in England and Wales were to women aged under 30, but by 2009 only half were to women in this age group.

Significant recent changes in the UK have of course been the introduction of civil partnerships in 2004, and then same-sex marriage in 2014. In 2014 there were 4,850 same-sex marriages in England and Wales, and in 2015 there were 1,671 in Scotland. These figures are similar for those relating to civil partnerships in previous years.[4] If these rates continue then over time same-sex marriages will constitute an increasing proportion of households in the UK.

A hundred years ago, extramarital births were comparatively rare, and the vast majority of marriages were ended by the death of one of the partners. Change has been substantial in both of these areas. In 1971, 8.4% of all live births were outside marriage; by 1991 it was 30.2%; and in 2011 it was 46.2%. Lone-parent families increased from 14.8% of the total in 2001 to 16.2% in 2010.[5] Patricia Morgan suggests that a major cause of this trend is the 'flexible employment market', which gives to men few prospects of secure employment, resulting in 'whole communities in which it is very difficult to establish and maintain families, with almost insuperable obstacles to family formation at the bottom of the socioeconomic ladder':[6] a ladder increasingly shaky and difficult to climb.[7]

One of the worst features of the current tax and benefits system in the UK is that it divides our society in two and imposes different sets of regulations on taxpayers and benefits recipients. Individuals pay Income Tax, but couples receive means-tested benefits such as Jobseeker's Allowance,[8] 'Tax Credits'[9] or 'Universal Credit'.[10] Why do more people not question this difference in treatment? If my wife's earned income was paid to me, or I needed to know her income in order to complete my tax return, or if a tax inspector were to come round to find out who I was living with, then I would be justifiably furious, and she might be too. But that is precisely how Jobseeker's Allowance, 'Tax Credits' and 'Universal Credit' operate. A joint claim has to be made, and whoever fills in the form has to know both partners' incomes. My wife chooses to tell me her income and I tell her mine, but that is a choice that we make. If we were claiming 'Tax Credits' then we would not have a choice to make: one of us would have to know the other's income; and if someone is claiming Income Support or 'Tax Credits' as an individual when they ought to be claiming as a couple, and someone who bears a grudge betrays them, then a fraud investigator might take a look at their relationship.

Calculating benefits on the basis of the household, rather than on an individual basis, reduces the employment incentive for the spouse of a full-time earner, reduces couples' incentive to live together, might reduce children's parents' incentive to live together,[11] and, alongside all of these difficulties, makes it necessary for benefits administrators to investigate the private lives of claimants in order to find out who is living with whom. Esam and Berthoud suggest that it would be possible to individualise current benefits, and that 'if the relationships between men and women ... continue to change at the pace of the last decade, the assumption of dependence built into the benefit system will have to be tackled eventually'.[12] When a government implements a Citizen's Basic Income, the individual must be the claimant, not one person on behalf of the household or family.[13]

To the objection that individualised benefits payments fail to promote marriage, we can say this: it is household-based payments that might be driving couples apart, and might be driving apart the parents of children. If a couple were to be allowed to keep the economies of scale generated by living together, if my employment incentives had nothing to do with my spouse's earnings, and if I were to receive the income to which I was entitled rather than my spouse getting it, then I would be *more* likely to stay in the marriage or the relationship, not less. It is the *current* system, which reserves to the government the economies of scale related to household composition,[14] and then calculates means-tested benefits accordingly, that corrodes marriage and long-term relationships.[15] A Citizen's Basic Income would be paid at the same rate to every individual of the same age, would be neutral between different household structures,[16] and would enable households to benefit from the economies of scale that they generate.[17] At the moment, someone living alone and receiving means-tested benefits who moves in with someone earning a living is likely to lose the whole of their independent income (apart from Child Benefit if they have children). This is a big risk for people to take;[18] and 'in this context, resisting economic dependency by retaining lone-parent status, by living apart from a partner or child's father, or by remaining unpartnered, can be seen as a means of managing and mitigating risk under conditions of economic and relationship uncertainty'.[19]

With a Citizen's Basic Income, the non-earning woman or man would lose their 'financial dependent' status[20] and would know that they would be able to leave any partnership with an independent income intact, thus making it more likely that they might form a new relationship; and the fact that a Citizen's Basic Income would not be withdrawn as earnings rose would make it more likely that they would seek employment once in the new relationship. Research has shown that children whose parents are in employment have a better experience of childhood than children whose parents are not, *and* that parental childcare has considerable benefits. Enabling parents to stay together and to balance both employment and sufficient time to care for their own children should therefore be a priority.[21]

As Paul Spicker puts it: 'We cannot ask claimants to live simpler, more orderly lives', so we need to rid the benefits system of its complexity by addressing its current 'conditionality, administrative rules and administrative procedures'.[22] Change in household and family structures can only accelerate. A benefits system containing a Citizen's Basic Income would go a long way towards meeting the needs of today's families and households, and also the needs of families and households of the future, whatever relational, employment market and economic structures they might turn out to have; and a Citizen's Basic Income would at the same time facilitate the kinds of stable families that children need, whatever other social changes might be taking place.

The changing role of women

While the changing role of women is of course bound up with the ways in which families and the employment market are changing, it is still important to discuss the ways in which the current tax and benefits systems affect women, and the ways in which a Citizen's Basic Income might also affect them.

The world for which William Beveridge designed the welfare state that we are still living with contained 'happily married, single-earner couples, widows (no widowers) and single people living either alone or with their parents ... in devising his Plan, Beveridge also assumed that virtually all poverty was and would continue to be due to interruption or loss of earnings, or to the presence of children in the family.'[23] Decreasing numbers of women live in the kinds of family that Beveridge envisaged; childcare and the care of older and disabled relatives are still mainly undertaken by women; and women are therefore more likely than men to take career breaks, pauses or decelerations. For this and other reasons, the average full-time earned income of women is well below that of men.[24] However, part-time hourly rates for women are higher than those for men.[25] This suggests that women are more likely to be working part time in the higher-paid occupations.[26] While the man in a marriage or partnership is not now the default claimant where claims have to be made on the basis of the couple rather than as individuals, the fact that claims are not made by individuals, and that distribution of money within the household is not always equitable,[27] means that women often do worse out of means-tested benefits than men do.[28], [29] Increasing Child Benefit would increase women's control over resources, as would individualising means-tested benefits. A Citizen's Basic Income would immediately help, of course, because each individual would be paid their own Citizen's Basic Income.[30]

Unfortunately, the inequality experienced by women persists into old age: a result of the increasing importance of private and occupational pension provision, and of the contributory nature of the Basic State Pension.[31] While more recent attempts to repair women's National Insurance Contributions records mean that younger women will now accrue records similar to those accrued by men, there are still women with lower Basic State Pensions because they do not possess full contributions records;[32] and because women tend to have fewer years in full-time employment, and their earned incomes tend on average to be below men's earned incomes, the pension rights that they build up are not as substantial as those accrued by men.[33]

We are beginning to build up a picture of continuing inequality, and of a scenario in which women in the UK are more likely to be poor than men. In the United States the picture is similar because adequate benefits, both publicly and privately provided, are closely tied to people's employment records.[34] Readers elsewhere will be aware of the situations in their own countries. I suspect that it will be similar, whether that country is more or less developed in terms of its economy and infrastructure.

But the world *is* changing, and many women now face three broad categories of lifestyle choice: 1. a life centred on career opportunities, 2. a life centred on family obligations, and 3. a role in which women adapt or compromise at various stages in their lifecycle depending on the opti ons available. Different social policy configurations will privilege or disadvantage different options.[35] Given that women are likely to want all three options to be available, an option-neutral policy bundle would clearly be preferable, and this suggests a benefits system based on a Citizen's Basic Income. Like Child Benefit, a Citizen's Basic Income would in no way constrain choice, and, in comparison with today's configuration, it would considerably enhance it.

A Citizen's Basic Income would not on its own generate equal status and equal net incomes for women and men,[36] and because it would enable women more easily to follow their lifestyle preferences, and because those preferences are to some extent constructed by an unjust society that ascribes an unpaid caring role to women, it is possible that a Citizen's Basic Income could entrench gender inequality by implicitly valuing the caring role.[37] However, because a Citizen's Basic Income would treat women and men equally, and because Child Citizen's Basic Incomes would normally be paid to the mother, every individual woman would experience at least some equalisation of their situation in relation to the gender division of income, and every mother would experience an even larger increase in unconditional income. The overall effect would be that women's financial positions would improve in relation to men's;[38] and because a Citizen's Basic Income of any size would reduce the marginal deduction rates that apply to additional earnings, it would be more worthwhile for a woman to seek employment or additional employment, and she would therefore be more likely to do so. A Citizen's Basic Income would therefore value both the caring and the earning roles, and because it would be more possible for two members of a couple to decide that they would both be employed part time, rather than one of them full time and one not at all, both their caring responsibilities and their earned incomes could be more equally distributed than they might be today, creating a greater gender equality in the home.[39] In the absence of such additional policies as the increased availability of childcare, and in the presence of continuing prejudice, we shall of course continue to see gender inequality:[40] but that is hardly the fault of a Citizen's Basic Income.

Should the state treat women as different from men, or should it treat them in the same way as it treats men? This question defines 'Wollstonecraft's dilemma', which in more practical terms asks this: should social policy recognise that typically male work and typically female work are in practice different, and find a way of rewarding them equally (the 'male breadwinner' model), or should it treat everyone the same, whatever activity they choose to undertake (the 'adult worker' model)?[41] A Citizen's Basic Income would make more possible for everyone a 'work-care' model, thus resolving the dilemma;[42] and because a Citizen's Basic Income would enhance women's financial independence,[43] recognise the value of care work, understand the rights of children,[44] make part-time jobs pay, redistribute somewhat from men to women,[45] and debureaucratise the state,[46] it would provide women and men with a more level playing field.[47]

The individual's dignity

Stigma is felt by a person who is stigmatised by another individual, by a community, or by society at large. Goffman lists three types of stigma: 'physical deformities', 'blemishes of individual character', and 'the tribal stigma of race, nation, and religion'.[48] It is the second of these that operates in the context of the benefits system. We stigmatise people who find themselves subject to means testing by ascribing their being in that situation to their weakness of character. At the root of stigma is the stigmatiser's fear of being in the situation of the person stigmatised, so if we are not on means-tested benefits ourselves then we might stigmatise people who find themselves on means-tested benefits because we fear being in their situation. This means that we might stigmatise ourselves if we are on means-tested benefits and have no wish to be. We experience shame: a global phenomenon among people who are poor relative to the economic norms of their societies.[49] Whether or not we are on means-tested benefits ourselves, the stigma attached to individuals who are on them results in the benefits themselves being stigmatised in the public mind, which is why it is easy for a government to reduce their levels[50] and to apply onerous sanctions to their recipients.

Both the overall structure and the detailed regulations of benefits communicate to us society's valuation of us,[51] and research shows that means-tested benefits impose a more negative image of the recipient and generate more stigma than either contributory or more universal benefits systems.[52] But why should we not wish to be on means-tested benefits, and why do we stigmatise people who are on them? Again, the cause is complex, but a factor must be the bureaucratic intrusion required by means testing: an intrusion into our lives by people whom we do not know and probably have no wish to know. A typical claim for a means-tested benefit might begin with a face-to-face interview with someone younger than ourselves who asks us for detailed personal information about our household, our living arrangements and the sources of our income. We have to provide them with evidence, which suggests that they do not believe us. Then a decision is made about how much benefit we will receive, and we do not know how that decision was made or who made it. 'Discretion' has been exercised in our direction,[53] setting up 'relationships of domination and subordination, within which supplication becomes a standard mode of conduct'.[54] All of this is demeaning, and it results in a self-stigmatising if we are going through it, or the stigmatising of someone else if they are going through it. Particularly demeaning are the often perfunctory 'work-related' interviews[55] integral to so-called 'active labour market policies'. Underlying such interviews is the assumption that the person interviewed will only seek employment if they are coerced into it, whereas the truth is that the increasingly onerous sanctions regime and the lack of employment opportunities have demotivated them, and the complexities of the benefits system make them hesitant about attempting any change in their employment market status.[56]

Given the aggravation and stigma attached to 'active labour market' policies, Hartley Dean wonders whether putting in-work and out-of-work means-tested benefits together into 'Universal Credit' might have the unintended consequence of increasing the stigma attached to means-tested benefits. At the moment, the 'virtuous worker', who believes that work is a virtuous taking of responsibility, can receive a means-tested benefit, Working Tax Credits, and still separate their self-image from their image of the out-of-work recipient of means-tested benefits. This is possible because Working Tax Credit was given a name different from Jobseeker's Allowance or Income Support in order to reduce stigma,[57] and because it operates with a different set of regulations. With 'Universal Credit' the employed worker will no longer be able to escape the stigma attaching to means-tested benefits paid to unemployed workers.[58]

The way round this problem is to provide exactly the same 'benefit' for everyone. No stigma attaches to Child Benefit: either to the benefit itself or to its recipients. The claim process is not intrusive, and everyone with a child receives Child Benefit. Similarly, receipt of a Citizen's Basic Income would be entirely without stigma,[59] and it would, as Tony Walter puts it, 'replace structural guilt with a universal structure of acceptance and forgiveness'.[60] If the non-earner, the low-wage earner and the highest-paid executive in the country, were all to receive the same income from the state, then receiving it could not possibly carry any stigma, and the benefits in terms of social cohesion could be considerable. A Norwegian research project has found that being on means-tested benefits reduces levels of interpersonal trust, but that universal benefits increase them,[61] presumably because they generate a kind of well-being that is collaborative rather than individual.[62] Because a Citizen's Basic Income would go to every individual, it would provide for every individual the 'recognition' that we need for good individual and social functioning;[63] it would create a whole new sense of social cohesion in place of increasing social fragmentation;[64] it would lay the foundation for a 'social citizenship' based on trust, inclusion, and reciprocity;[65] and it would foster the kind of trust, cooperation and social capital exchange required to sustain a welfare state. [66] No longer would we be divided into resentful workers (subject to tax regulations) and supplicant non-workers (subject to benefits regulations), and no longer into a 'them and us' defined by whether or not we receive means-tested benefits.[67]

As well as social cohesion, we would find social welfare,[68] individual welfare, and productivity enhanced,[69] not to mention the significant increase in self-worth that would be experienced by individuals and households able to come off means-tested benefits.[70] While a means-tested system imposes substantial loss of self-worth on everyone involved (including the civil servants who have to operate the system: something that this author discovered when engaged in administering means-tested benefits), a Citizen's Basic Income would positively enhance self-worth; and because a Citizen's Basic Income would impose no stigma or complexity, and because no benefit could be easier to understand, take-up would be almost 100%[71] – unlike the current means-tested system, in which stigma leads to low take-up that not only exacerbates, but also masks poverty.[72]

As Richard Titmuss has suggested, 'poor quality selective services for poor people were the product of a society that saw "welfare" as a residual, as a public burden'.[73] Universal and unconditional benefits, on the other hand, go to everyone, and so are more likely to remain of high quality;[74] and because they benefit everyone, they make 'welfare' into something that we share, something that we ensure that everyone experiences, and something to which everyone contributes according to their means. If a system is based on support for everyone, poor people will also be helped. If it supports only the poor, some are likely to be excluded.[75] Selective schemes generate stigma, whereas universal provision does not.[76] The way to get rid of stigma, and to ensure that everyone receives the income that they need, is obvious.

Conclusion

Households can find themselves in multiple traps. We have already met the unemployment trap, the poverty trap, the part-time trap, and the lack-of-skills trap in the previous chapter. The 'invalidity trap' refers to a situation where, because of disability or long-term illness, someone's 'earnings potential net of tax is low in relation to out-of-work benefits'.[77] Employment market entry can require a flexible approach to the number of hours worked, but this can be administratively difficult under the present benefits system. It would be a lot easier with a Citizen's Basic Income, because the Citizen's Basic Income would never change. The 'lone-parent trap' – the additional costs associated with employment that make it less feasible for lone parents to seek employment – is not as serious now as it was in 1995 when Hermione Parker was writing about the many traps that households suffer, [78] because the way in which childcare costs are now taken into account when benefits are calculated gives more recognition to the level of childcare costs incurred. However, the 'lone-parent trap' can, as we have seen, have another meaning as well: that the benefits system can impose penalties on marriage and other relationships.[79]

We have already met in Chapter 2 the new Single Tier State Pension, which will help to ameliorate the 'savings trap'. Many retired people today might be receiving a Basic State Pension, a State Second Pension (if they worked for an employer that was not contracted out), one or more occupational pensions, and a private pension: and they might also have personal savings. If that is not enough to live on then they will receive a means-tested pension – Pension Credit – made up of a Guarantee Credit and a Savings Credit.[80] It is the Pension Credit that causes the problem. Any gap between pension income and a specified minimum (in 2017, £159.35 for single people, and £243.25 for couples) is filled by a Guarantee Credit, which takes into account personal savings. A separate Savings Credit used to be paid, but it is no longer paid for new claims. Instead, the new Single Tier State Pension is being rolled out.[81] This will raise the Basic State Pension to the specified minimum, and will take numerous elderly households off means-tested Pension Credit.[82] No longer will savings reduce the value of the state pension, so many elderly households will find it more worthwhile to save for retirement.

While the 'savings trap' is normally understood in relation to saving for old age, there is of course a more general savings trap.[83] All means-tested benefits take savings into account when benefits are calculated: which means that for any household that might potentially find itself on means-tested benefits, saving is disincentivised. This is counterproductive because saving reduces the risk of poverty.[84] Just as the savings trap in relation to pension provision would be substantially solved by a Single Tier State Pension, so the same trap more generally, and other traps as well, would be substantially or completely solved by a Citizen's Basic Income. Because the Citizen's Basic Income would not be withdrawn as other income rose, any element of a trap currently related to the withdrawal of benefits (including the withdrawal of 'Tax Credits' or 'Universal Credit') would disappear. Even a small Citizen's Basic Income would reduce marginal deduction rates for households that are able to come off means-tested benefits, either because their Citizen's Basic Incomes take them off means-tested benefits, or because their Citizen's Basic Incomes bring them within striking distance of coming off them and they add the necessary additional earned income to complete the process. An increase in Child Benefit would ameliorate the poverty trap for all families with children, [85] and a Citizen's Basic Income would do it for everyone.

We have done enough to show that a Citizen's Basic Income would not disincentivise enterprise, training, long-term relationships among parents of children, and providing for oneself and one's dependents both financially and in terms of personal availability: so in comparison with our present benefits system, a Citizen's Basic Income would positively incentivise these public goods.[86] Significantly, a Citizen's Basic Income would benefit the well-being of both individuals and society. There is no contradiction here. While means-tested benefits can disbenefit the individual by stigmatising them, by intruding into their personal relationships, and by controlling their employment and other options,[87] a Citizen's Basic Income would be a social provision that enhances the freedom and dignity of the individual.[88]

Hermione Parker's words are as relevant today as when she wrote them over 20 years ago:

> Many of the changes taking place, especially increased life expectancy, drudgery-avoiding automation and women's emancipation, could add to the sum of human happiness, but only if we quickly adapt to the new conditions they

impose. If we do not, if we cling to institutions handed down from the past, then there are dangers of accelerating relative economic decline, continuing mass unemployment, further destabilisation of family life, and social discord. … Only governments can ensure that the tax and benefit systems match the economic and social conditions under which people actually live.[89]

We recognised in Chapter 2 that government recognition of some of the issues that we have discussed has led to the combining of in-work and out-of-work means-tested benefits into 'Universal Credit': but it is still the case that the current system both is now and will remain a nightmare to administer, and a nightmare for households to manage when they are in transition from one employment configuration to another. If a couple receiving 'Tax Credits' or 'Universal Credit' separates, and the mother takes the young children and is no longer employed, then she needs to make a new Income Support, Jobseeker's Allowance, or 'Universal Credit' claim, and her husband needs his 'Tax Credits' or 'Universal Credit' recalculated. Her boyfriend moves in. He is employed, and receiving 'Tax Credits'. Her benefit stops, and his 'Tax Credits' increase. He leaves. She seeks and finds employment, only to discover that she is no better off than when she was on benefits because most of her benefits are withdrawn and she now has fares and childcare to pay for. [90] … Alternatively, the woman knows how complicated it will get if she tells the office that her boyfriend has moved in, so she fails to tell them. Her neighbour does it for her, and there is a fraud investigation, at great cost.

Who benefits from all of this? [91]

A Citizen's Basic Income of any size would begin to tackle these problems, and would continue to make sense as households and families continue to change in the future.

Notes

[1] Torry, 1996.
[2] Centre for the Modern Family, 2011: 4; Hughes, 2010: 14; Office for National Statistics, 2014.
[3] Office for National Statistics, 2014.
[4] National Records of Scotland, 2016; Office for National Statistics, 2017c.
[5] Beaumont, 2011: 2, 16.
[6] Morgan, 1995: 61.
[7] Brittan, 1995.
[8] www.gov.uk/jobseekers-allowance/eligibility, 03/05/2017.
[9] www.gov.uk/claim-tax-credits/joint-claims, 03/05/2017.

10 www.gov.uk/government/publications/universal-credit-and-couples-an-introduction/universal-credit-further-information-for-couples, 03/05/2017.

11 There is some controversy over whether the regulations do in fact favour the separation of a child's parents. The benefits and child support regime regulations would suggest that there is no advantage to separation. What the figures cannot show is the advantage to a couple of the father moving out, the mother receiving Income Support, Jobseeker's Allowance, 'Tax Credits', or 'Universal Credit', and the father continuing to earn (and maybe receiving his own 'Tax Credits' and 'Universal Credit') and supplementing the mother's income with undeclared payments.

12 Esam and Berthoud, 1991: 71.

13 Brittan and Webb, 1990: 1.

14 Piachaud, 2016: 11.

15 On the 'couple penalty', see an open letter from Baroness Stroud: www.centreforsocialjustice.org.uk/library/open-letter-chancellor-exchequer-baroness-stroud, 10/06/2017.

16 Kirnan and Wicks, 1990: 31.

17 Miller, 2016: 169.

18 Jane Lewis at a seminar at the London School of Economics on 15 February 2012 on Bennett and Sutherland, 2011.

19 Griffiths, 2017: 555.

20 Miller, 2016: 173.

21 Cusworth, 2009: 195–7.

22 Spicker, 2011: 145.

23 Parker, 1993: 14, 16; Parker, 1989: 22–30.

24 The OECD reports a gender pay gap of 16.9% of median male earnings, https://data.oecd.org/earnwage/gender-wage-gap.htm, 03/05/2017; the Office for National Statistics (2016) reports a gender pay gap of 9.4% of median hourly earnings.

25 Office for National Statistics, 2016: figure 6.

26 Office for National Statistics, 2010.

27 Pahl, 1983; Adelman, Middleton and Ashworth, 1999.

28 Addabbo, Arrizabalaga, Borderias and Owens, 2010.

29 The author served in the Church of England's full-time ministry from 1980 to 2014, during which time he had quite enough experience of men who waste a family's resources on their addictions and obsessions to know that this is a problem.

30 Pahl, 1986; Zelleke, 2008.

31 Rein and Schmähl, 2004; Ginn, 2003; Twine, 1996: 16–17.

32 Workers in this position can pay voluntary contributions if they wish, but few do so. Sainsbury, 1996: 55–8.

33 Ginn, 1993: 47.

34 Alstott, 2001.

35 Hakim, 2003.

36 Baker, 2008.

37 Gheaus, 2008.

38 Elgarte, 2008.

39 Vollenweider, 2013.

40 O'Reilly, 2008.

41 On the relationship between feminism and Citizen's Basic Income, see Widerquist, Noguera, Vanderborght and De Wispelaere, 2013: 141–88.

[42] Bambrick, 2006: 9; Parker, 1993: 10.

[43] Parker, 1993: 21.

[44] Mullarney, 1999: 32.

[45] Torry, 2016g.

[46] Yamamori, 2014.

[47] Fitzpatrick, 1999: 174.

[48] Goffman, 1990: 13–14.

[49] Walker et al, 2013.

[50] Hirsch, 2015: 4–5.

[51] Tonkens, Grootegoed and Duyvendak, 2013.

[52] Larsen, 2006: 141; Baumberg, Bell, Gaffney, Deacon, Hood and Sage, 2013: 4, 11. The three welfare state regimes are those listed in Esping-Andersen, 1990: see Mayes and Michalski, 2013: 50 for a suggestion that the situation is more diverse than the three-fold model suggests; Kuitto, 2016: 38–81 for a diversified version of Esping-Andersen's categorisation; West and Nikolai, 2013, for evidence for the robustness of Esping-Andersen's categorisation in relation to education provision; and *Social Policy and Society*, April 2015, 14(2) for several articles on the influence of Esping-Andersen's categorisation.

[53] Hill, 1990: 110.

[54] Wagner, 2007: 196.

[55] Handler, 2005: 117.

[56] Welfare Reform Team, Oxford City Council, 2016: 51; Patrick, 2017b: 123–44.

[57] Baumberg, 2016: 196.

[58] Dean, 2012a: 355.

[59] Hirsch, 2015: 4–5.

[60] Walter, 1989: 133.

[61] Hyggen, 2006: 507.

[62] Searle, 2008: 129.

[63] Mulligan, 2013.

[64] O'Hara, 2014: 15.

[65] Taylor-Gooby, 2009.

[66] Svendsen and Svendsen, 2016.

[67] Gamble, 2016: 109; O'Hara, 2014: 5.

[68] Jordan, 2010.

[69] Lundvall and Lorenz, 2012: 347.

[70] Birnbaum, 2012: 48–51.

[71] Spicker, 2011: 14–15; Darton, Hirsch and Strelitz, 2003: 33; Walker, 2011: 149–50.

[72] Prady, Bloor, Bradshaw, Tunstall, Petherick and Pickett, 2016.

[73] Titmuss, 1968: 134.

[74] Walker, 2011: 149–50.

[75] Spicker, 2007: 136.

[76] Baumberg, 2016: 196.

[77] Parker, 1995: 35.

[78] Parker, 1995: 43.

[79] Evans and Harkness, 2010.

[80] www.gov.uk/pension-credit, 08/05/2017.

[81] www.gov.uk/government/uploads/system/uploads/attachment_data/file/181229/single-tier-pension.pdf, 08/05/2017. And see Chapter 2 for further material on the Single Tier State Pension.

[82] Pensions Policy Institute, 2013a: 3–4.

[83] Wind-Cowie, 2013: 59–60.
[84] Jameson, 2016: 32–4.
[85] Brown, 1988: 20.
[86] Morel, Palier and Palme, 2012; White, 2014: 93.
[87] Harrison and Sanders, 2014.
[88] Spicker, 2013: 23, 99, 156, 173.
[89] Parker, 1989: 20, 21.
[90] Owen and Mogridge, 1986.
[91] McGinnity, 2004: 185.

FIVE

Administrative efficiency

In Chapter 1 we recognised that there are two ways to argue towards benefits system reform: we can invent tax and benefits systems on the basis of a set of criteria, and then compare our current systems with the systems that we have invented; or we can ask how we might solve the problems that the current systems have bequeathed to us. In practice we have followed both methods, by constructing a benefits system appropriate to changing employment markets and changing families, and by showing that a Citizen's Basic Income would do this better than our current system. Both methods will be in evidence in this chapter as well as we seek a benefits system that is coherent, simple to administer, and avoids error and fraud, and show that a Citizen's Basic Income would be a considerable improvement on means-tested benefits in these respects.

Our tax and benefits structure should be coherent: its parts should fit together

As things stand, our tax and benefits structure does *not* fit together. Indeed, the tax system on its own is 'unnecessarily complex and distorting'.[1] When we add the benefits system, the resultant tax and benefits structure is a very long way from coherent, with different sets of rules for means-tested benefits, National Insurance benefits, Income Tax, National Insurance Contributions, and such universal benefits as Child Benefit. This would not matter if the different sets of rules did not cause problems when people are subject to several of them, but they do. The only regulations that do not cause problems when in combination with other regulations are those for Child Benefit. Similarly, the regulations for a Citizen's Basic Income would not cause problems for the administration of any other parts of the system. This is one of many good reasons for saying that a Citizen's Basic Income would make a good basis for a future benefits and tax structure. (If an unconditional benefit like Child Benefit is taken into account when means-tested benefits are calculated – which it usually is not – then any complication is the fault of the means-tested benefit, and not of the unconditional one.)

Now let us suppose that we establish a Citizen's Basic Income. If there is no additional money available, and revenue neutrality is essential, then we shall need to pay for the Citizen's Basic Income by reducing tax allowances and means-tested benefits. If there is extra money available (for instance, through a tax on financial transactions), then the Citizen's Basic Income could be paid on top of the current system. In either case, the fact that a Citizen's Basic Income was being paid would create no additional incoherence in the current system. If it were decided that means-tested benefits should be reduced by the amount of a Citizen's Basic Income, then if the Citizen's Basic Income rose, and individuals and households found their Citizen's Basic Incomes either equal to or approaching the value of their means-tested benefits, they would come off means-tested benefits, their lives would be a great deal simpler, and they would be able to make choices about employment patterns without taking into account their decisions' effects on their benefits. They would also begin to experience the tax and benefits structure as coherent, rather than as a complex tangle. The same would be true if a combination of Citizen's Basic Income and earned income enabled them to come off means-tested benefits.

There is no need to see 'means-tested' and 'unconditional' as an either/or choice,[2] nor to see adding a Citizen's Basic Income to the current system as an increase in incoherence. If we take the coherence of the system to mean the sum of individuals' and households' experiences of the coherence of the system, then a Citizen's Basic Income of any size would create greater coherence because more people would be able to leave means-tested benefits behind. The higher the Citizen's Basic Income, the greater the coherence. This is very different from the effect of means-tested benefits, where higher means-tested benefits, or means-tested benefits to which more people become entitled, tend to increase incoherence.

Our tax and benefits structure should be simple to administer[3]

Our current system is not,[4] and Members of Parliament have noticed. The last two paragraphs of a report from the House of Commons Work and Pensions Committee read as follows:

> We do not underestimate the difficulty of the task facing decision makers across DWP's businesses. The complex rules that govern the social security system increase the scope for both customer and official error and the

challenge of decision making accuracy. We have previously recommended that the Department establish a body to examine complexity in the benefits system ... .

We reiterate a previous recommendation of this Committee, that the Government should establish a Welfare Commission to examine the existing benefits system and model possible alternative structures with the aim of creating a fair but simpler system that claimants and their representatives are able to understand more easily and DWP staff are able to administer more accurately.[5]

It would be nice to think that a means-tested system, which adjusts the amounts of benefit paid as people's circumstances change, could be simple to administer: but it cannot be. As research published by the Joseph Rowntree Foundation has shown:

[I]ncome testing can never be both simple and responsive in practice. There is always a trade-off between a simple system that does not reflect exactly the current circumstances of the recipient and a more complex system that adjusts to the detailed profile of a recipient's needs. The challenge is to decide when the trade-off is worthwhile.[6]

It is bad enough that duplication and complexity impose substantial administrative costs: it is much worse that the multi-dimensional complexity of means-tested benefits[7] blights the lives of so many families and individuals. With means-tested benefits, a small change in circumstances can throw a household's income maintenance system into disarray. Adding self-employment to employment, for instance, can cause complexities for both claimants and benefits staff alike: so either the new enterprise is not attempted, or it is attempted and not reported. A Citizen's Basic Income would achieve the opposite. It would be a secure financial platform on which to build self-employment as well as employment, and, whatever happened, a household's Citizen's Basic Incomes would not change.[8] But the clear benefits to households and individuals are by no means the only reason for valuing the extreme simplicity of a Citizen's Basic Income's administration. Equally important would be a substantial saving in administrative costs.[9] Means-tested in-work benefits cost a full 10 times as much as Child Benefit to administer,[10] mainly because means-tested benefits require complex and expensive administration throughout the claim, whereas universal benefits do not.[11] This is not simply a waste of money: it is a waste of the time and skills of the civil servants administering means-tested systems: time and skills that ought to be used on more productive activity.[12] And it is not just the government that suffers the expense of administering means-tested benefits. The National Audit Office lists the costs borne by claimants: 'financial, such as the cost of calling a government benefits hotline from a mobile phone, which can be as much as 40p per minute; time, such as the costs of filling in forms; and psychological, including the "stigma" and uncertainty of claiming benefits'.[13]

Unfortunately, when, from the best of motives, attempts are made to simplify the administration of means-tested benefits, the situation only gets worse. 'Universal Credit' is a genuine attempt to combine different means-tested benefits into a single benefit in order to facilitate employment market transitions; and the attempt to computerise the entire process, from the employer's computer, through HMRC's computer, to the Department for Work and Pensions' computer,[14] is designed to simplify administration: but this can only work smoothly for a stable household with a simple and stable employment pattern. The system is not designed to cope with situations in which there is little clarity about relationships within a household, or where someone has a part-time employment alongside occasional self-employment, or they move frequently between employers. Flexible employment patterns are becoming more common and I do not envy Department for Work and Pensions' staff, or HMRC, as they attempt to administer changes in claimants' circumstances in relation to a benefit involving both departments, the two departments' computer systems, and complex relationships between claimants, departmental staff, departmental computers, and employers.

It costs £7.75 per annum to administer a claim for Child Benefit. A Citizen's Basic Income would be as easy and cheap to administer as Child Benefit and could be even cheaper for households with no children. For argument's sake, let us suppose a Citizen's Basic Income of £60 per week for each adult citizen. The administrative cost would then be less than 0.26% of the total budget. The government might occasionally need to update someone's bank account details, and might decide that it wanted proof of address when someone declared a change of address: but this would be the only administration that a Citizen's Basic Income would require. A simpler benefit could not be possible.

The basic inefficiency in the current system is that a task is being done twice, millions of times a year. If I am earning an income and also receiving 'Tax Credits' or 'Universal Credit', then my earned income is being taxed on the basis of calculations undertaken by my employer and by HMRC, and my 'Tax Credits' or 'Universal Credit' are being calculated by HMRC or the Department for Work and Pensions on the basis of information about my household's earnings. The first calculation is designed to take money away from me, and the second to pay me the right amount of benefit. As Atkinson and Sutherland put it, 'a number of benefits are based on income tests, in effect operating a parallel system of taxation. If an extra £1 of earnings leads to the loss of 25p of a social security benefit, then this is no different, as far as cash receipts are concerned, from paying 25p extra income tax.'[15] Why do the same job twice? Why not simply pay a universal benefit that is never withdrawn, and then tax all earned income? Two sets of calculations would then be replaced by just one, and everyone would experience the single set of calculations, thus improving social cohesion.[16]

This would be genuine 'integration' – which is interesting, because it might not look like it. Schemes that *look* like integration are those that combine all of the operations in a single system to produce a single payment or deduction, such as a Negative Income Tax (which we shall discuss in Chapter 11); but, as we saw with the Heath Government's attempt at Tax Credits, complexity can be the result, particularly where an employer's administrative systems are being used to make payments or deductions, and where workers move between employers. A Citizen's Basic Income, by making payments directly to every citizen, and by leaving the tax system as the only form of calculation relating to earnings, efficiently integrates the tax and benefits systems without integrating their administration. Keeping the administration of the unconditional benefit and of the tax system separate is the most efficient thing to do.[17]

An increasingly important factor relating to the administration of the benefits system is the ease with which a system can be computerised. The current means-tested benefits system has proved difficult to computerise. As computer companies and civil servants are discovering, the greater the complexity of a system, the greater the difficulty of computerising it, leading to the strong possibility that companies that win contracts to computerise tax and benefits systems will suggest policy changes that would make the system easier for them to automate, particularly if they are already in the middle of a fixed-price contract. Once a contract has started, it is difficult for the government to resist such pressure, because no department wishes to see a computerisation project fail. The National Audit Office always has something damning and public to say when that happens. The extent to which the convenience of software companies is driving tax and benefits policy, and thus subverting the democratic process, would be an interesting issue to study. 'Tax Credits' computerisation was flawed,[18] as is 'Universal Credit' computerisation:[19] but there appear to be no flawed computer systems in relation to Child Benefit.[20] A Citizen's Basic Income would be equally easy to computerise successfully.

Increasing numbers of benefits and 'Tax Credits' claimants receive their benefits into their bank accounts; although, for various reasons, such as women's reluctance to see Child Benefit disappear into a joint account effectively controlled by their husbands, appreciable amounts of Child Benefit are still collected from Post Offices.[21] People could easily be offered the same range of options for payment of a Citizen's Basic Income as they are currently offered for the payment of Child Benefit. Because someone's Citizen's Basic Income would never alter from one end of a financial year to the other, whether payment would be made weekly or monthly could be an entirely individual choice.

Just in case you might leave this section with the idea that the simplicity of a Citizens Income is its most important characteristic, and the characteristic most likely to recommend it to politicians and public alike (although not necessarily to civil servants, as we have already recognised), there are at least two counterarguments, and it is only fair to explain them.

As Tony Walter puts it: 'Simplicity may not be a vote catcher.'[22] People not receiving 'Tax Credits' or other means-tested benefits might not wish to know how much redistribution is being achieved, and, if they did know, they might not like it. With a Citizen's Basic Income, taxpayers might not like the fact that they were paying for everyone's Citizen's Basic Income, and that some other people were choosing not to seek employment and were thus making no effort to contribute to the pot out of which Citizen's Basic Incomes were being paid. We have to recognise that taxpayers might not be rational. They might not understand the argument that currently their taxes are paying people means-tested benefits that impose high marginal deduction rates and complex administrative problems that between them make it less likely that claimants will seek employment, whereas a Citizen's Basic Income would lower marginal deduction rates and simplify administration and so would make it more likely that people currently not earning a living would seek to earn one. All one can say to this is that public education is a necessity.

A second argument for not emphasising too much a Citizen's Basic Income's simplicity is that reform schemes rarely reach the statute book in their original form. A Citizen's Basic Income could well be implemented in a corrupted form, and if that happened then it would not be a Citizen's Basic Income,[23] and it would not be simple to administer. As De Wispelaere and Stirton point out, identifying those people entitled to a Citizen's Basic Income would be a necessary administrative task, and a variety of payment methods might be needed in order to reach the maximum number of payees: so administration of a Citizen's Basic Income might not be as simple as some might think, even if a genuine Citizen's Basic Income were to be implemented. Equally, a small Citizen's Basic Income, which is the only form that we are likely to see initially,[24] would leave in place many existing means-tested benefits. The higher the Citizen's Basic Income, the more households would no longer receive means-tested benefits: but there would still be large numbers of people still being means-tested, and therefore large numbers giving rise to *increased* administrative costs because they would be receiving both the Citizen's Basic Income and means-tested benefits.[25] In order to save money, attempts might be made to impose conditions, or to withdraw the Citizen's Basic Income from some sections of society as their earnings rose; or a household scheme rather than an individualised one might be attempted, which would impose all kinds of complex administrative consequences. Any Citizen's Basic Income that ceased to be a genuine Citizen's Basic Income would add substantially to the complexity of the whole system and thus to administrative costs.

While there is legitimate debate about the level of administrative savings likely to accrue from establishing a Citizen's Basic Income,[26] and equally legitimate debate about whether a smaller Citizen's Basic Income's ability to remove a large number of households from a range of means-tested benefits constitutes a simplification of the system,[27] there can be no doubt about a Citizen's Basic Income's simplicity: so the hope must be that a genuine Citizen's Basic Income will one day be implemented, that its level will rise over time, that it will eventually take everyone off means-tested benefits, and that it will therefore reap the maximum administrative savings possible.

Error, fraud and criminalisation

A benefits system with increased administrative simplicity would, of course, reduce some of the consequences of the complexity that characterises the current system. In particular, it would reduce administrative error, reduce fraud and reduce criminalisation.

In relation to 'Tax Credits', 'error and fraud resulting in overpayments in 2014–15 is 4.8% of total spending on Personal Tax Credits (4.7% in 2013–14) and … error resulting in underpayments is 0.7% of total spending on Personal Tax Credits. This equates to overpayments of

£1.37 billion and underpayments of £0.19 billion.'[28] HMRC estimates that error and fraud in relation to Child Benefit costs £170m, which is 1.4% of total spending: but the National Audit Office criticises the method for obtaining this estimate, which is to assume that anyone who does not respond to a letter from HMRC is claiming Child Benefit fraudulently or in error. The true figure must be a lot lower than 1.4%.[29]

Material levels of fraud and error in the payment of benefits have led to the Department for Work and Pensions' accounts being qualified for 27 consecutive years. The National Audit Office estimates that the total amount overpaid of all benefits administered by the department, apart from Basic State Pension, amounts to 3.6% of total expenditure on those benefits, and underpayments amount to 1.8% of total expenditure, whereas overpayments of Basic State Pension, which operates in a similar way to unconditional benefits, amount to 0.1% of total expenditure, and underpayments amount to 0.3%. The comparable figures for the means-tested Pension Credit are 5.6% and 2.3%.[30]

While a book of this nature would not normally quote from *Private Eye*, there is one quote that I cannot resist:

> After reporting changes in her childcare arrangements, one *Eye* reader had the temerity to question a demand for repayment of a tax credit overpayment. Not only did HM Revenue and Customs customer support unit respond that 'it is not possible to explain how the figure of [£x] per week was calculated', but she was also told the demand would stand as 'we do not think it was reasonable for you to expect that your payments were correct'.[31]

The serious point being made, of course, is that the greater the complexity of a tax and benefits structure, the greater the likelihood that mistakes will be made.

Overpayment of benefits can result in anxiety for the claimants who have been overpaid, additional administrative costs as the government attempts to recover the debt, and an additional cost to the Exchequer when it fails to achieve that. If the anxiety generated by a letter telling a family that they have been overpaid and that they have to pay back money that they no longer have were to be quantifiable, then the cost of errors would be astronomical.

The National Audit Office recognises that fraud and error have different causes, but does not distinguish between them in its report. This is surely correct. In the context of a complex system, whether an error made by the claimant is fraud or simply an error will often be difficult to determine. But there is genuine fraud, and the Department for Work and Pensions and HMRC have to spend money detecting it, proving it, prosecuting it and recovering the benefits paid out. The Department for Work and Pensions estimates that overpayments of Jobseeker's Allowance during 2015–16 constituted 4.3% of total expenditure, made up of 0.1% claimant error, 1.3% official error, and 2.9% fraud, mainly related to non-declaration of earnings. Comparable figures for 'Universal Credit' are 4.0%, 0.1%, 1.2% and 2.7%.[32]

Fraud is theft: but as we have recognised, it might be rational for someone on means-tested benefits not to declare occasional earnings, because declaring them can have serious consequences for a household's financial stability. So claimants are often left with an irresolvable dilemma: earn occasional or additional income in order to improve the well-being of one's family, and not report the additional earnings; earn occasional or additional income and risk domestic budgetary chaos by reporting the earnings; or not earn occasional or additional income. Fraud thus finds itself as one of a series of wrong answers in a context without a right answer.

During the 1980s, Bill Jordan and his colleagues studied the employment market decisions of low-income families on a housing estate in Exeter. They found that each household had put together a financial strategy made up of a variety of employments and self-employments, with casual cash earnings not declared to benefits authorities if they remained below a certain level. Both a pragmatic moral sense and a community consensus permitted such non-declaration as long as it did not go too far.[33] This was all very sensible, but it meant that legitimate businesses could suffer from the unfair competition provided by those not paying tax and not needing to provide subsistence incomes,[34] and that criminal activity had become a community norm. It does nobody any good for crime to be both rational and acceptable. It brings the law into disrepute, it lowers the psychological barrier to other criminal activity, and it encourages criminal non-declaration of income to become a habit, depriving the Exchequer of tax revenue in the longer term. And there are further problems with a system that incentivises fraud: it can result in criminal records, compromising workers' ability to earn a living; and it enables journalists to write stories that then generate an anti-claimant agenda that enables the government to cut benefits.[35]

The only answer is to remove the possibility of fraud. A Citizen's Basic Income would probably attract a level of fraud similar to that experienced by the State Pension and Child Benefit. If someone's Citizen's Basic Income was simply a follow-on from their Child Benefit, then the only way in which fraud could occur would be for there to be two Child Benefit claims related to the child. This would have to have happened at birth, which would be unlikely to occur. If, on the other hand, a new Citizen's Basic Income claim had to be made at the age of 16 or 18, then a normal check of identity and address would be sufficient to prevent multiple claims.[36] When in payment, someone's Citizen's Basic Income would be of an unchanging amount, whatever their circumstances. Earnings would never affect the amount of Citizen's Basic Income paid, household structure would not affect it, and savings would not affect it. The vast majority of fraud related to means-tested benefits results from non-declaration of earnings, changed household structure or savings. None of this would be a problem with a Citizen's Basic Income; and because a Citizen's Basic Income would remove numerous individuals and households from means-tested benefits, overall levels of fraud and criminalisation would drop.[37]

Conclusion

In 2007, the House of Commons Work and Pensions Committee made the following recommendations (I make no apology for quoting at length):

> There is a direct correlation between the amount of means-testing and the complexity of the system. We recommend that the Government specifically evaluates the current caseload of means-testing in the system as part of its simplification efforts and, where possible, reduces it. ...
>
> The contributory principle adds an additional layer to the current system and research suggests it is no longer as relevant to the benefits system as it once was. We therefore recommend that the Government reviews whether or not the contributory principle remains a relevant part of the modern benefit structure. ...
>
> There is no Government Minister, department or unit that is attempting to address the combined and overlapping complexities of the benefits and tax credits systems. This omission must be urgently addressed. ...
>
> We recommend that the Government undertakes research to investigate whether there remain some groups of claimants for whom work does not offer the best route out of poverty, and more detailed analysis of the impact

of high Marginal Deduction Rates in parts of the benefits system on overall work incentives. ...

It is not enough to rely on 'masking' complexity; there is a need to go further and address the rules of the different benefits and the structure of the system itself. ...

The Government should establish a Welfare Commission, similar in format and remit to the Pensions Commission, which can take a holistic view, model alternative systems, and come up with a considered blueprint for a way forward. A benefits system that DWP staff, claimants and welfare rights advisers have a hope of understanding is in everyone's best interests.[38]

This is the suggestion for a Welfare Commission that the quotation in italic type at the beginning of the section titled 'Our tax and benefits structure should be simple to administer' from three years later criticises the government for doing nothing about. If such a commission were to be established then it might or might not find that abolishing the means-tested and contributory systems would be a good idea: but if it took seriously the evidence for the desirability and feasibility of a Citizen's Basic Income then it would find it to be well worth studying as a possible basis for the benefits system. In particular, a Citizen's Basic Income would pass the simplicity test, it would be radically simple to administer, it would attract almost no error or fraud, and it would reduce criminality, alongside the economic, social and employment market advantages that we have already discovered in the previous two chapters.

Notes

[1]   Adam et al, 2011: 7.
[2]   Bennett, 1988.
[3]   Parker, 1989: 285–6.
[4]   Morris, 1982: 210.
[5]   House of Commons Work and Pensions Committee, 2010: 44, original emphasis.
[6]   Whiteford, Mendelson and Millar, 2003: 27.
[7]   Spicker, 2005.
[8]   Van Parijs, 1996: 65.
[9]   National Audit Office, 2011: 19.
[10]   In 2015/16, the cost of administering Child Benefit was 0.49p per £1 paid out. Net expenditure was £11.7bn p.a. paid out to 7.4m families. Total administration cost was £57.3m p.a., and administrative cost per family was £7.75 p.a. The cost of administering 'Tax Credits' was 1.60p per £1 paid out. Net expenditure was £20.45bn p.a. paid out to 4.4m families. Total administration was £327m p.a.,

and administrative cost per family was £74.32 p.a. (National Audit Office, 2016a: 36, 52, 148, 180, R60).

[11] National Audit Office, 2011: 19.
[12] Jameson, 2016: 23–4.
[13] National Audit Office, 2011: 22.
[14] www.publications.parliament.uk/pa/cm201213/cmselect/cmworpen/576/576vw32.htm, 03/05/2017.
[15] Atkinson and Sutherland, 1988a: 1; Atkinson and Sutherland, 1988b.
[16] Spicker, 2011: 117; Spicker, 2017: 69.
[17] Parker and Dilnot, 1988.
[18] Craig and Brooks, 2006: 7–11.
[19] www.publications.parliament.uk/pa/cm201011/cmselect/cmworpen/writev/whitepap/uc52.htm, 03/05/2017.
[20] Craig and Brooks, 2006.
[21] Lott, 2017.
[22] Walter, 1989: 59.
[23] Walter, 1989: 59–61.
[24] Parker, 1988.
[25] De Wispelaere and Stirton, 2011: 122.
[26] Stirton and De Wispelaere, 2009; Miller, 2009a.
[27] Piachaud, 2016: 3–4.
[28] National Audit Office, 2016a: R12.
[29] National Audit Office, 2016a: R12.
[30] National Audit Office, 2016b: §§7, 34, 35, annex 1.
[31] *Private Eye*, September 2006.
[32] Department for Work and Pensions, 2016a: 7, 8.
[33] Jordan, James, Kay and Redley, 1992: 277.
[34] Noteboom, 1987.
[35] Baillie, 2011: 67–70.
[36] In Chapter 10 we explore the possibility of paying Citizen's Basic Incomes to everyone on the electoral register.
[37] Rodger, 2012: 429.
[38] House of Commons Work and Pensions Committee Report, 2007: §§51, 55, 148, 176, 262, 381.

SIX

Reducing poverty and inequality

Poverty

Consider two fictional people:

- Edna lives in a housing association flat. Her only income is means-tested Pension Credit as her husband, who is now dead, worked in the building industry and never paid National Insurance Contributions. She is now 70; she belongs to pottery and singing classes at the local adult education centre; her children – all of them in low-paid employment, and sometimes unemployed – come to see her once a week; and she tells her grandchildren about family hop-picking holidays spent living in wooden sheds and working from dawn to dusk in the fields. She will tell you how her mother helped to start the local co-op, and how she now has rheumatism but still enjoys visiting her old school at the end of the road: though it is now very different from the way it was when she left it at 14 to work in a shop.
- And there is Paul, 35, who works in the design industry. He is single; he can just about keep up with the mortgage payments; and he earns £35,000 a year, but is not sure how long his job will last. He has a first-class degree and a master's degree, but his field is being taken over by younger people who can cope with the software better than he can. He is depressed, he never has any money, and he has started to drink too much.

Which of these two people is poor? Which of them is in poverty? The housing association tenant on Pension Credit who left school at 14? Or the owner-occupier who earns an above-average salary and has two degrees.

Might we be better off without the word 'poverty'?[1] Different authors use it in different and often undefined ways; sometimes it means 'income poverty,[2] and sometimes it means something broader;[3] such definitions of income poverty as 'sixty per cent of median household income' can lead to misleading conclusions (if median income falls, and more households have incomes above the median, then it can look as if income poverty has fallen when it hasn't);[4] debates about the meaning of 'poverty', and whether it should be understood as relative poverty or absolute poverty, can distract attention from particular instances of poverty, such as child malnutrition during school holidays; any definition of poverty assumes an agreed understanding of what human beings need, whereas human need is always specific to an individual or situation;[5] and the word 'poverty' can lead us to categorise people in ways in which they might not wish to be categorised. Edna does not regard herself as 'poor'. Bill Jordan's work on how residents of an Exeter housing estate think about themselves[6] is perhaps the most useful piece of evidence yet that we have no right to categorise any group as 'poor', or any particular bundle of circumstances as 'poverty', without first asking whether the people we have in mind wish to categorise themselves in this way. Those Exeter residents did as Runciman's research suggests that they would: they compared themselves with people socially and geographically close to themselves, rather than with people living different kinds of lives.[7]

We can combine these problems with 'poverty' into a statement that poverty is 'socially constructed': that is, that we create the category and then we put people into it: either ourselves, or other people.[8] We also create 'mechanisms for the relief or prevention of poverty … [that] make poverty an object of definition and regulation … social policies calculated to relieve or prevent poverty in fact sustain poverty as a definable and manageable phenomenon …'. [9] This suggests that individuals will understand themselves to be poor if their income arrives via a claim submitted to a government department and on which they await a decision with some anxiety, and particularly if their income derives from a 'safety net' that does not lift people out of poverty.[10] Nobody feels themselves to be poor because they receive Child Benefit, use the NHS, or send their children to a state school.

There are thus substantial problems with the word 'poverty', and these lead to problems with the measurement of the extent of poverty. For instance, we have too little information about transfers within the family, or about the informal economy, to be able to make an accurate estimate of the extent of income poverty. So rather than trying to measure something that we cannot define, perhaps we should instead be measuring what we *can* define and *can* measure: for instance, the number of households suffering marginal deduction rates greater than 80%, the number of individuals with no qualifications at the end of their secondary schooling, or growth in the inequality of disposable incomes. These things we are able to measure because we can define them with a reasonable degree of clarity. We can then develop policies and strategies to solve the problems thus defined and measured.

But whatever the problems with the word 'poverty', the consequences of abandoning it would probably be worse than the consequences of keeping it. Families and individuals often do face a bundle of difficulties: low or non-existent earned income, low disposable income, poor-quality housing, low educational achievement, poor health and so on. For such multiple deprivations the word 'poverty' might still be helpful, and to abandon it might be to suggest that multiple deprivations do not exist. However, if we are going to keep the concept, then we shall need to discuss whether poverty is relative or absolute. If a school makes a charge for a school journey, and one family cannot afford to pay and so makes an excuse and their child stays at home, then that family is in relative poverty[11] – that is, relative to other families whose children go to that school. 'Relative poverty' is 'exclusion from ordinary living patterns' because of a lack of resources:[12] hence the idea of 'social exclusion',[13] and now 'disadvantage'.[14] On the other hand, the concept of absolute poverty is a recognition that for a family to fall below certain defined levels (such as a level of net income defined by Jobseeker's Allowance scale rates) will mean that they and others will regard them as poor.

Ruth Lister suggests that such notions of absolute and relative poverty are rather static ideas, and that to understand poverty as social exclusion is to understand poverty as a process rather than as a state. This is a more dynamic definition of poverty, within which individuals and families are regarded as agents, that is, as actively seeking ways out of poverty. We might therefore define poverty as 'an inability, either through the nature of social structures or personal resources or both, to climb out of a variety of deprivations'. If we experience a variety of deprivations but are able to climb out of them – by our own agency, and/or by utilising social structures and processes – then we would be less likely to call ourselves poor than somebody unable to do that. We are only socially excluded and disadvantaged if routes into advantage and social inclusion are closed to us.

Such a dynamic definition of poverty and social exclusion rather changes the debate about how poverty and social exclusion are to be tackled because what we now need to do is remove barriers to social inclusion rather than provide additional resources to people regarded as poor. In the income maintenance field, one policy change surely required by a dynamic approach to social inclusion is a reduction in the prevalence of means-tested benefits. As we have seen, these imprison people in low disposable incomes (because benefits are withdrawn as earned incomes rise), they structure people's relationships and household arrangements, and they define people into social categories ('benefits recipients', 'free school meals recipients', and so on). All of these social processes constrain people's psychological motivation. The replacement of all or some means-tested benefits with a structure of unconditional benefits would provide low-earning and no-earning families with a secure income, which would help to prevent families falling into poverty in the first place; and the lower marginal deduction rates would make possible new routes out of social exclusion and into social inclusion via new employment and self-employment opportunities.[15] Similarly, the NHS, Child Benefit, and free education keep people out of poverty in the first place, and enable them to climb out if they fall into it.[16]

There are of course Citizen's Basic Income schemes that could exacerbate poverty.[17] To replace means-tested benefits entirely with a revenue-neutral Citizen's Basic Income would impose initial losses on low-income households, and poverty levels would rise (although the effect might be short-lived, as many households would be able to make up losses more easily than they can make up benefits losses now).[18] However, as the illustrative scheme in the appendix shows, it is also possible to implement a Citizen's Basic Income scheme that reduces poverty at the point of implementation, and in both its static and dynamic forms.

Additional unconditional social provision could reduce poverty, whether understood as absolute, as relative, or as social exclusion,[19] and would represent the 'process' freedom that Amartya Sen discusses alongside the 'capabilities' freedom experienced in the situation to which process freedom will take us. A Citizen's Basic Income would not necessarily add to households' disposable incomes, but it would provide people with a wide variety of new processes from which they could choose, and by which they could release themselves into the new situations of freedom that they might wish to experience.[20]

Inequality

Income inequality has risen during the past 30 years because people with the highest earnings have seen their earnings increase in real terms, while those with the lowest earnings have seen their earnings fall.[21] Behind this change lie globalisation and technological change, resulting in an increase in the proportion of the proceeds of production going to capital, and a decrease in the proportion going to labour,[22] and in a bifurcation of the employment market into high-skilled well-paid jobs and low-skilled badly paid jobs. Compounding factors are a reduced role for trades unions and less income redistribution.[23]

In 2009, Richard Wilkinson and Kate Pickett wrote *The Spirit Level*,[24] which suggested that higher income inequality caused a higher incidence of other social ills, such as mental illness and imprisonment. An alternative explanation of the correlations that they find – and one that Wilkinson and Pickett begin to recognise in the foreword to the second edition of Danny Dorling's *Injustice* – is that deep social structures influence a variety of inequalities, including income inequality.[25] If this is the case, then only tackling the deeper social structures that constitute the 'social ladder' will affect income, health, educational and other inequalities.

If income inequality is the cause of other social ills, then reducing income inequality *by any available means* would begin to put things right. The available means could include an increase in means testing. But if it is deeper social inequality that causes both income inequality and other social ills, then attention needs to be paid to the deeper rifts in society, and not just to the amounts of money that households receive. Means testing divides society into the means-tested and the non-means-tested; into those whose household structures are subject to examination by civil servants, and those whose household structures are entirely their own business; into those subject to sanctions and those not; into those whose choices in the employment market are constrained by means-tested benefits regulations (including 'Tax Credit' and 'Universal Credit' regulations), and those whose choices in the employment market are relatively unconstrained; into those who have to report changes in personal circumstances to civil servants, and those who do not; into those who have to use foodbanks, and those who volunteer for them.[26] These divisions in our society add up to a serious social rift that is 'undermining the effectiveness, inalienability and universality of social citizenship in the UK',[27] and that needs to be repaired if we are to experience ourselves as a single society,[28] and social citizenship as emancipatory[29] – for only on the basis of knowing ourselves to belong together shall we begin to tackle the particular inequalities from which we suffer. Means-testing makes the rift worse, whereas unconditional benefits repair it, so it matters whether it is deeper social inequality that is causing a variety of inequalities, or whether it is income inequality that is the culprit.

Wilkinson and Pickett call for a Citizen's Basic Income.[30] They are right to do so, whether or not they are right about the causal link between income inequality and other inequalities. A Citizen's Basic

Income could reduce net income inequality if implemented in a context of progressive taxation,[31] and it would increase social mobility by reducing employment disincentives. But if deeper social structures are the roots of all of our society's inequalities, then a Citizen's Basic Income would have an even more significant effect because it would help to repair social rifts and thus the deeper social structures that generate a variety of inequalities. Changing the *structure* of welfare provision would change the ways in which the system redistributes income, would change the national culture, would increase social mobility, and would therefore reduce income inequality and other inequalities. Changing only what might be a symptom – income inequality – could make matters worse if additional means testing were to be used to redistribute income: for that would increase marginal deduction rates (as more benefits would be withdrawn as earned income rose) and it would dig people deeper into poverty. In this, as in all other policy areas, it is the structure that requires attention as well as the symptom. A Citizen's Basic Income would do that.[32]

If inequalities continue to increase, then our social fabric could find itself irreparably damaged,[33] so we need to take to heart the conclusion of Evans and Williams' survey of social change: 'We have lost and gained … and we are mostly all hugely better off, but the losers and the gainers are further apart than ever.'[34] A Citizen's Basic Income cannot reduce inequality on its own. A more progressive tax system encompassing both wealth and earned income will be required, and other institutions will need to change as well:[35] but we have seen that for a variety of reasons a Citizen's Basic Income would make a significant contribution to reducing the level of inequality in our society.

Redistribution

First of all, *can* we redistribute income? As Income Tax rates rise, tax revenue plateaus (because each hour of employment is now worth less, and additional free time might therefore be preferred), so there is a limit to the amount of redistribution that is possible. A limit is also imposed by the connection between inequality and social mobility. Social mobility can reduce inequality by enabling people earning less to earn more: but unfortunately, the greater the inequality in a country, the less social mobility there will be.[36] A further limit is political: loss of income will be of interest to wealthier members of society, and wealthier members of society tend to be more influential politically. There will therefore be political limits to the range of possible redistributions.[37] There would appear to be no self-righting tendencies within inequality, but only tendencies that exacerbate the situation: which means that redistribution of income, wealth or opportunities, will need to be by purposeful policy change, will rarely happen of its own accord, and will only happen at all within some significant constraints.

Perhaps a prior question should have been: *should* we redistribute income? Do we do it because we share convictions about liberty, equality, fraternity, justice or human rights? Because the poor have sufficient political power to extract money from the rich? Because the social consequences of not redistributing income are too awful to contemplate? Because a religious or ethical tradition still informs our social policy? Because the same sum of money added to the net income of a poorer person is likely to increase their welfare more than that sum's loss will reduce the welfare of the wealthier person from whom it has been redistributed?[38] Or for all of those reasons?

Any tax and benefits structure *does* redistribute income, and in a variety of ways. Redistribution from rich to poor or from poor to rich is 'vertical' redistribution; redistribution between differently constituted households receiving the same earned income is 'horizontal' redistribution; and redistribution across the lifecycle is precisely that: we tend to be net recipients when we are young and when we are old, and net contributors during the years in between.[39] This section will concentrate on vertical redistribution.

The reason that income maintenance mechanisms have not created greater equality is that the majority of people do not want to see very much redistribution. Provided nobody is starving, and we ourselves are protected from ill fortune, many of us are generally quite content to allow substantial inequality to persist. We only object when its levels are obscene and appear to be the result of redistribution from ourselves to the wealthy (hence recent objections to bonuses for bankers). Only if the public at large wants additional redistribution can it occur without authoritarian coercion.[40] R.H. Tawney recognised that public opinion was unlikely to support equality of income, even though 'those who dread a dead-level of income or wealth, which is not at the moment a very pressing danger in England, do not dread, it seems, a dead-level of law and order, and of security for life and property'.[41] Tawney believed that it was worth working towards greater equality of opportunity in the hope that greater equality of outcome would be the result,[42] perhaps recognising that there will always be more people who do not want greater equality than people who do; and that many of the people with power will be among those who want to see just enough equality to head off social unrest, but no more than that. All of this means that those who wish to pursue equality are doomed to pursue it by policies for which they have to argue on other grounds.

Inequality is rising, and if the shaky foundations under a minimal consensus about redistribution give way, then we can look forward to accelerating inequality, greater absolute and relative poverty, untapped human potential, and multiple deprivations affecting more families, more children, and therefore more future adults. We now live in a plural society, so it is not easy to see how an ethical consensus is to be rebuilt once the old foundation has started to crumble and the social policy house is still on top of it.[43] David Collard's attempt to establish an economics on the basis of altruism – a natural human inclination to cooperate and to be generous – is a brave one:[44] but altruism is nothing like strong enough to combat individuals' and nations' inclinations to compete in a world in which the winners are wealthy and the losers are increasingly left behind. Within communities, people will continue to cooperate, but I see little hope that the wealthy and the poor will cooperate across our society when the income differences between them are large and growing.

We shall only be able to maintain policies that redistribute income if those policies can be shown to improve the efficiency of a market economy, to relieve poverty and to redistribute resources across the lifecycle. If they improve equality, liberty and justice (however defined) then that will be a bonus: but this will not be the reason for the acceptability of such policies. A Citizen's Basic Income could make the market economy more efficient as well as improving equality, liberty and justice,[45] and it is that combination that is perhaps the idea's greatest virtue.[46] To introduce a Citizen's Basic Income would redistribute from rich to poor more efficiently than means-tested benefits,[47] and in such a way that poorer families would gain significant amounts and wealthier families would lose insignificant amounts.[48] A universal scheme in which everyone had an interest would be far more likely to retain its value than means-tested benefits in which fewer people have an interest, and it would be more likely to redistribute from rich to poor:[49] so such a scheme would have a more significant impact on inequality.

Maybe we should put the question the other way around: is there any reason for *not* redistributing income? If the response is given: 'because greater income inequality damages economic growth', then we can refute that charge on the basis of empirical findings that 'income equality does not harm economic growth',[50] on the basis that the evidence base for concluding that income inequality drives economic growth is weak,[51] and on the logical and empirical basis that people with lower net incomes spend higher proportions of their incomes on consumption of local goods and services than do people with higher net incomes.[52]

Redistributing the ability to raise one's net income

The decision as to whether we should or should not redistribute income has to be a political one: but just as we have already asked whether 'poverty' should be discussed in static or in dynamic terms, so now we surely need to ask whether it might be more important to redistribute the opportunity to increase one's income than to redistribute income.

As we have discovered, numerous households find it difficult to increase their net incomes, not because they are lazy – most people are not – or because they do not wish to do so,[53] but because initial conditions mean that they have few personal and financial resources on which to draw, and because the UK's benefits system (including 'Tax Credits' and 'Universal Credit') makes it very difficult to turn additional paid employment into additional disposable income. Marginal deduction rates of 75% or over are not unusual,[54] meaning that for every extra £1 that someone earns they might keep only 25p of it. Among the highest earners, Income Tax is paid at 45% and National Insurance Contributions at 2%, so for every additional £1 earned, the individual keeps 53p.[55] This hardly seems just.[56] We might wish to discuss whether or not someone should be earning a great deal more than someone else, and we might wish to discuss whether the tax system should redistribute income by imposing higher tax rates on higher earners: but for the government to be taking away from many of the lowest earners three quarters of additional earnings, but only half of the additional earnings of the highest earners, has got to be wrong. On 7 September 2011, 20 economists wrote to the *Financial Times* to say that the 50% tax rate should be abolished because it inhibits economic growth.[57] There was no suggestion that the marginal deduction rates suffered by low earners might be damaging growth: but, as we have seen, there is little financial incentive for people on low or no earnings to improve their skills, or to seek additional or more lucrative employment.

It is equally unacceptable that the lowest earners, and those on no earnings, experience far higher costs than higher earners when they interact with the tax and benefits structure. The smallest change in circumstances (it might be an increase in the weekly amount charged by a childminder) can cost hours in administrative hassle, particularly if 'Tax Credits', 'Universal Credit' or Housing Benefit staff make a mistake. I am not here blaming the staff for making mistakes: it is the system that they are working with that is the problem. Civil servants do an amazing job getting right as many claims as they do.

Growing inequality of gross and net incomes is bad enough, but inequality in the ability to increase one's net income is arguably worse. The system will only be fair when high earners, low earners, and those earning nothing, can experience equal administrative burdens and equal marginal deduction rates. If that were to happen, then unequal earned incomes would be less of a problem, and unequal disposable incomes would be less of a problem, because it would be easier for people with no or low earnings to increase their disposable incomes. We might then begin to worry less about income inequality because far more people would have the ability to earn their way out of poverty, and would thus have the ability to reduce inequality for themselves without anyone else having to do it for them.

Conclusion

A Citizen's Basic Income, of whatever size, would reduce marginal deduction rates for anyone on means-tested benefits, and for those able to escape from means testing it would reduce their administrative burdens as well.

Depending on the precise Citizen's Basic Income scheme, we might of course see some immediate redistribution of income:[58] preferably with the lowest earners gaining net income, and the highest earners losing not too large amounts (say no greater loss than 5% for the highest 10% of earners).

It thus appears that we can achieve multiple redistributions: of net income, of the ability to increase one's earned income, and of administrative burden, and all without imposing too much pain on high-earning households. This has to be good for low-earning households, it has to be good for society, and it has to be good for the economy.

Notes

[1] For a longer discussion of the meaning of 'poverty', see Torry, 2013: 161–8.
[2] Abel-Smith and Townsend, 1965.
[3] Donnison, 1982.
[4] Cribb, Joyce and Phillips, 2012.
[5] Dean, 2010: 24–6, 46–7.
[6] Jordan, James, Kay and Redley, 1992.
[7] Runciman, 1966: 18.
[8] See Sinclair, 2016: 21 on all social problems being socially constructed.

[9]   Dean and Melrose, 1999: 27, 48.

[10]   Bahle, Hubl and Pfeifer, 2011: 233, 236.

[11]   Stouffer, Suchman, DeVinney, Star and Williams, 1949; Runciman, 1966; Fahey, 2010.

[12]   Townsend, 1979: 131.

[13]   Hills, Le Grand and Piachaud, 2002; Lister, 2004: 94–7, 145–6, 178–83.

[14]   Dean and Platt, 2016.

[15]   Belfield, Cribb, Hood and Joyce, 2016: 72–3.

[16]   Rosner, 2003: xiv–xv.

[17]   Piachaud, 2016: 15.

[18]   Stapenhurst, 2014; Torry, 2014a; Torry, 2015a.

[19]   Dean and Melrose, 1999: 172.

[20]   Sen, 2009: 225–52, 370–1; Burchardt and Vizard, 2007; Walter, 1988: 3–5.

[21]   Atkinson, 2015: 105.

[22]   Piketty, 2014.

[23]   Atkinson, 2015: 82; Evans and Williams, 2009: 313; Jin, Joyce, Phillips and Sibieta, 2011: 2.

[24]   Wilkinson and Pickett, 2009.

[25]   Torry, 2010; Dorling, 2010; Bergh, Bilsson and Waldenström, 2016: 70.

[26]   Garthwaite, 2017.

[27]   Edmiston, 2017: 267.

[28]   Dorling, 2017: 245.

[29]   Patrick, 2017a: 301.

[30]   Wilkinson and Pickett, 2009: 263–4. Cf Jones, 2012: 27, where reforms to the tax system are expected to reduce inequality, and the benefits system is ignored.

[31]   Lo Vuolo, 2015: 35.

[32]   White, 2007b: 84, 93.

[33]   Dore, 2001: 84; Dorling, 2017.

[34]   Evans and Williams, 2009: 315.

[35]   Lo Vuolo, 2015; Haagh, 2015.

[36]   Dorling, 2012: 47–8; Dickens and McKnight, 2008a.

[37]   Atkinson, 1995: 5–11.

[38]   Arneson, 2002.

[39]   Parker, 1989: 303–17.

[40]   George and Wilding, 1984: 117.

[41]   Tawney, 1964: 86.

[42]   Tawney, 1964: 42.

[43]   Marshall, 1981: 109.

[44]   Collard, 1978.

[45]   Van Parijs, 1990b: 12.

[46]   Horton and Gregory, 2009.

[47]   Bryan, 2005: 39.

[48]   Parker and Sutherland, 1994: 6–13.

[49]   Harrop, 2012: 9.

[50]   Pressman, 2005: 97.

[51]   Rowlingson, 2011: 35–6.

[52]   Irvin, Byrne, Murphy, Reed and Ruane, 2009: 15; Hobijn and Nussbacher, 2015; Ehrenfreund, 2015.

[53]   Hills, 2014.

[54]   For the calculations, see notes 5 and 6 in chapter 1.

55 www.gov.uk/government/organisations/hm-revenue-customs, 06/05/2017.

56 Standing, 2017: 36.

57 'Coalition must ditch 50p tax rate for growth', letter, *Financial Times*, 7 September 2011: www.ft.com/cms/s/0/d92b0bc4-d7e9-11e0-a5d9-00144feabdc0. html#axzz1cje51OoH, 06/05/2017.

58 See the appendix for an illustrative scheme that redistributes from rich to poor with significant gains for lower disposable income deciles and manageable losses for the higher ones.

SEVEN

Is it feasible?[1]

Here 'feasible' means 'capable of being done, effected, or accomplished'.[2] So the question that we are asking here is this: is a Citizen's Basic Income capable of being legislated and implemented? – which implies that context has to be prescribed. As with the other chapters in this book, the context that this chapter will assume will the UK. Readers in other countries will need to adapt the material to their own contexts and then make their own decisions about feasibility.

The question 'is Citizen's Basic Income feasible?' requires a complex answer because there will always be multiple feasibilities to consider:

- *Financial* (Would it be possible to finance a Citizen's Basic Income? And would implementation impose substantial financial losses on any households or individuals?)
- *Psychological* (Is the idea readily understood, and understood to be beneficial?)
- *Administrative* (Would it be possible to administer a Citizen's Basic Income? And would it be possible to manage the transition?)
- *Behavioural* (Would a Citizen's Basic Income work for households and individuals once it was implemented?)
- *Political* (Would the idea cohere with existing political ideologies?)
- *Policy process* (Would the political process be able to process the idea through to implementation?)

An important question is whether the feasibilities are 1. additive, 2. conjunctive, or 3. disjunctive: that is, 1. will the strength of each feasibility contribute to the strength of a more generalised feasibility? 2. will the strength of the feasibility with the least strength determine the strength of a more general feasibility? or 3. will the strength of the strongest feasibility determine the strength of a more general feasibility? (Analogies: a tug of war team is additive; a relay race is conjunctive; and a pub quiz team is disjunctive.)[3]

I shall draw conclusions relating to each of the feasibilities and to the relationships between them.

Financial feasibility

The obvious answer to the question 'would a Citizen's Basic Income be financially feasible?' is of course 'yes' if we mean by the question 'could a Citizen's Basic Income be funded by reducing tax allowances and means-tested and contributory benefits?' The appendix contains an illustrative scheme of this nature. With different kinds of scheme, the answer might be more problematic. To the question 'would a Citizen's Basic Income large enough to live on be financially feasible?' the answer might be 'no' in the current political context.[4]

The concept of financial feasibility might also relate to the number of individuals who would suffer significant losses if a revenue-neutral Citizen's Basic Income were to be implemented. We might somewhat arbitrarily decide that feasibility in this sense might be defined as: 'no more than 2% of households should suffer a loss of disposable income of more than 10%, and no more than 4% of households in the lowest original income quintile should suffer a loss of disposable income of more than 5%.'[5] The illustrative scheme in the appendix fulfils these conditions.

It might be thought that a loss of disposable income of any size would be problematic. A household that suffers a loss in means-tested benefits will often find it difficult to make up that loss because additional earned income will be withdrawn at a high rate and little additional disposable income would be generated. For any household enabled by their Citizen's Basic Incomes to escape from means-tested benefits, making up a loss in disposable income by earning additional income would be much easier.

Only one illustrative scheme that passes the two financial feasibility tests needs to be available for Citizen's Basic Income to be declared financially feasible in a particular context. The illustrative scheme in the appendix is such a scheme.

Psychological feasibility

There are some public policy fields in which public opinion plays only a small part in policy making:[6] but in the benefits sphere public opinion might matter, the idea that the state should provide an unconditional income for every individual, paid for by increasing Income Tax rates, would represent a sizeable shift in public opinion,[7] and it might be in relation to the public mindset that a Citizen's Basic Income will be less feasible than in relation to any of the other kinds of feasibility.

My experience of explaining a Citizen's Basic Income to groups of intelligent people is that, at the beginning of the conversation, at the forefront of people's minds are such understandable presuppositions as 'to reduce poverty we need to give money to the poor', 'to reduce inequality we need to give more money to the poor', 'if you give more money to the poor then they might not work', 'the rich don't need benefits'. I might draw the group's attention to Child Benefit. This gives the same amount of money to every family with the same number of children, it reduces poverty because it provides additional income for families with the lowest incomes, it reduces inequality because it constitutes a higher proportion of total income for those with low incomes than it does for those with high incomes, and because it is not withdrawn as earned income rises it does not act as an employment disincentive and so is more likely to encourage additional gainful employment than means-tested benefits are. I might also draw the group's attention to means-tested benefits. These give more to the poor than to the rich, but because the benefits are withdrawn as earnings rise, they prevent families from earning their way out of poverty, they make it less likely that people will seek gainful employment, and they therefore tend to increase inequality. When I suggest that the intentions behind the group's presuppositions are better served by Child Benefit than by means-tested benefits, and that a Citizen's Basic Income would also serve those intentions better than means-tested benefits currently do, I can see the penny drop for some of the group's members. They have understood. But by the end of the session there will still be some members of the group who cannot see beyond the idea that if the poor need more money then means testing is the obvious way to make sure that they get the money that they need.

This presupposition is so difficult to shake off because we have been means-testing benefits for 400 years. Four centuries ago this might have been the only option, but, in the context of a progressive tax system, unconditional and nonwithdrawable benefits are the administratively efficient way to provide those with low incomes with additional income, and at the same time to ensure that they experience no employment disincentives.

The important question in relation to the psychological feasibility test is this: is it possible to shift the public mindset? Is it possible to achieve a widespread grasp of the fact that means-testing 'is inefficient because it is administratively costly, because it typically fails in its objective of securing adequate welfare to those in need, and because it nurtures poverty traps'?[8] Is it possible for enough people to understand that preventing poverty 'is not about how we spend our next pound bringing about the largest possible reduction in poverty, but rather about getting the underlying institutional design right'?[9] Is it possible to educate large numbers of individuals who are used to thinking round issues rather than judging an issue in relation to their existing conceptual structure, and for them to begin to shift the mindsets of individuals not used to having their mindsets shifted?[10]

Shifting public opinion is certainly possible. For instance, 'public attitudes towards those experiencing poverty are harshly judgemental or view poverty and inequality as inevitable. But when people are better informed about inequality and life on a low income, they are more supportive of measures to reduce poverty and inequality,'[11] they are happy to support a welfare state, and they are 'willing to contribute to the collective good as long as the distributions of burdens and benefits are regarded as just'.[12]

Since William James wrote *The Varieties of Religious Experience*[13] we have known quite a lot about individual conversion experiences, both religious and otherwise;[14] and, of more relevance here, Serge Moscovici has shown how a minority within a group can convert the majority to their viewpoint:

> A minority, which by definition expresses a deviant judgment, a judgment contrary to the norms respected by the social group, convinces some members of the group, who may accept its judgment in private. They will be reluctant to do so publicly, however, either for fear of losing face or to avoid the risk of speaking or acting in a deviant fashion in the presence of others.[15]

If individual but unexpressed conversions then occur, public compliance with the view expressed by the majority can for a long time coexist with an increasing minority thinking differently. Then one act of courage can reveal how opinion is shifting, and a snowball effect can then occur because 'a consistent minority can exert an influence to the same extent as a consistent majority, and ... the former will generally have a greater effect on a deeper level, while the latter often has less, or none, at that level'.[16]

Moscovici researched groups and institutions, and we ought not to assume that a whole society will function in the same way: but the UK's recent experience of a rapid shift of public opinion in relation to sexuality in general,[17] and towards same-sex marriage in particular, suggests that the same process might also occur on a societal level. Within just 60 years the UK has seen the decriminalisation of homosexual activity, anti-discrimination legislation, equalities legislation, civil partnerships, and now same-sex marriage. The same process has occurred with equalities legislation generally. Starting with the Race Discrimination Act in 1965 and the Equal Pay Act in 1970, the UK government has legislated for various equalities when doing so has been somewhat ahead of public opinion. Each legislative step changed public behaviour and propelled an already changing public opinion more quickly along its trajectory, and thus prepared the ground for the next legislative step that was slightly ahead of public opinion. The public opinion trajectory was always clear, so although it might have looked as if the government was taking a risk, in fact it was not.

There are loud voices opposed to unconditional benefits, particularly in the press. This is why party leaders sometimes feel a need to express opposition to universal benefits, why during a speech made on 6 June 2013 Ed Miliband MP said that 'it doesn't make sense to continue sending a cheque every year for Winter Fuel Allowance to the richest pensioners in the country',[18] and why in its 2017 General Election manifesto the Conservative Party promised to means-test the Winter Fuel Allowance,[19] presumably either by paying it only to pensioners receiving the already means-tested Pension Credit, or by implementing a new stigmatising means test that will reduce take-up among the pensioners most in need of the payment. However, the silent majority know both how efficient Child Benefit is, and how well it serves those on the lowest incomes: and households containing children, and with at least one adult paying higher rate tax, would now appreciate not having the value of Child Benefit withdrawn through the tax system. Now Miliband is willing to say that Citizen's Basic Income is 'an admirable idea because it thinks big about our society. It says we want to give people much greater freedom in their lives, much greater freedom to learn, to care for others, to work as well. I'd put myself in the category of someone willing to be convinced, but there are obstacles.'[20] Might there now be a silent majority in favour of unconditional benefits, but perhaps not knowing that they are a majority?

The only way to test this would be for the government to argue for Citizen's Basic Income and then to implement the policy. *How* it argues the case will of course be crucial.[21] There are many ways of 'framing' Citizen's Basic Income. A 'benefits' vocabulary could confuse the idea with means-tested benefits; and a 'money for everyone' slogan might not be attractive to individuals keen on reciprocity. One way of framing a Citizen's Basic Income would be as a 'Fair Personal Allowance': or, if that's too long, a 'Fair Allowance'. Or perhaps 'Universal Allowance', which, unlike Universal Credit, really would be universal.[22] Once the reframing of the argument has begun to educate the public, implementation could be attempted for an age group that the majority could regard as deserving in some way, so that the experiment becomes a test of public appreciation of unconditional benefits rather than a test of public attitudes towards groups within society. There is a precedent. As we have seen, during the 1970s Child Tax Allowances were abolished and Family Allowance was extended to the first child in each family and became Child Benefit. The change was achieved with almost no public opposition.[23] There is therefore no reason for not making similar attempts, and there is every reason for doing so.

Groups regarded by the public as deserving, and for whom the government might therefore attempt transitions from tax allowances and means-tested benefits towards unconditional and nonwithdrawable benefits, might be young adults and pre-retirement working-age adults (perhaps with National Insurance contribution records functioning as a gateway for the latter group, as they do for the Single Tier State Pension).

My hunch is that we would see the same process as we have seen for same-sex marriage, and that the popularity of the changes for young adults and for pre-retirement adults would reveal and embed an existing public opinion shift towards understanding the advantages of unconditional and nonwithdrawable benefits. The silent majority will have become conscious of their approval and might have become vocal about it, and the minority willing and able to express the advantages of unconditional and nonwithdrawable benefits will have converted the rest of society.

Important causes of public opinion at the moment are a neoliberal public discourse,[24] an increasingly culturally embedded vilification of poor people by politicians and the media,[25] and the current state and direction of social policy.[26] In such a context a market-oriented discourse and an increasingly means-tested benefits system will embed approval of means testing and at the same time will stigmatise it. Similarly, new unconditional benefits, alongside a discourse to match, would generate increasing approval of unconditionality: so if ever a small Citizen's Basic Income, or a Citizen's Basic Income for a particular age cohort, were to be established, its existence would build the necessary positive public opinion on the basis of which the policy could be extended.[27]

But perhaps none of this will be required. In six European countries, opinion polls have shown that both understanding and approval of Citizen's Basic Income are increasing and are already at high levels, with 63% of polled individuals being familiar with the idea of a Citizen's

Basic Income (up 5% on a year previously), and 68% of the sample saying that they would vote for it (up 4% on a year previously).[28] A European survey conducted in 2016 that correctly described a Citizen's Basic Income, but did not explain the idea if the interviewee had not previously heard of it, found that in the UK 50.8% agreed or agreed strongly that a Citizen's Basic Income should be implemented and that 49.2% disagreed or disagreed strongly.[29] So perhaps a Citizen's Basic Income does not need to be rolled out gradually after all, and implementing an unconditional income for every legally resident individual might not be as difficult as we might have thought.

Administrative feasibility

We have already discussed the administrative efficiency of Citizen's Basic Income in Chapter 5. It is enough to say here that the UK has been paying Family Allowance to every family with more than one child since 1946; and it has been paying Child Benefit for every child since the 1970s. Administration is simple and efficient, almost no fraud occurs, and error rates are negligible. To pay a Citizen's Basic Income to every adult would be even easier, with each child's Child Benefit becoming a Citizen's Basic Income at the age of 16 along with the issuing of their unique National Insurance number. Just as importantly, it would be easy to administer an unconditional and nonwithdrawable benefit for any particular age cohort; and whether for the entire population, or for a particular age cohort, the unconditional and nonwithdrawable nature of the benefit would make computerisation simple in the extreme. We shall be looking at implementation options in the next chapter. They are all feasible in administrative terms. And the illustrative scheme in the appendix shows just how easy it would be to manage the transition. We can therefore see that a Citizen's Basic Income can pass both parts of the administrative feasibility test: the Citizen's Basic Incomes would be simple to administer, and the transition would be as well.

Behavioural feasibility

We might think that in order to demonstrate behavioural feasibility we would need to show that a Citizen's Basic Income would work for households in the sense of providing them with an ideal income maintenance system, somehow defined. Such a demonstration would not be possible. Take the case of housing costs. In London in particular, but also across much of the UK, housing is becoming unaffordable for large sections of the population, forcing households into living some distance from their workplaces, in accommodation too small for their needs, or with too insecure a tenure. An unconditional income high enough to enable every household to pay for the accommodation that it needs, as well as other living expenses, would be unaffordable without politically unsustainable increases in Income Tax rates. For the time being, Housing Benefit, calculated in relation to both housing costs and ability to pay, will be required; and because it is households that live in houses and flats, Housing Benefit will need to continue to be paid on the basis of the household as the claimant unit, unlike the Citizen's Basic Income, which will be paid equally to every individual of the same age.[30] Much the same applies to Council Tax Reduction: the now localised assistance that the government gives to those with too low an income to pay Council Tax, the local tax that pays for local services. (Each Local Authority can now set its own regulations for Council Tax Reduction, imposing some seriously difficult new complexities on the relationships between different means-tested benefits and on the resulting marginal deduction rates.[31])

Although there would be plenty of problems that a Citizen's Basic Income would not solve, the payment of an unconditional income would make a considerable difference to many households because it would provide them with new options in relation to employment patterns. Take the example of a household in which the male adult has been unemployed for more than six months and the female adult is in low-paying employment. Currently, most of the value of the woman's earnings is deducted from the household's means-tested Jobseeker's Allowance or 'Universal Credit'; and if the man finds a job then much of the value of the woman's earnings will be deducted from the household's 'Tax Credits' or 'Universal Credit'.[32] If the payment of a Citizen's Basic Income enabled the household to come off means-tested benefits then the female partner could earn as much as she wished and the household's Citizen's Basic Incomes would not change. The household would be in a radically different position. If their Citizen's Basic Incomes were not enough to live on, and Housing Benefit was still in payment, then both partners would have a substantial incentive to earn sufficient income to enable the household to escape from means testing altogether.

While we cannot test behavioural feasibility before a Citizen's Basic Income has been established, we can employ the behavioural sciences to make some useful predictions. Research has shown that cognitive functioning is impaired by scarcity and insecurity, creating the kinds of behaviour that governments then attempt to control by employing sanctions of various kinds. What the research suggests is that a more secure income that created additional opportunities for escaping from scarcity would reap considerable rewards for families currently facing insecure low incomes: in terms of cognitive functioning, rational decision making, and behaviour patterns beneficial to them and to society in general. This in turn suggests that a Citizen's Basic Income would facilitate better cognitive functioning, better decisions and more beneficial behaviour patterns.[33]

We can also predict that households would either experience no major change in their economic and employment circumstances if a Citizen's Basic Income were to be implemented, or that they would find themselves in a better position: not necessarily in terms of net income on the day of implementation (because for some households net income might go down slightly), but in terms of employment options, and the disposable income possibilities attached to those options. If attempts at new behaviours were to produce advantageous outcomes – whether in terms of work–life balance, or increasing net income, or both – then the Citizen's Basic Income will have been behaviourally feasible.

A further and perhaps somewhat surprising behaviour change that implementing a Citizen's Basic Income paid for by reducing or eliminating the Income Tax Personal Allowance would bring about would be that people's engagement with the democratic process might change. Research has shown that if people believe that more income should be redistributed from rich to poor, and they pay more income tax, then they are more likely to vote according to their convictions.[34] This suggests that raising the Income Tax Personal Allowance, which takes low-earning families out of paying Income Tax, results in people being less likely to vote according to their redistributive convictions. (Another significant effect of the accompanying rise of other tax thresholds in tandem with the Personal Allowance is that gains are concentrated among mid-range income deciles, and not among the lowest earners:[35] a fact somewhat under-expressed by the statement that the policy takes the poorest families out of paying Income Tax.) If we want an engaged democracy that will tackle growing inequality then we shall need to reduce tax allowances and increase the number of people paying Income Tax. A revenue-neutral Citizen's Basic Income scheme would achieve this.

A potential problem with behavioural feasibility is that while we might be able to predict behavioural feasibility, it will not be possible to demonstrate it in advance. This is not necessarily a problem, particularly if implementation of a Citizen's Basic Income is phased in, either by providing every citizen with a small Citizen's Basic Income and then increasing it, or by establishing a Citizen's Basic Income for one demographic group at a time. For instance, if an unconditional and nonwithdrawable Pre-Retirement Income were to be paid to adults between the age of 55 and state retirement age, then that group would experience behavioural changes, and policy makers would be able to evaluate both the changes and their acceptability. This would provide valuable evidence about the behavioural feasibility that might follow the implementation of Citizen's Basic Incomes for other demographic groups.

Behavioural feasibility matters, but not initially. Implementation of a Citizen's Basic Income can begin without behavioural feasibility having been demonstrated for every recipient. This means that behavioural feasibility functions rather like psychological feasibility. They are both requirements for successful implementation of a Citizen's Basic Income, but neither are required prior to the commencement of Citizen's Basic Income implementation.

Political feasibility

The question is this: does a Citizen's Basic Income cohere with the ideological positions of the UK's major political parties? – parties in the plural, because a Citizen's Basic Income's implementation would require all-party support; and parties in particular, because the political configuration in one country will not necessarily mesh with political configurations elsewhere, suggesting that any discussion of the political feasibility of Citizen's Basic Income will need to be country specific.[36]

In *Money for Everyone*[37] I show that for the main political ideologies in the UK – the New Right, Socialism, One Nation Conservatism, Liberalism, Social Democracy, and a Green perspective – the ideology itself generates arguments for a Citizen's Basic Income, arguments for a Citizen's Basic Income have in fact been developed by proponents of the different ideologies, and any arguments against a Citizen's Basic Income developed by proponents of the ideologies are generic: that is, whatever the ideology espoused by the objector, the objections are always of the form 'A Citizen's Basic Income would be too expensive', 'We should not pay people to do nothing', 'Rich people don't need it', and 'A Citizen's Basic Income would discourage people from seeking employment'.[38]

This all suggests that a Citizen's Basic Income would be politically feasible in the sense that every mainstream UK political ideology, and every proponent of these ideologies, would be able to find reasons to support the implementation of a Citizen's Basic Income; and that any arguments against implementation would not be related to those political ideologies.[39]

At the time of writing, the UK's Green Party remains committed to implementing a Citizen's Basic Income, the Scottish National Party has voted in favour, the Labour Party's leadership is asking the Party to think about it,[40] and there is increasing interest among trades unions.[41] Political events during 2016 and 2017 suggest that we should not predict with too much confidence what political parties might decide about Citizen's Basic Income: but neither should we predict with too much confidence what they might not decide to do.

Policy process feasibility

It might be important to be able to show that no mainstream UK political ideology would necessarily be a barrier to the implementation of a Citizen's Basic Income: but if the ways in which policy is made in the UK would preclude the implementation of a Citizen's Basic Income, then ideological acceptability would be irrelevant. So the question that needs to be answered is this: given the way in which social policy achieves implementation in the UK, is it possible for a Citizen's Basic Income to be implemented? 'The policy process is a complex and multi-layered one. It is ... a complex political process in which there are many actors: politicians, pressure groups, civil servants, publicly employed professionals, and even sometimes those who see themselves as the passive recipients of policy.'[42]

Crucial to the policy process are the institutions for which ideas and evidence are inputs, and legislation and implementation are outputs. In the case of the UK's social security benefits this means ministers, government departments and Parliament. Any one part of this tripartite system can block or delay policy change, and all three parts have to co-operate to enable change to occur.[43] Also essential to the policy process will be a policy community, or policy network, concerned about a particular issue, or perhaps about a variety of issues. Such networks (around which information passes) and communities (groups of organisations more intimately engaged in the policy process)[44] will often be complex, with some members more concerned about one aspect of an issue, and some more concerned about another; and they will overlap with other networks and communities.[45] In relation to a Citizen's Basic Income, networks concerned with poverty alleviation, poverty abolition, employment incentives, individual freedom, and the voluntary sector, will all be relevant, as will be the already quite well-developed network gathered around the idea of a Citizen's Basic Income.

But however effective interest groups might appear to be, however well organised policy networks and policy communities might be, and however adequate the general public's understanding and approval of a policy proposal, only if all the parts of the policy community – including the government, the civil service and parliamentary institutions – line up behind a proposal, will the policy change occur.[46]

As Hill suggests, institutions relate to institutions, which means that as well as individual proponents of a policy change relating to individuals within the policy system, it is important that institutions within policy networks and communities should relate to other institutions.[47] Think tanks are important because they are institutions that can relate to institutions, so recent think tank engagement with the Citizen's Basic Income debate is a significant development.[48]

Important to both individual and institutional relationships with the government, the civil service and Parliament will be a recognition that every actor in the system is to some extent self-interested. Each Member of Parliament, each minister and each civil servant will to some extent be influenced by their own interests; and if supporting a proposal would be clearly against their own interests then they would be unlikely to support it. So, for instance, civil servants would be unlikely to support proposals that might reduce the size of their departments.[49] They might also be somewhat unenthusiastic about a policy change that might be impossible to implement. Successful implementation of a policy can enhance a civil service career, whereas impending implementation failure will lead to capable civil servants seeking transfer from the department or section involved.

But would Parliament approve? If ever a UK government were to publish a consultation paper on a radical overhaul of the benefits system in the direction of universal benefits, then ministers might be surprised at the extent to which Parliament would welcome the idea. Research has revealed considerable support for a major review of income maintenance policy, and for serious consideration to be given to a Citizen's Basic Income.[50] Similarly, Bochel and Defty have found a diversity of views on social policy issues among Members of Parliament, and an interesting willingness to question previous policy positions.[51] As we discovered when we discussed psychological feasibility, there might be more support for unconditional benefits among MPs than we might think.

What I have said so far about the policy process makes it look as if it might be orderly and rational, but that is sometimes far from the truth. Hill describes the policy environment as like a soup within which problems (which are socially constructed[52]), policy options (again, socially constructed), and political factors (constantly influenced by societal pressures) swirl in unpredictable ways. This makes incremental change[53] look like the safest option, even in the midst of a financial crisis.[54] Because complex systems adapt as circumstances change,[55] incremental change is the only kind that looks feasible within a complex environment;[56] incremental change enables learning and adaptation to occur,[57] and political pressures in a variety of directions will often only allow minor policy changes, and will frequently result in a pendulum effect: for instance, between means testing and unconditionality.[58] Another reason for change generally being incremental are that we have a permanent civil service in the UK, so civil servants have to serve consecutive ministers with often very different ideological positions, and seeking consensus is the most likely way to avoid turbulence as governments change.[59] Additional reasons are that evidence can only be collected from existing systems; that it is often easier to implement changes to existing systems than to build entirely new systems;[60] that small incremental changes are generally easier for the different parties within a policy network to understand than major system changes would be; and that the media[61] will often not be capable of expressing simply and accurately small policy changes, let alone large ones.[62] Every one of these pressures favours incremental change.

The policy process is often described as a series of steps – for instance: 1. precise definition of policy objectives; 2. instruments chosen; 3. implementation arrangements formulated; and 4. rules for implementation[63] – whereas in practice 'policy formulation is a piecemeal activity'[64] within which the different theoretical steps merge into each other.[65] Take the example of changes to the benefits system. Theoretically the minister will take to Parliament a Bill prepared by civil servants according to instructions given by the minister; Parliament will turn the Bill into an Act; and the new policy will then be implemented by civil servants. Things are rarely as simple as that. For instance: if new computer software is required to implement the benefits changes, then the computer company writing the software will be an interested party, will attempt to influence both the policy and its regulations, and will often succeed in doing so because their statement that computerisation would be cheaper or easier if changes were made, or that computerisation would be impossible if changes were not made, would be difficult to contradict. The computer company possesses 'expert power' in the situation,[66] even if it is not very expert. And once a policy has been legislated, implementation can be complex and problematic.[67]

We can draw some initial conclusions in relation to the feasibility of a Citizen's Basic Income:

- Institutional representation of the policy idea is essential: that is, broadly based think tanks and academic departments actively involved in research, dissemination and education.
- A policy network or community is required in which institutions and individuals representing the media, community groups, academia, political parties, trades unions, employers' organisations, and generally as wide a range of interests as possible, will relate well to each other, will relate consistently to the issues of poverty, the poverty trap, and a Citizen's Basic Income, and will together relate to Parliament, the government and the civil service.
- An important task will be to prepare draft legislation, regulations and implementation strategies because these will make it clear that some of the complexities related to other policy options would not apply to a Citizen's Basic Income – and, in particular, that computerisation would be simple, that institutional arrangements for implementation would be radically simple, and that there would be no street-level bureaucrats to worry about.[68]
- Implementation of a Citizen's Basic Income might need to be incremental: that is, implementation for one demographic group at a time rather than as a single project for the entire age range.[69] Implementation might also need to ensure that current benefits systems remain in place. Not only would this cohere with the normal additive method by which new benefits have been implemented, but it would also enable the scheme implemented to avoid significant numbers of losses for low-income households at the point of implementation.[70]
- Careful study of current government priorities will be required throughout. Current themes are the disaggregation of the public sector (which suggests that the Citizen's Basic Income should be managed by a separate agency); explicit standards; output controls; and discipline and parsimony in relation to resources (all easy to achieve with a Citizen's Basic Income).[71]
- The policy process is a complex web of individuals and institutions, and successful negotiation of a policy from idea to implementation will normally involve the whole of that web: so any individual or institution interested in seeing a Citizen's Basic Income will need

to pay attention to the whole of it and not just to one or two elements of it.[72]

Our discussion and its conclusions suggest a range of criteria by which we might judge whether or not a Citizen's Basic Income is likely to be policy process feasible:

- it will need to address poverty, inequality, and a variety of other social problems, in a way that is generally understood;
- it will need to garner government, parliamentary, and civil service support, and this will require a measure of public understanding and support;[73]
- an active policy community will need to include trades unions and other social institutions;
- policy change will need to be, and been seen to be, an incremental change or a series of incremental changes (and the existence of pilot projects of some kind might be useful to represent the incremental and proven nature of the change envisaged);
- it will be essential to build sufficient consensus across all of the various players, and particularly between political parties, so that when a government attempts implementation the necessary political commitment will be present;[74]
- implementation will need to be, and be seen to be, feasible, both in relation to transition, and in relation to ongoing administration;
- the media will need to be actively involved in the policy network, and both this and public understanding will depend on clearly deserving social groups benefiting from the proposed change or changes – which is again an argument for incremental implementation.

A final word must be said here about a frequent characteristic of the policy process: compromise.[75] Any compromise over the characteristics of unconditional and nonwithdrawable benefits – for instance, by applying conditions of any kind to their receipt – would destroy the policy proposal, would not deliver the benefits that an unconditional and nonwithdrawable benefit would offer, and would make it more difficult to establish an unconditional and nonwithdrawable benefit for the next demographic group. Here commitment to unconditionality and nonwithdrawability by individual and institutional members of relevant policy networks and communities, and their carefully and consistently expressed arguments for these characteristics, will be essential.

Conclusion

At the beginning of this chapter I outlined Ivan Steiner's categorisation of group tasks: 1. additive, 2. conjunctive, and 3. disjunctive: that is, 1. will the strength of each feasibility contribute to the strength of a more generalised feasibility? 2. will the strength of the feasibility with the least strength determine the strength of a more general feasibility? or 3. will the strength of the strongest feasibility determine the strength of a more general feasibility?[76] I shall ask how this categorisation might relate to the different kinds of feasibility that have been discussed.

If the pre-implementation feasibilities required for the establishment of an unconditional and nonwithdrawable benefit for a demographic group are the financial, administrative, psychological, political and policy process feasibilities, then the argument of this chapter suggests that if one of the feasibilities is absent or weak then it is difficult to see how implementation is likely to be possible. This means that the relationships are not disjunctive. Some of the feasibilities relate to each other (for instance, psychological and policy process feasibilities form a circular, or possibly a spiral, process), so here an element of additivity might be present: but generally the feasibilities are independent of each other;[77] and, because they are all required, it would appear that we are looking at conjunctive feasibilities. The order in which the feasibilities would be established is important: for instance, financial and administrative feasibilities, and a certain amount of psychological feasibility, would need to be in place before the political and policy process feasibilities for a Citizen's Basic Income could be tested, and a Citizen's Basic Income for a demographic group tested; and behavioural feasibility would then need to generate the next tranche of psychological feasibility, so that the next demographic group could be tackled. This makes the relay race analogy even more relevant.

The conjunctive nature of the feasibilities that we have been studying has practical importance because it means that for the implementation of a Citizen's Basic Income to be feasible for a single demographic group, sufficient work will need to be done on all of the feasibilities, and that none can be neglected. Once Citizen's Basic Incomes have been established for successive demographic groups (a Citizen's Pension, a Pre-Retirement Income, an Education and Training Income for young adults,[78] and an enhanced Child Benefit – not necessarily in that order), we would find the age range without a Citizen's Basic Income sufficiently narrowed to enable a Citizen's Basic Income to be considered for working-age adults, and for the policy process to embrace the idea as a necessary completion of a task already nearly complete.

It would appear that the only way forward for the UK might be the implementation of a Citizen's Basic Income for one demographic group at a time, and this chapter has shown that this would be entirely feasible, provided that at every stage we have put the necessary work into all of the different feasibilities required. But having said that: the UK found itself with Family Allowance because Juliet Rhys Williams wrote a book, William Beveridge read it and was then asked to chair a committee, and Members of Parliament could find reasons to vote for the proposal. The feasibility tests were cursorily attempted or entirely bypassed. Accidents happen.

While it might look as if the 'policy process' and 'accidents happen' understandings of how policy change occurs are very different perspectives, they are in practice quite similar in their structure. Both conform to the requirement that 'agency, structure, institutions and discourses'[79] must be moving in the same direction. Relevant individuals must be persuaded that a particular reform is required, and they must take action; structures and institutions must be moving in the direction of the reform, or they must be able to do so; and the reform must be coherent with a possible trajectory of public discourse.

A Citizen's Basic Income is an unusual proposal. It is both a whole new way of seeing the way that we live together, and a relatively minor change in the way in which tax and benefits are administered.[80] This suggests that lessons drawn from previous examples of policy change might not be easy to apply, that a policy accident could be more likely than we might think, and that, as with Family Allowance, we might see agency, structures, institutions and discourse moving in the same direction towards the implementation of a Citizen's Basic Income scheme.

Notes

[1]   This chapter is based on a paper delivered to the BIEN Congress in Montreal in June 2014. The paper built on the work of Jürgen De Wispelaere and his colleagues: De Wispelaere and Stirton, 2005; De Wispelaere and Stirton, 2008; De Wispelaere and Stirton, 2011; De Wispelaere and Noguera, 2012; De Wispelaere and Stirton, 2012. For a thorough discussion of the feasibility of Citizen's Basic Income, see Torry, 2016a.

[2]   www.dictionary.reference.com, 02/06/2017.

[3]   Steiner, 1972.

[4]   Blix, 2017: 161.

[5]   Torry, 2016c; 2017c.

[6] Cf Richardson, 1969, about the Restrictive Trade Practices Act 1956. The general public was largely unaware of the effects of the ways in which trade associations policed resale price maintenance. The motive for change was the UK government's need to make the economy more efficient.

[7] Hirsch, 2015: 5.

[8] Esping-Andersen, 1996: 262.

[9] Horton and Gregory, 2009: 98.

[10] Smith, 1992.

[11] Hanley, 2009.

[12] Mau and Veghte, 2007: 13.

[13] James, 2012/1902.

[14] James, 2012; cf Sargant, 1976.

[15] Moscovici, 1980: 211.

[16] Moscovici, 1980: 214–16.

[17] Sinclair, 2016: 137.

[18] http://labourlist.org/2013/06/full-text-ed-miliband-speech-a-one-nation-plan-for-social-security-reform/ 15/05/2017.

[19] Conservative Party, 2017: 66.

[20] www.bbc.com/news/uk-politics-36782832, 06/06/2017.

[21] Perkiö, 2012.

[22] Citizen's Income Trust, 2017d: 2.

[23] Torry, 2013: 22–5.

[24] Humpage, 2015: 143, 227.

[25] Walker and Chase, 2014: 151.

[26] Kumlin and Stadelmann-Steffen, 2014.

[27] Humpage, 2015: 228, 240.

[28] https://daliaresearch.com/wp-content/uploads/2017/05/basic_income_2017-2.pdf, 15/06/2017, 16/06/2017.

[29] Result presented at a briefing at the House of Commons on 16 November 2017: http://www.europeansocialsurvey.org/about/singlenew.html?a=/about/news/essnews0037.html.

[30] Torry, 2013: 268–70.

[31] Emmerson, Johnson and Miller, 2013: 215; Finch, 2016: 15–16; Born, Bushe, MacInnes and Tinson, 2015: 4.

[32] Atkinson, 1984: 33.

[33] Curchin, 2017.

[34] Gingrich, 2014: 109.

[35] Belfield, Cribb, Hood and Joyce, 2015: 41; Adam, Browne, Emmerson, Hood, Johnson, Joyce, Miller, Phillips, Pope and Roantree, 2015: 17.

[36] For discussions on political aspects of the Citizen's Basic Income debate based in a variety of other contexts, see Widerquist, Noguera, Vanderborght and De Wispelaere, 2013: 471–561.

[37] Torry, 2013: 211–30.

[38] Torry, 2013: 228; Martinelli, 2017c: 3–4.

[39] For responses to the generic objections, see Chapter 10.

[40] www.greenparty.org.uk/assets/files/gp2017/greenguaranteepdf.pdf; http://citizensincome.org/news/jeremy-corbyn-on-citizens-income-in-a-huffington-post-interview/, 11/06/2017.

[41] www.unitetheunion.org/news/unite-in-fight-against-poverty-do-not-rule-out-a-basic-income/; www.unitetheunion.org/uploaded/documents/Policy%20

Conference%202016%20Special%20Report11-27789.pdf; http://citizensincome.
org/news/the-tuc-votes-for-a-resolution-on-in-work-benefits-and-universal-
basic-income/, 11/06/2017.

42 Hill, 2009: 4.
43 Hill, 2009: 68, 73.
44 Smith, 1993: 76–7.
45 Hill, 2009: 58–66.
46 Hill, 2009: 87; Smith, 1993: 82–3.
47 Hill, 2009: 88.
48 Painter and Thoung, 2015; Reed and Lansley, 2016; Story, 2015; www.adamsmith.
    org/free-market-welfar/, 02/06/2017.
49 Hill, 2009: 90, 102. Rational choice theory is generally understood as integrated
    with a particular ideological position, but that does mean that it cannot be a useful
    tool for understanding the behaviour of public servants.
50 Citizen's Income Trust, 2007.
51 Bochel, 2011: 13; Bochel and Defty, 2007.
52 Anglund, 1999: 151.
53 Martin, 2016.
54 Marchal, Marx and van Mechelen, 2014.
55 Room, 2011.
56 Hill, 2009: 157, 164.
57 Richardson, 1999: 67.
58 Barkai, 1998.
59 Hill, 2009: 186. The permanent civil service's consensual methods have now been
    somewhat diluted by the presence of increasing numbers of externally recruited
    civil servants and of ministers' political advisers.
60 Hill, 2009: 188.
61 Hill, 2009: 167.
62 Jacobs and Shapiro, 1999: 136.
63 Hill, 2009: 174.
64 Hill, 2009: 173.
65 Hill, 2009: 191.
66 Hill, 2009: 191; French and Raven, 1959.
67 Hill, 2009: 299.
68 Hill, 2009: 212.
69 Torry, 2013: 49–52; Torry, 2016e.
70 Torry, 2015a.
71 Hill, 2009: 291.
72 De Wispelaere, 2016: 626–7.
73 A point made by John McDonnell MP at a meeting at the House of Commons
    on 4 March 2014. As we have seen, such support might be growing.
74 Koistinen and Perkiö, 2014.
75 Richardson, 1969: 107.
76 Steiner, 1972.
77 Pasquali, 2012: 60, 188.
78 Torry, 2016e; OECD, 2017: 8.
79 Deacon, 2013: 143.
80 Roebroek and Hogenboom, 1990.

EIGHT

Options for implementation

We have already begun our discussion of implementation by recognising in the last chapter that it might be preferable to implement Citizen's Basic Income one demographic group at a time, starting with the groups that the public might regard as more 'deserving', so that each age group's roll-out can pass the behavioural feasibility test and therefore build the psychological feasibility required for subsequent roll-outs.

This chapter studies four different implementation methods discussed in a report prepared for the Institute for Chartered Accountants for England and Wales and explored during a consultation organised by the Institute.[1] The implementation methods will be studied in turn.

Four implementation methods

All in one go, and abolishes means-tested benefits

> A Citizen's Basic Income for every UK citizen, large enough to take every household off means-tested benefits (including Working Tax Credits, Child Tax Credits, and Universal Credit), and large enough to ensure that no household with low earned income would suffer a financial loss at the point of implementation. This scheme would be implemented all in one go.[2]

This option would require levels of Citizen's Basic Income high enough to ensure that no household would be worse off following the implementation of the Citizen's Basic Income and the abolition of the relevant means-tested benefits. It would not be possible for such a scheme to be revenue neutral without infeasible increases in Income Tax rates,[3] which suggests that the scheme would not be financially feasible. If it could be funded, then the advantages of the scheme would be the abolition of the main means-tested benefits (although Housing Benefit might need to be retained in areas of high housing costs); if the scheme could be funded from outside the current tax and benefits system, so that no increase in Income Tax rates would be required, then most households would experience a substantial cut in their marginal deduction rates; the scheme would release most households from the stigma, bureaucratic intrusion, errors and sanctions that accompany means-tested benefits; the large Citizen's Basic Income would offer considerable personal freedom, and would provide lots of opportunity to start new businesses, do voluntary work, or care for relatives and neighbours; and the scheme would redistribute from rich to poor.[4] However, a very large Citizen's Basic Income could generate employment market disincentives, and it would be difficult to know whether these would be larger or smaller than the incentive effect of lower marginal deduction rates; and such a large change to the tax and benefits system implemented all in one go would generate considerable uncertainty as to its possible effects.

The scheme's financial feasibility would depend on where the funding came from, and whether the funding would compromise the economy's productive capacity without generating inflation. In a highly mechanised economy in which the government was able to tax profits effectively, funding such a Citizen's Basic Income scheme might be possible; and in such an economy a reduction in employment market incentives might not be too much of a problem: but it would only be in such an economy, and with efficient taxation of profits, that such a scheme could pass all of the feasibility tests.[5]

All in one go, and retains means-tested benefits

> A Citizen's Basic Income for every UK citizen, funded from within the current tax and benefits system. Current means-tested benefits would be left in place, and each household's means-tested benefits would be recalculated to take into account household members' Citizen's Basic Incomes in the same way as earned income is taken into account. Again, implementation all in one go.[6]

This is the kind of scheme that is tested for financial feasibility, poverty and inequality reduction, and marginal deduction rates, in the appendix. A Citizen's Basic Income of £61 per week for each working-age adult, £20 for each child (on top of Child Benefit), £50 for each young adult (up to age 25), and £40 for each pensioner (on top of current state pension provision), could be paid for by adjusting Income Tax and National Insurance Contribution rates and thresholds.

The advantages of the scheme are that anyone currently on means-tested benefits (including Working Tax Credits, Child Tax Credits and 'Universal Credit') would either be taken off them or would be receiving less of them (and so would have a greater opportunity to come off them by reducing costs or seeking additional earned income); that any household no longer on means-tested benefits would no longer experience the stigma, bureaucratic intrusion, errors and sanctions that accompany them; that because existing tax and benefits structures would not change, the scheme could be implemented almost overnight; that the scheme would reduce poverty and inequality, and redistribute from rich to poor; and that the more limited nature of the scheme would mean that any net employment market effects would be likely to be small: but having said that, the microsimulation results in the appendix show that although marginal deduction rates relating to household disposable incomes would change very little, there could be more of an impact on marginal deduction rates where disposable income is understood as wage and benefits payments made to individuals. Means-tested benefits are paid to one member of the household, and if both the payment recipient and their partner increase their earned income then those benefits payments can be considerably reduced or might cease entirely. If the recipient of those payments understands benefits payments as their personal income, then they might experience a substantial marginal deduction rate. What is of interest is that this particular implementation method for a Citizen's Basic Income reduces this effect. If we can assume that actual experience of benefits payments lies somewhere between the 'individual income' and 'household income' models, then with the current tax and benefits system the payment recipient can experience a substantial marginal deduction rate if their own and their partner's earned incomes increase, and a lower marginal deduction rate in the context of the Citizen's Basic Income scheme.

Disadvantages of this implementation method are that lots of households would still be on means-tested benefits; Income Tax would be payable on all earned income; Income Tax rates would need to rise by 3%; and National Insurance Contributions would be payable at 12% on all earned income.[7] Any household not in receipt of means-tested benefits might see a small reduction in their disposable income, and higher earners would see a larger reduction. Whether the fact that the means-tested benefits structure would be retained should in itself be regarded as compromising the simplicity claimed for a Citizen's Basic Income is an interesting question.[8] 'Simplicity' is as much a household issue as it is a structural one. Any household taken off means-tested benefits by their Citizen's Basic Incomes, or brought sufficiently close to coming off them to enable them to earn sufficient additional earned income to come off them, would experience their Citizen's Basic Incomes as a simplification; and given that the administration of a Citizen's Basic Income would be radically simple, it is doubtful that any household still on means-tested benefits would regard receiving Citizen's Basic Incomes alongside their means-tested benefits as a complication. Nobody regards Child Benefit as complicated.

Because the scheme could be funded from within the current tax and benefits system, would not generate losses of any significance for low-income households, and would generate few losses for other households, this scheme could pass most of the feasibility tests. Difficulty might occur over psychological feasibility. Because tax rates would rise, there might be resistance to giving money to working-age adults.[9]

Gradual roll-out, starting with enhanced Child Benefit and then beginning with 16-year-olds

> This scheme would start with an increase in Child Benefit. A Citizen's Basic Income would then be paid to all 16-year-olds, and they would be allowed to keep it as they grew older, with each new cohort of 16-year-olds receiving the same Citizen's Basic Income and being allowed to keep it.[10]

This is the gradual roll-out for which microsimulation results are given in the appendix.[11] Child Benefit would no longer be payable beyond the 16th birthday; the 16-year-olds would receive no Income Tax Personal Allowance; and their Income Tax Personal Allowance would remain at zero as they grew older. Because parents and other carers often remain responsible for the care costs of young adults up to the age of 18, a phased approach to the payment mechanism might be required, with the Citizen's Basic Income at age 16 being paid to parents or carers, as Child Benefit is now, then half each to parents and young adults at age 17 (this would not be an administrative problem), and payment to the young adult from age 18. As the appendix shows, the scheme could be funded by raising National Insurance Contributions to 12% above the Upper Earnings Limit, and increasing Income Tax rates by 1%.

Advantages of these fairly minor changes are that they would reduce poverty and inequality, would reduce an important marginal deduction rate, would begin to take households off means-tested benefits, and would reduce the amounts of means-tested benefits being claimed. The increase in unconditional benefits coming into every household with children would provide a solid financial platform on which to build, and would therefore offer many of the effects of a Citizen's Basic Income. The young adult's Citizen's Basic Income would provide a valuable contribution to maintenance costs during education and training, would reduce student debt, and would therefore encourage education and training.[12]

A disadvantage of the scheme might be that two individuals with only one day's difference in their ages could find themselves on very different tax and benefits systems: but this is not a new problem. The new Single Tier State Pension will treat differently people whose state retirement ages falls either side of April 2016;[13] and under the arrangements for raising state retirement age, a woman born on 6 April will have to wait four months longer for their state pension than someone born the day before:[14] but such anomalies have not prevented policy implementation. In any case, if the Citizen's Basic Income scheme were to avoid significant gains and losses at the point of implementation then there would be no unfairness in relation to the amount of money received.[15] However, if the unconditionality of the Citizen's Basic Income *were to* be experienced as an advantage – which it should be – an initial unfairness might generate pressure to extend the scheme to additional cohorts, and so could be counted as an advantage. A possible disadvantage is that it could take between 40 and 50 years for the whole population to benefit from a Citizen's Basic Income implemented in this way: but again, the advantages of the scheme could easily cause extension to additional age cohorts earlier than planned.

As to whether the changes are feasible, much would depend on public opinion related to the increase in National Insurance Contributions above the Upper Earnings Limit. The current National Insurance Contributions configuration is highly regressive, as individuals with low earnings can be paying National Insurance Contributions at 12% of additional earned income, whereas higher earners can be paying just 2%. To equalise all National Insurance Contributions at 12% would be entirely just: but that is not necessarily how a government dependent on the votes of high earners would see it. A government not so dependent would argue for equalising National Insurance Contribution rates on the basis of the reduction in child poverty that would be achieved. To remove the Child Benefit tax charge on higher-rate taxpayers could help to render the proposal acceptable.

The young adult's Citizen's Basic Income would be popular both with the young adults who would receive it and with their parents; and the fact that once beyond the age of 19 each one-year cohort's Citizen's Basic Income would not require any additional funding (because it would replace their Income Tax Personal Allowance if they were employed, and means-tested benefits, or most of them, if they were not) would mean that it would not be difficult for the scheme to pass financial feasibility tests.[16]

Starting with volunteers

> Inviting volunteers among the pre-retired, between the age of 60 and the state pension age.[17]

Anyone above the age of 60 would be able to exchange their Income Tax Personal Allowance, their National Insurance Contribution Lower Earnings Threshold, and their ability to claim means-tested benefits for a Citizen's Basic Income of the same value as the Personal Allowance and the Lower Earnings Threshold. (If it was agreed that means-tested benefits would still be payable, then these would be recalculated so as to take into account the value of the Citizen's Basic Income.) Backing out would not be possible once the pre-retirement Citizen's Basic Income was in payment.

For the vast majority of such volunteers, disposable incomes would not change. For a couple not receiving means-tested benefits and in which one partner had not been earning an income, additional funding would be required to pay for their Citizen's Basic Incomes. The government would need to decide whether to claw back these Citizen's Basic Incomes from high-earning households via an additional tax charge, as with Child Benefit. Anomalous cases might generate either a requirement for additional funding or a saving to the Exchequer.

An interesting advantage would be that take-up of the scheme would constitute a clear measure of the scheme's popularity. A further advantage would be that the scheme would offer maximum freedom as to whether to receive a Citizen's Basic Income and to pay more Income Tax and National Insurance Contributions on earned income, or to remain in the current system. Many of those who volunteered who had been on means-tested benefits (including Working Tax Credits, Child Tax Credits and 'Universal Credit') would find themselves on reduced means-tested benefits, or on none at all. They would therefore experience increased incentives in the employment market: and anyone who came off means-tested benefits would no longer suffer from sanctions, errors, stigma or the bureaucratic intrusion associated with means-tested benefits. If means-tested benefits remained in payment for the volunteers, then the solid financial floor provided by the household's Citizen's Basic Income would enable many pre-retired individuals to reduce their costs, or to accept part-time or occasional employment, in order to come off means-tested benefits: something currently impossible for many pre-retired people.

There would be at least three disadvantages: in the absence of a clawback mechanism for high earners, granting a Citizen's Basic Income to the non-earning spouse of a high earner might prove to be generally unpopular; two tax and benefits systems would be running alongside each other for the same age cohort; and because means-tested benefits, including Pension Credit, are based on a household claimant unit, couples rather than individuals would need to volunteer for the scheme. This might cause difficulties if one member of a couple wished to volunteer and another did not.

The scheme could pass all of the feasibility tests. In particular, it would pass the psychological feasibility test because only those persuaded of the scheme's virtues would be on it.[18]

The 20 years between 55 and 75 constitute a time of transition for many people, and also a time of opportunity, in which many would prefer a mixture of paid, caring and voluntary activity. A 'Third Age income' or 'Pre-retirement income', a Citizen's Basic Income for this age group, would reduce the stigma experienced by those in the 'netherworld' between work and retirement:[19] that is, no longer in full-time employment, and with little chance of finding another full-time job. It would also make part-time employment more viable, it would make it easier for people to care for older parents or for grandchildren, it would encourage the kind of sustained community involvement to which people in their Third Age have so much to contribute, and it would value all of this as socially useful work. Charles Handy suggests that the Third Age 'provides an opportunity for pilot testing. It is a discrete section of society but one that will increasingly set norms and fashions for the rest. ... We could experiment with them, at moderate cost, and so make the idea [of a Citizen's Basic Income] workable and practicable to the rest.'[20]

An evaluation of the four implementation methods

The first implementation method would require substantial additional public funding and so in the short term is not feasible. However, if sufficient additional funding were to become available to enable a Citizen's Basic Income to be paid that would be large enough to float every household off both in-work and out-of-work means-tested benefits, then implementation would not be a problem. Psychological feasibility might be a problem, though.

The second implementation method would be financially feasible, and it would not impose significant losses at the point of implementation: but that method too might prove to be psychologically infeasible.

The third implementation method could potentially satisfy all of the feasibility tests, as could the fourth method.

Particularly important in this connection are the lessons that we have drawn from the history of the UK's tax and benefits systems:

- The proposals that have changed the system have been for identifiable groups of people.
- Those proposals that have changed the system have generally benefited from long-standing and widespread debate and a reasonable level of public understanding of what was intended.
- Those proposals that have become Acts of Parliament are those that have not reduced the number of civil servants, and those that have not become Acts of Parliament would have done.

This suggests that whatever feasibility tests might be passed, the two proposals for gradual roll-out would probably be the most feasible; and given the complexities that might result from implementing option 4, option 3 might be where future research effort should be concentrated.

An implementation scenario based on the third implementation method

Matters might proceed as follows: Enhanced Child Benefit (paid for by equalising all National Insurance Contributions above the Primary Earnings Threshold at 12%) and a 1% rise in all Income Tax rates could be followed by a Citizen's Basic Income for everyone aged 16, 17 and 18 (which would enable the easiest transition from Child Benefit). This three-year age cohort would then keep its Citizen's Basic Income as it grew older, and every new single-year cohort of 16-year-olds would receive a Citizen's Basic Income (and no Income Tax Personal Allowance). As the roll-out progressed, the National Insurance Contribution Primary Earnings Threshold would slowly reduce to zero, and Income Tax rates would slowly rise to 3% above current levels. The Single Tier State Pension might at some point be detached from National Insurance Contribution records and become a Citizen's Pension; and public pressure might result in a pre-retirement Citizen's Basic Income for everyone between the ages of 55 or 60 and State Retirement Age – perhaps along the lines of the fourth implementation option. If sufficient public approval of Citizen's Basic

Income was then generated we might see the gap between the Pre-retirement income and the age cohort reached by the gradual roll-out to one-year cohorts filled in by a Citizen's Basic Income for every working-age adult.

An additional implementation option

A further possibility that we have not so far considered is the introduction of a very small Citizen's Basic Income, with an agreement that it will rise slowly as Income Tax and National Insurance Contribution rates and thresholds and means-tested benefits slowly adapt. Such a gradual introduction would enable individuals and households to adapt slowly to the new employment market incentives, to additional options for household employment patterns, and to new options for household structure; would enable adjustments to net income, and to the higher net incomes that lower marginal deduction rates would make possible, to be handled more easily; and would enable the employment market to become gradually more flexible. None of us have ever known an employment market without rigidities imposed by the tax and benefits systems, so such a major new experience might be best tackled slowly.

A small Citizen's Basic Income would not create major changes in people's marginal deduction rates, it would not increase employment market options in a major way, it would not redistribute very much, and it would not reduce poverty very much: so would the implementation of a small universal payment give us genuine experience of a Citizen's Basic Income? The answer to that question is 'yes'. However small it is, the Citizen's Basic Income would reduce the marginal deduction rates for any household enabled to escape from means-tested benefits or brought within striking distance of doing so. If a household were to receive a Citizen's Basic Income of just half of the value of any means-tested benefits which they currently receive, then they would find themselves suffering from high marginal deduction rates across just half of the earnings range across which they suffer them now. As earnings rose, they would much more quickly reach a position from which net income could increase rapidly as earnings rose. This could have a major effect on a household's employment pattern and net income.

Tony Atkinson's verdict was that an initially small Citizen's Basic Income 'represents a definite and practicable scheme … and the results … indicate that it could be introduced without having major distributional consequences'.[21] This absence of redistributional effects would enable a Citizen's Basic Income to be introduced without major transitional arrangements being required; and such a small Citizen's

Basic Income[22] would still reduce disincentives, reduce the effects of the unemployment and poverty traps, and bind us together as a society because everybody would receive it.

Conclusion

While all that we require for debate about a Citizen's Basic Income to be realistic is one viable route from the current situation to the payment of a Citizen's Basic Income, we are in the fortunate position of being able to choose between a number of possibilities that would have some chance of passing the feasibility tests.

But a word of caution: the implementation methods that we have discussed are themselves ideal types, for, as Bill Jordan has pointed out, social policy reform is rarely so orderly. It is more a 'winding country lane' than a 'majestic highway'. Taking the UK as an example, and employing a slightly different metaphor, Jordan compares the 'high road', represented by a Citizen's Basic Income, to the 'low road', motivated by the need to fix the current benefits system: a road well represented by 'Universal Credit'.[23] The problem is that if, for instance, we started to reduce the taper rate on Working Tax Credits and 'Universal Credit', increased the work allowances (the amount of earnings permitted before the benefit starts to be reduced),[24] and extended the constituency to which they were paid, then first of all a lot more people would find themselves on means-tested benefits, and secondly, 'if progress towards a true basic income (more generous, with individual rather than household eligibility, and without work enforcement) stalled at this point, the other gains associated with it, in terms of liberty and equality, would remain out of reach'.[25] So a small Citizen's Basic Income, designed to make employment markets more flexible, might remain small and fulfil only its initial purpose rather than growing and therefore reaping the wider benefits of a Citizen's Basic Income. The first steps towards a genuine Citizen's Basic Income might become politically feasible for a variety of reasons, and all of those steps would be perilous for the principle in various ways: but those steps should not for that reason be rejected: 'Social policy can seldom deal in pure principles or utopian solutions, and basic income is no exception. It cannot resolve all the challenges of globalisation … in a single reform, but these [first steps] may be a step in the right direction.'[26]

We have already noted in Chapter 7 that every mainstream political ideology can generate arguments for a Citizen's Basic Income, and that any ideology's arguments against a Citizen's Basic Income relate more to general anxieties rather than to the political ideology itself. There is no harm in regarding 'Universal Credit' as a step along the 'winding country lane' towards a Citizen's Basic Income: but there is no reason to think that a next step will be taken.[27] That would require an all-party commitment to lower marginal deduction rates and the individualisation of the benefits system: both worthwhile objectives in their own right, as well as steps along the lane towards a Citizen's Basic Income. Gradual convergence of benefit rates and the cash values of the Income Tax Personal Allowance would also contribute towards ease of transition when tax allowances are turned into cash payments in order to establish a Citizen's Basic Income.[28] The Personal Allowance is moving in the right direction.

At each step along the way we shall need to be sure not only that individual households' gains or losses are not too great, but also that the administrative steps required are easy to achieve; and we shall also need to ensure that the direction in which we are travelling is in fact towards a Citizen's Basic Income: an unconditional and nonwithdrawable income for every individual. While it is true that the details of a Citizen's Basic Income will be context specific (for instance, in terms of the frequency of payment, or in terms of precisely how the regular sum is paid to each individual), what we must never do is declare that a Citizen's Basic Income has been implemented if its unconditionality, nonwithdrawability or payment to individuals have in any way been compromised.[29]

Before we leave unchallenged the idea that the 'pure principles or utopian solutions'[30] of the 'full automation, … reduction of the working week, … provision of a basic income, … diminishment of the work ethic'[31] variety are not a realistic way to do social policy, we ought at least consider Eleanor Rathbone's explicit attempt to create a utopia in which child poverty had been abolished in the UK. That was the intention behind the Family Allowance, and she got her way. Ruth Levitas suggests that we might do more useful social policy if we had in our own minds the kind of society that we want, rather than identify problems in today's society and then try to fix them.[32] Similarly, an editorial on Citizen's Basic Income in *The Guardian* has suggested that we should 'dream big, and then proceed with care'.[33]

This chapter has studied some very practical implementation options for a Citizen's Basic Income in the UK. If we were serious utopians then we might want to add a further step: a global Citizen's Basic Income.[34] I suspect that we shall need to see a number of national schemes established before such an idea gets anywhere near to serious consideration, although because, in spite of Brexit, a substantial level of social solidarity already exists across Europe,[35] a European Citizen's Basic Income is not beyond the bounds of possibility in the medium term,[36] and a European Citizen's Basic Income for Children could be the first step.[37] Whether the UK will have rejoined the European Union in time to join in is an interesting question.

Notes

[1]   Some of this chapter paraphrases or quotes from the ICAEW report, Torry, 2016e, which can be found at www.icaew.com/-/media/corporate/files/technical/sustainability/outside-insights/citizens-income-web---final.ashx?la=en, 02/06/2017. Permission from the ICAEW to use the material here is gratefully acknowledged. For details of the consultation, see http://citizensincome.org/news/icaew-report-on-implementing-citizens-income/, 15/05/2017.

[2]   Torry, 2016e: 13.

[3]   Torry, 2014a; Torry, 2015a.

[4]   Torry, 2015a.

[5]   Torry, 2016a: 13–14.

[6]   Torry, 2016e: 14.

[7]   Piachaud, 2016: 4.

[8]   Piachaud, 2016: 4.

[9]   Torry, 2016e: 14–15.

[10]   Torry, 2016e: 15.

[11]   The scheme researched in the appendix is based on Torry, 2017c, and is not quite the same as the scheme described in Torry, 2016e, which is based on Torry, 2016c.

[12]   Smith, 1985: 16; Morley, 1985; BIRG youth group, 1985; Lewis, 1986.

[13]   Pensions Policy Institute, 2013b.

[14]   Thurley and Keen, 2017: 12; www.gov.uk/state-pension-age, 07/10/2017.

[15]   Van Parijs and Vanderborght, 2017: 160.

[16]   Torry, 2016e: 15–16.

[17]   Torry, 2016e: 17.

[18]   Torry, 2016e: 17.

[19]   McGann, Kimberley, Bowman and Biggs, 2016.

[20]   Handy, 1990: 4.

[21]   Atkinson, 1989b: 334.

[22]   Parker and Sutherland, 1995. For other possibilities see Brittan, 2001, on slowly reducing the taper on 'Tax Credits' and extending the number of households claiming 'Tax Credits', and Bennett and Sutherland, 2011, on slowly universalising National Insurance benefits.

[23]   Jordan, 2012; Jordan, Agulnik, Burbidge and Duffin, 2000: 126.

[24]   Judge, 2015: 38.

[25]   Jordan, 2012: 3.

[26]   Jordan, 2011: 112.

[27]   De Wispelaere, 2016: 622.

[28]   Jordan, Agulnik, Burbidge and Duffin, 2000: 11, 28, 42, 56.

[29]   De Wispelaere and Stirton, 2005. In my view, De Wispelaere and Stirton allow too much potential conditionality into their definition of 'Universal Basic Income'.

[30]   Jordan, 2011: 112.

[31]   Srnicek and Williams, 2015: 127.

[32] Levitas, 2012.
[33] www.theguardian.com/commentisfree/2016/jun/06/the-guardian-view-on-a-universal-income-the-high-price-of-free-money, 10/06/2017.
[34] See Torry, 2013: 61–3 for discussion of national, regional and global options, and also see a website appendix for Torry, 2013.
[35] Ellison, 2011.
[36] Van Parijs and Vanderborght, 2017: 230–41; McKnight, Duque and Rucci, 2016: 67–8, 80.
[37] Levy, Matsaganis and Sutherland, 2014.

NINE

Pilot projects and experiments

In the UK we already have Child Benefit, which functions as a universal benefit for children. We have already discussed the UK's NHS: a universal, unconditional, nonwithdrawable and highly efficient public service. In this chapter I shall discuss the social dividend (a form of Citizen's Basic Income) distributed in Alaska, Citizen's Basic Income pilot projects conducted in Namibia and India, Iran's cash benefit, and a number of other experiments.

Alaska[1]

Since 1977 the State of Alaska has been receiving royalties from oil extraction on state-owned land at Prudhoe Bay, and about 20% of the royalties have been saved in the Alaska Permanent Fund. When the fund was established in 1976, the state legislature decided that the principal of the fund should accumulate, so that future generations could benefit from what was bound to be a temporary income stream. No decision was made about how income from the fund's investments should be used, except that sufficient was to be added to the capital to inflation-proof the fund. When in 1979 Governor Jay Hammond[2] proposed that some of the surplus interest might be distributed to Alaska's citizens, the idea was warmly received. The initial proposal was that the dividend received by each citizen should be proportional to the number of years that they had lived there, but a legal challenge on the basis that this would discriminate against recent arrivals succeeded, and the outcome was an equal annual payment to every citizen of Alaska who had lived in the state for at least a year.[3] In 2017 the Alaska Permanent Fund had a total value of $58.9 bn,[4] and the annual dividend paid in 2016 was $1,022 to each eligible resident.[5] The world had its first Citizen's Basic Income: although in some ways it has not behaved like one because the payments are made annually, so the income does not function as a regular income, and the amount fluctuates with the profits generated by the Permanent Fund, meaning that the dividend cannot be relied upon to provide a firm income floor.[6]

When he had been Mayor of Bristol Bay Borough, Hammond had tried unsuccessfully to establish a social dividend on the basis of fishing revenues. When he became Governor of Alaska in 1974, he decided to try again, on a larger scale, and for the same reasons: to prevent resources being squandered on public projects driven by interest groups, to help the poor, and to reflect the common ownership of the state's natural resources. This time he succeeded. The Alaska Permanent Fund owes its existence to the right person being in the right place at the right time. It also owes its existence to public opinion. In 1966 Alaska sold oil drilling rights and spent all of the money. Public perception was that the proceeds had been wasted. Suggesting that a proportion of oil revenues should be saved for future generations was therefore a popular move, and legislators of a variety of political views could support it, so the fund was relatively easy to establish. The dividend, however, divided opinion, and was eventually achieved only slowly by making compromises, and by building a coalition of policy makers. Unlike the Fund, the dividend is not protected by a constitutional amendment.[7] It is protected by the fact that every resident receives it, and none of them would wish to lose it.

The dividend has increased personal income, and therefore consumption, and has thus increased employment. In 1990 it was estimated that for every $1m distributed, 13 Alaskan jobs, mainly in the service and trade sectors, were created. The dividend has had an anti-inflationary effect,[8] and it has helped the poor. Alaska is the only state in the US in which inequality has decreased during the past twenty years.[9] Whereas in 1980 Alaska's net income inequality was the highest in the United States, in 2013 it was the lowest.[10]

Can the model be exported? Such dividends are popular once they are in place. Even with its oil revenues, Alaska is not among the states with the highest per capita income, and it uses only a small and now declining proportion of the interest generated by the Alaska Permanent Fund to pay the dividend.[11] If 'resources' were to be sufficiently broadly defined to include land values, then most countries could establish resource dividends if they wished to do so. The Alaska model could therefore be tried elsewhere,[12] and dividends established elsewhere would be at least as secure as Alaska's. A change of government can easily lead to the abolition of targeted programmes, but a change of political ethos cannot damage the Alaska Permanent Fund or the dividend. The dividend has no enemies so there is no opposition movement in which a politician can make a home.[13]

Iran[14]

Iran now has a cash transfer programme that looks remarkably like a Citizen's Basic Income. In 2010 the Iranian government replaced subsidies on food and fuel with an unconditional cash payment of 455,000 rials per month (about US$40) to every individual.[15]

Before the reform, 70% of the food and fuel subsidies went to 30% of the population, and resulted in wasteful consumption of energy and foodstuffs, lack of investment, pollution and smuggling to countries that did not benefit from such subsidies.[16] When the replacement of subsidies by cash transfers was first discussed, the plan was to provide additional cash to poorer members of society via a means test, and 17 million households completed means-test questionnaires. It was the public unrest resulting from that exercise that led to the abandonment of the means test. As soon as the suggestion was made that the money should be given to everyone (since the wealthy are taxed more than they would receive from the cash transfer), it just seemed obvious. Most of the households that had not applied for the payment then did so. The only requirement was that those who received the cash transfer had to complete tax returns. 96% of the population received the payments.[17]

In one respect the Iranian cash subsidy (the official designation) is not a Citizen's Basic Income. The head of the household receives all of the household's individual entitlements, so although the individual is the claimant unit in relation to the income's calculation, the individual is not the claimant unit in relation to the income's payment. The transfer is not truly universal either. Afghan refugees, many of whom have lived in Iran for decades, do not receive the cash subsidy, but do suffer price rises related to the withdrawal of commodity subsidies. Neither is it clear how sustainable the cash subsidy would be if oil revenues were to decline because the total value of the unconditional incomes has been above the savings from the abolition of fuel and food subsidies, giving rise to inflation, and because the language of rights has played no part in the establishment of the scheme, which both the government and the population regard as a pragmatic measure, and not necessarily a permanent one.[18] An interesting question is the extent to which a universal payment will itself generate a concept of rights and a broader acceptance of democratic government. The scheme is enshrined in law, and it is possible that the resulting economic efficiencies, new investment, poverty reduction, and particularly income security, will recommend the scheme to both government and public as a longer-term necessity.[19]

While the cash subsidy does not constitute a subsistence income, it is a substantial start. For a family of five, it comes to something like two thirds of subsistence. If the research opportunity that the Iranian scheme might offer is taken up then we shall have available to us information that we do not yet have on how a Citizen's Basic Income affects employment, consumption and household patterns.

The Iranian scheme is hugely important. We had thought that the widespread European debate on the benefits of a Citizen's Basic Income[20] might one day result in a Citizen's Basic Income being established in a European country, so that Europe would be the first continent to see a genuine unconditional and nonwithdrawable income for every legal resident. But it was not to be. Alaska has now paid a Citizen's Basic Income (an annual one) for 30 years; and now Iran has something very close to a Citizen's Basic Income. A possible conclusion to draw is that this is one more signal of the end of US-European hegemony. The empire is dying and new empires are taking shape, doing what new empires always do: doing things in new ways, and in ways that the old empires (therefore) refuse, thus hastening their decline.

Namibia [21]

On 27 January 2009 I attended a seminar at the School of Oriental and African Studies (SOAS) in the University of London. In the audience were academics, staff members of non-governmental organisations working in Africa, and people like me, all wanting to know how successful a Citizen's Basic Income pilot project had been.

Guy Standing[22] started his presentation with the heart of his message: poverty is primarily a lack of money, so what people need is a means of providing economic security that is not paternalistic, is based on rights and not charity, benefits the most disadvantaged, encourages ecological restraint and promotes dignified work.[23] Of the three types of cash transfers available:

- universalistic and unconditional;
- targeted (usually on groups deemed to be the poorest, often by means-testing); and
- selective (for instance: in Latin America, cash transfers are received by poorer families who send their children to school, again requiring means-testing);

means-tested systems suffer from problems familiar to developed countries, such as unemployment traps, poverty traps and savings traps:

so in Africa new methods must be sought. At a BIEN Congress in Cape Town in 2006 much support was expressed for unconditional cash transfers, especially among trades unionists and community and church representatives – and now a pilot project involving two Namibian villages had answered some common criticisms of unconditional transfers: that they would reduce labour supply, would go to the rich as well as the poor, would be wasted on alcohol and other undesirable expenditure, would be unaffordable and would lower incentives to save.

The pilot project ran from 2007 to 2009. It built on an existing debate about the possibility of a Citizen's Basic Income in Namibia,[24] and also on the existing Namibian universal pension. It gave to each of a thousand inhabitants of two villages a Basic Income Grant (a Citizen's Basic Income) of N$100 a month for every man, woman and child (100 Namibian dollars is about US$12). The costs were borne by donors, mostly in the form of voluntary contributions, and the project was carefully watched by potential donors, including the World Bank.

The team organising the pilot conducted a benchmark survey and an evaluation survey. The results were significant:[25]

- Household poverty dropped. In November 2007, 76% of residents of the two villages fell below a food poverty line. Within a year, this was reduced to 37%. Those households that were not joined by family members from outside the project villages (an understandable migration) saw poverty levels reduced from 76% to just 16%.
- The proportion of people engaged in economic activity rose from 44% to 55%, often through own-account work of various kinds: and especially through such initiatives as the tending of vegetable plots and the building of latrines, which directly led to an increase in the community's health.
- Far from leading to idleness and a decrease in economic activity, the economic security that a Citizen's Basic Income offered to people gave them the confidence to take the economic risks necessary for new productive activity.
- Child malnutrition fell. Children's weight-for-age improved in just six months from 42% of underweight children to just 10% by the end of the project.
- Before the pilot project, almost half of the villages' children did not attend school regularly. Pass rates were at 40%, and drop-out rates were high. This was mainly because parents had to pay fees for their children to attend school. By the end of the project, 90% of parents were paying school fees, and most children now attend school. Drop-out rates fell from 40% to almost zero during the project.

- The clinic, like the school, is funded by attendees' payments. During the project, residents could pay the attendance fee, use of the clinic increased six-fold, and the income of the clinic increased five-fold.
- During the first year of the project, average household debt fell from N\$1,215 to N\$772. Savings increased, as did ownership of livestock.
- Crime rates fell by 42% during the project. Theft of stock fell by a similar amount, giving people the confidence to invest in assets.
- The Citizen's Basic Income gave to women a new economic independence, and paid-for sex was reduced accordingly.
- There was no evidence that the Citizen's Basic Income led to an increase in alcoholism.
- Administrative costs were just 3–4% of the total outlay.[26]
- The villages of their own volition elected an advisory committee of 18 residents, and among its achievements were the opening of a post office, the establishment of savings accounts, and the closure of shebeens on the day of the monthly distribution of the grants.
- New shops were opened.
- The number of people experiencing daily food shortages fell from 30% to 12% of the population in just six months.
- The number of people who rarely experienced food shortages rose from 20% to 60% of the population.
- Economic activity rose fastest among women.
- Average income rose in every earnings quintile, and proportionately more for lower quintiles.
- Average income rose a staggering 200% in the lowest quintile *excluding* the N\$100 (US\$12) Citizen's Basic Income, because people could now purchase the means for making an income, and they did.
- Low-wage employment was in many cases replaced by better-paid self-employment.

Following the end of the two-year pilot project, additional small unconditional grants had similar effects.[27]

The pilot project passed all of the tests: it was based on rights, not charity; it was not paternalistic; it benefited the poorest most; it promoted dignified work; and the kind of activity that it promoted cared for the environment: and the project refuted the critics of unconditional cash transfers. Far from encouraging dependency, the Citizen's Basic Income increased enterprise; far from leading to waste of resources, it encouraged productive use of resources; and far from being unaffordable, the level of Citizen's Basic Income employed in the pilot project would, if extended to the country as a whole, cost just

2.2% to 3.8% of GDP, and the increased economic activity generated by the Citizen's Basic Income would by itself pay the entire cost.

Additional findings of the pilot project were that the Citizen's Basic Income was not inflationary; that women's economic status had risen relative to men's; that the Citizen's Basic Income was more effective than conditional transfers partly because it could not be removed by a local bureaucrat if someone upset them, as a conditional cash transfer could be; that because unconditional payments limit the power of bureaucrats, more of the money reached the poor; that in the context of today's more flexible employment markets, trades unions are more willing to support a Citizen's Basic Income; and that surveys in Africa have found that 80% of people favour unconditionality.

Standing speculated that one reason why policy makers in Africa and elsewhere do not like the idea of a Citizen's Basic Income is that the scheme is emancipatory:[28] it allows people to make choices for themselves, and it does not allow policy makers to interfere in people's lives by imposing conditions on cash transfers.

The most vigorous, and to some extent hostile, questioning at the seminar came from people who worked for non-governmental organisations committed to providing goods and services in Africa and elsewhere. Is it not better to build schools for people than to give them money? Well, no, not necessarily: because if they are given the money then they will build the kind of school that they need, not the kind that someone outside the situation thinks that they need. The main achievement of the pilot project was that it proved that people do not waste money – they invest it wisely: in their children's nourishment, health and education, in income-generating activity, and in the infrastructure that their community needs.

The seminar ran out of time.

After the end of the pilot project, Namibia's government showed no interest in the results, and the Prime Minister dismissed the Citizen's Basic Income idea: 'We can't dish out money for free to people who do nothing.' Initially the trades union movement followed the government's lead and withdrew from the alliance that had sponsored the pilot project. A vociferous public reaction provoked trades union re-engagement, and for the first time the movement found itself in opposition to the government. Subsequently more interest has been shown, and in 2015 the Namibian president included a Citizen's Basic Income in his anti-poverty strategy: but so far nothing has come of that stated interest.[29]

India

In January 2011 two more pilot projects began: one in West Delhi's Raghubir Nagar slum, and the other in eight rural villages in Madhya Pradesh. The Self-Employed Women's Association (SEWA) began planning and raising money for the rural project in 2008. The Delhi government joined in and worked with SEWA to organise the urban project. In the urban project 100 households received 1,000 rupees per month (about US$22) and were deprived of permission to use the subsidised ration shop. Another 100 households got a bank account and continued use of the ration shop; a third group of 150 families received neither cash nor a bank account, and continued to use the ration shop; and a fourth group of 150 families did not wish to receive the cash transfers. All cash transfers were made to the woman of the family. In the rural project, adults received 200 rupees a month (between 30% and 40% of subsistence income) and 100 rupees a month was given for each child under the age of 14. The economic and social effects were studied in relation to control groups.[30] A further project involving tribal villages was added later.

Interim results were announced at the 2012 BIEN Congress in Munich, and final results in a report.[31] Families mainly spent their unconditional cash transfers on food, healthcare and education. School attendance increased three-fold, school performance two-fold, and more girls were in secondary school. Spending on alcohol declined.[32] Especially where SEWA was active, communities pooled their benefits to create roads, drains and toilets, with benefits to community health.[33] Economic activity increased, new businesses were founded, and families worked together to improve their housing.[34] A significant benefit identified by the researchers and by SEWA was the empowerment of women. Because they received cash transfers of their own, they were able to start their own businesses, and they were no longer entirely dependent on their husbands for income. This applied as much to wealthier women as to poorer ones. This effect, along with the ability to escape from debt that the Citizen's Basic Incomes gave to many families, represented a considerable emancipatory effect.[35]

SEWA's intention was to give to women greater financial security, and this was achieved. The government's interest was to find a way to replace numerous corrupt and inefficient social welfare programmes[36] with a new scheme in which money would reach those for whom it was intended, and the pilot project results suggest that unconditional cash transfers could achieve that goal.[37] The authors of the report suggest that the combination of effects generated by the Citizen's Basic

Income – welfare, equity, economic growth and emancipation – shows the policy to be transformative.[38]

Both the Namibian and Indian pilot projects were for limited periods (two years and eighteen months respectively), so it might be difficult to draw conclusions about long-term behavioural effects from the behavioural effects evidenced during the projects: but all the same, the effects on nutrition, education, health, economic activity, income and emancipation have been considerable. The effects of longer-term Citizen's Basic Incomes would probably be greater, but until we try a permanent Citizen's Basic Income we won't know that.

Social transfers in Latin America and elsewhere

A number of countries, particularly in Latin America, run social transfer programmes for children and older people.[39] Some of these, such as the *Bolsa Familia* in Brazil, are conditional (only for poor families, and conditional on children attending school and health clinics):[40] but the stated intention is universality and unconditionality,[41] and in that cause coverage is being extended and conditionalities are being whittled away.[42] It was regional experiments that gave rise to the *Bolsa Familia*, and regions are again innovating.[43] Similarly, Argentina's Universal Child Benefit is not in fact universal, but the intention is continual extension to new recipients,[44] and in 2009 a scheme previously only for families with a worker in the formal employment market was extended to the unemployed and to informal workers.[45] Some schemes are becoming more conditional on attendance at school or for health checks,[46] but some new benefits have been a bit of a surprise, such as Greece's new near-universal pension established in the midst of its financial crisis.[47]

A study by the International Labour Organization has found that the Latin American Conditional Cash Transfers for families with children result in numerous positive outcomes for recipients, including new economic activity,[48] higher net incomes, reduced amounts of child labour,[49] increased school attendance, higher educational achievement, increasing productive activity, and better nutrition: but research has also shown that short-term results might be more positive than longer-term ones; that for the children involved the schooling conditionality does not necessarily result in better life chances; and that the programmes make little impact on intergenerational poverty transmission.[50] Conditional Cash Transfers have become a default position in many countries,[51] and there are not enough unconditional social transfer programmes designed for working-age adults to enable researchers to draw conclusions as to their effects: but Orton can still legitimately draw the conclusion that 'the results of social pensions and a number of other unconditional transfers support the expectation that a [Citizen's Basic Income] could generate similarly positive social and micro-economic effects';[52] and more recent evidence on Bolivian cash transfers that are not dependent on employment status has supported the view that unconditional cash transfer schemes can generate as much additional school attendance as conditional ones.[53] Standing's conclusion, following a survey of cash transfers with varying degrees of conditionality, is that

> now conditional cash transfers are legitimised. But the flaws of all forms of targeting, selectivity and conditionality, as well as their unnecessary costs, are making more people question the need for them. What we can say is that only universalistic transfers, ... where they have been tried, including in some of the world's poorest countries, ... have proved an effective means to combat poverty and income insecurity while promoting livelihoods and work.[54]

The World Bank has evaluated unconditional schemes and discovered how effective they can be,[55] but we still await the kind of permanent unconditional cash transfer programmes that will tell us whether a Citizen's Basic Income can create the long-term change in poverty levels hoped for but imperfectly realised in relation to conditional schemes.[56]

Further experiments

At the time of writing, there are several experiments at various stages of planning or implementation.

In Finland, a random sample of 2,000 unemployed individuals are receiving €560 per month for a period of two years in place of existing benefits.[57] If they find employment then they keep the payment. This experiment will, it is hoped, deliver some useful information about the employment market effects of turning conditional benefits into unconditional incomes. However, it is not a Citizen's Basic Income pilot project.[58] It shares with all other experiments so far the characteristic that the experiment is limited to two years, which means that long-term behavioural effects cannot be evaluated: but even more importantly, payment is conditional on being unemployed, so conclusions will not be able to be drawn about broader effects; the sample is a random one across the whole country rather than being geographically localised, so community effects, like those found in Namibia and India, cannot be evaluated; and the way in which the project has been designed will generate an important injustice: if one of the individuals receiving the unconditional income finds employment, then they keep their unconditional €560 per month, and they will probably be working alongside someone who is not part of the experiment: so two people in identical circumstances could find their net monthly incomes to be different by €560. The only solution to this would be a Citizen's Basic Income across the entire population.

A project planned for Ontario, in Canada, will be testing payments that do not look as if they are going to be Citizen's Basic Incomes at all;[59] and it looked as if experiments similar to the Finland project might take off in the Netherlands, but these are still under discussion, and what they might look like is far from clear.[60] The same is true for Glasgow, in Scotland.[61] Plans for a 'saturation' pilot project in a small town in Fife, Scotland, look rather more like a genuine Citizen's Basic Income experiment, but plans are still at an early stage.[62] Further details are awaited with interest: as are details of an experiment planned for Oakland, California.[63] A project involving 95 participants in a village in Kenya is exhibiting results similar to the projects in Namibia and India, but the sample is very small, and evaluation methods appear to be nothing like as robust as those in the Indian project.[64] A larger project is planned.[65]

A rather different and particularly innovative project is a crowd-funded Citizen's Basic Income paid to individuals selected at random from individuals who have applied. €1,000 per month is paid for a period of one year, and so far 89 such incomes have been paid.[66] Other experiments of various kinds have happened. For instance, in 2009, 13 homeless men in London were given £3,000 each, and most of them used it to turn their lives around.[67] And experiments of various kinds are planned. No doubt there will be more.[68] What is essential is to be clear exactly what each experiment is and what it is not. Only if a regular income is paid, and it is entirely unconditional, is the experiment a Citizen's Basic Income pilot project. Impermissible conditions are homelessness, unemployment, choice by random selection, number of previous payments and, arguably, location. The only permissible condition is age. This means that only a permanent national trial involving everyone of the same age can be a genuine Citizen's Basic Income pilot project. This does not mean that other experiments are not worth doing: they are, because they can produce some valuable data, but the fact that they are not genuine Citizen's Basic Income pilot projects means we need to be careful how we interpret the results. The nearest we've got to a Citizen's Basic Income is Iran; and the nearest we've got to Citizen's Basic Income pilot projects are the Namibian and Indian experiments. Future projects need to learn from those.

An interesting additional example to study is an equal annual distribution of casino profits to Cherokee Indians. Health and educational benefits similar to those noticed in India and Namibia have been discovered, along with a significant increase in the quality of parenting.[69] Whether varying annual payments to Alaskans and Cherokee Indians should be counted as Citizen's Basic Incomes is an interesting question. Probably not, as varying annual payments function very differently from unvarying weekly or monthly payments.

Not exactly a pilot, but more a test of public opinion, Switzerland has held a referendum on Citizen's Basic Income. It is unfortunate that even though the referendum resolution was a request to the Swiss government to implement a Citizen's Basic Income, to decide on the level at which it would be paid, and to determine the funding mechanism, the resolution's proposers put out material that asked for a Citizen's Basic Income of 2,500 Swiss francs a month. It was this suggestion, rather than the resolution, that took centre stage in the media and in political and public debate, leading to the resolution being defeated.[70]

A pilot project in the UK?[71]

Might it be possible to run a Citizen's Basic Income pilot project in the UK? A genuine *Citizen's Basic Income* pilot project? The project would have to be permanent for each individual involved, or at least for a sufficiently long period for the payments to be experienced as permanent; the payments would have to be funded by changing Income Tax and National Insurance Contribution levels and thresholds, which would require government departments to make those adjustments for the individuals involved in the project, and to recycle the savings into project participants' Citizen's Basic Incomes; and the project would need to involve a cross-section of the population, as well as involving the whole of a community, if it were to stand some chance of modelling a genuine Citizen's Basic Income.

One possibility would be for residents of a single large community to be the sample group. If the community were sufficiently isolated, if all of its members lived and worked in the community, and if nobody worked in the community who did not live there, then the injustice generated by the Finnish project – in which two people could be working together, one with a Citizen's Basic Income, and one not – would not occur. A Hebridean island comes to mind: although whether such a community could be regarded as representative is an interesting question. Somewhat less isolated but probably more representative would be the Isle of Wight.

Either participants would give up their right to claim means-tested benefits (including Working Tax Credits, Child Tax Credits, and 'Universal Credit', but not Housing Benefit and Council Tax Reduction, which would continue to be paid), or means-tested benefits would continue to be paid, and the Department for Work and Pensions and HMRC would recalculate them for the participant group. National Insurance Benefits and Child Benefit would continue to be paid. If the scheme in this book's appendix were to provide the model, then participants' Income Tax Personal Allowances and National Insurance Contribution Primary Earnings Thresholds would be reduced to zero, and National Insurance Contributions would be paid at 12% on all earnings and the additional government revenue would be paid into a dedicated fund out of which the Citizen's Basic Incomes would be paid. After administrative costs, any annual surplus in the fund would be paid to HM Government, and any shortfall would be met by HM Government.

Such an experiment would constitute a genuine pilot project. It would take a lot of work on the part of two government departments and a local authority, and it would require the government and Parliament to approve changes to Income Tax, National Insurance and means-tested benefits legislation for the project community, which could be a complex task: but a genuine pilot project of this nature could reap considerable rewards. It would test a genuine Citizen's Basic Income scheme and could propel the UK into establishing a nationwide scheme and experiencing the benefits of being a first mover. It would be a pleasure to see the UK being the first to implement a constructive and future-directed way of organising our society, economy and employment market.

Conclusion

Given the runaway success of the UK's NHS and Child Benefit, the popularity and beneficial effects of the Alaska Permanent Fund dividend, the rapidity with which Iran has established an unconditional cash benefit as an entirely pragmatic measure, and the stunning results seen by those evaluating the Namibian and Indian pilot projects, is it not time for a developed country to establish a genuine pilot project? There would be a difference. The Namibian and Indian pilot projects have been funded by donations, the Alaskan dividend has been funded by the proceeds of a permanent fund into which oil extraction royalties have been paid, and the Iranian incomes have been funded by redirecting oil revenues previously spent on subsidies, whereas in a country like the UK any Citizen's Basic Income would need to be funded in the first instance by reducing tax allowances and means-tested and contributory benefits, so any meaningful pilot project would have to be funded in that way. Organising such a pilot project in a developed country would not be easy, and, as we have seen, it would be all too easy for a project to cease to be a genuine Citizen's Basic Income pilot project: but that is no reason for not attempting a genuine pilot project in a developed country.[72] As David Purdy suggests:

> [D]esirability, viability and achievability, though logically distinct, must ultimately be considered together. Until and unless [a Citizen's Basic Income] is actually tried, its advocates can only speculate about how people would respond to its introduction, just as in the early nineteenth century, advocates of universal suffrage could only speculate about how government and society would be affected if all adults acquired the right to vote.[73]

Lively debate around the world is of course important,[74] but there comes a point when theory must give way to verification via experiment. The only way to find out whether a Citizen's Basic Income will benefit individuals, families, society, the economy and the employment market is to try it; and the only way to find out whether there will be detrimental effects on the employment market will be to try it.[75] The Namibian and Indian experiments offer us tried and tested ways of conducting pilot projects,[76] so nobody will need to start from scratch. Particularly important is to keep the design of the project clear and constant. If it is a Citizen's Basic Income that is to be tested, then it must be a genuine Citizen's Basic Income that is experienced by pilot project participants, and not something similar or changing; and the pilot will need to be long enough for behavioural trends to emerge. Two years is not long enough.

If the results from the Namibian and Indian experiments are as significant as we think they are, then a Citizen's Basic Income is an opportunity for social and economic change that the UK must not neglect. If we do neglect it then other countries will not, countries across the world will follow Iran's lead, and it will be those countries that will reap the economic and social benefits. Namibia's government might extend their pilot project to other villages and towns, and then establish a nationwide Citizen's Basic Income; the Indian government could well see a Citizen's Basic Income as a way out of numerous current problems; a country like East Timor, that is in the process of developing its economic infrastructure, might use resources revenues to pay for a Citizen's Basic Income;[77] Citizen's Basic Incomes might be found to be the best mechanism for enabling communities to recover from natural and other disasters;[78] Latin America could turn more of its conditional transfers into unconditional ones; and Central and Eastern Europe could be next.[79]

Seventy years ago, the UK was a world leader in social policy innovation. The inventions of that time have served us well. We now need to innovate in a new context. The rapid changes affecting our economy, our employment market and our society demand a new approach to the tax and benefits systems. If we get this wrong then we shall all suffer, rich as well as poor. If we get it right then we could achieve the economy, employment market and society that we shall need in this still quite new millennium.

A substantial UK Citizen's Basic Income pilot project is not a lot to ask, given the extent of our current economic and social problems, and the possibly substantial benefits of a Citizen's Basic Income.

What are we afraid of?

Notes

[1] Citizen's Income Trust, 2000; Widerquist, 2010; Widerquist and Howard, 2012b.
[2] Hammond, 1994.
[3] O'Brien and Olson, 1991.
[4] www.apfc.org/home/Content/home/index.cfm, 16/05/2017.
[5] https://pfd.alaska.gov/Payments/Tax-Information, 16/05/2017.
[6] Zelleke, 2012: 150.
[7] Rose and Wohlforth, 2008.
[8] Goldsmith, 2012.
[9] Widerquist, 2010.
[10] Goldsmith, 2012: 53; Sommeiller, Price and Wazeter, 2016.
[11] www.adn.com/politics/2016/09/23/gov-walkers-veto-shaves-alaska-permanent-fund-dividends-to-1022/, 16/05/2017.
[12] Lansley, 2016.
[13] Widerquist, 2010; Widerquist and Howard, 2012a.
[14] Tabatabai, 2011a; Tabatabai, 2011b.
[15] Salehi-Isfahani, 2014.
[16] Hamid Tabatabai, presentation on 15 September 2012 at the 14th BIEN Congress in Munich.
[17] Tabatabai, 2012a: 295; Salehi-Isfahani, 2014.
[18] Tabatabai, 2012b; De Wispelaere, 2016: 625.

[19] Salehi-Isfahani, 2014.
[20] Blaschke, 2012.
[21] Torry, 2009.
[22] Standing, 1999; 2002; 2004; 2005; 2009; 2011b; 2012b; 2014; 2016; 2017; Standing and Samson, 2003; Davala, Jhabvala, Mehta and Standing, 2015.
[23] Casassas and Bailón, 2007.
[24] Haarman and Haarmann, 2007.
[25] Basic Income Grant Coalition, 2009: 13–17.
[26] The following results were given at the seminar.
[27] Standing, 2017: 232.
[28] Standing, 2015.
[29] Haarmann and Haarmann, 2012; Standing, 2017: 232.
[30] Davala, Jhabvala, Mehta and Standing, 2015: 34: unlike the Namibian pilot project, which exhibited a less rigorous methodology (Osterkamp, 2013).
[31] Davala, Jhabvala, Mehta and Standing, 2015.
[32] Davala, Jhabvala, Mehta and Standing, 2015: 96, 113, 134, 154.
[33] Davala, Jhabvala, Mehta and Standing, 2015: 73, 76, 92–5.
[34] Davala, Jhabvala, Mehta and Standing, 2015: 153–5.
[35] Davala, Jhabvala, Mehta and Standing, 2015: 69–70; Standing, 2017: 236.
[36] Standing, 2013.
[37] Interim results announced at the 14th BIEN Congress in Munich on 15 September 2012. See also Standing, 2012b.
[38] Davala, Jhabvala, Mehta and Standing, 2015: 195–214; Standing, 2012a; 2017: 237.
[39] Papers presented at conferences of the United States Basic Income Guarantee network, which explore moves towards Citizen's Basic Income in various parts of the world. An early collection of papers can be found in Widerquist, Lewis and Pressman, 2005.
[40] Barrientos and Pellissery, 2011: 6; Coêlho, 2012.
[41] Suplicy, 1995; 2012.
[42] Britto and Soares, 2011; Standinga, 2012: 6.
[43] Senator Eduardo Suplicy, a presentation given on 14 September 2012 at the 14th BIEN Congress.
[44] Roca, 2010: 18.
[45] Gasparini and Cruces, 2010.
[46] Lund, 2011; Barrientos, 2011; Standing, 2011a.
[47] Matsaganis and Leventi, 2011.
[48] Standing, 2017: 228–9.
[49] Orton, 2009.
[50] Jones, 2016.
[51] Cobham, 2014.
[52] Orton, 2011: 6.
[53] Standing, 2017: 228.
[54] Standing, 2008: 26.
[55] Garcia and Moore, 2012: 8.
[56] Papadopoulos and Valázquez Leyer, 2016a; Padopoulos and Valázquez Leyer, 2016b.
[57] Kangas, 2016; https://helda.helsinki.fi/handle/10138/167728, 17/05/2017.
[58] http://blogi.kansanelakelaitos.fi/arkisto/3316, 13/06/2017.
[59] www.ontario.ca/page/ontario-basic-income-pilot, 17/05/2017; Standing, 2017: 266–8.

60 McFarland, 2017a.
61 McFarland, 2017b.
62 McFarland, 2017c.
63 Altman, 2016; https://blog.ycombinator.com/hiring-for-basic-income/, 17/05/2017.
64 Douillard, 2017; Bregman, 2017: 28–30.
65 Standing, 2017: 270–71.
66 Offe, 2014; www.mein-grundeinkommen.de/, 17/05/2017.
67 Bregman, 2017: 25–7.
68 Standing, 2017: 260–74.
69 Akee, Simeonova, Costello and Copeland, 2015: 9; Bregman, 2017: 51–4.
70 www.theguardian.com/world/2016/jun/05/swiss-vote-give-basic-income-every-adult-child-marxist-dream, 02/06/2017; http://citizensincome.org/opinion/referenda/, 17/05/2017.
71 This section is based on a paper submitted to the trustees of the Citizen's Income Trust following interviews undertaken by a French postgraduate student, Lucas Delattre, in the London Borough of Tower Hamlets, and subsequent research by the author.
72 Standing, 2017: 310–15.
73 Purdy, 2007.
74 Caputo, 2012.
75 Groot, 2004: 93–114; Groot, 2005; Groot, 2006; Widerquist, 2006; Peters and Marks, 2006; Noguera and De Wispelaere, 2006; Virjo, 2006.
76 Standing, 2012b.
77 Casassas, Raventós and Wark, 2010.
78 International Social Security Association, 2014.
79 Huber, 1996; Standing, 1996.

TEN

Objections

In this chapter we shall study a number of objections commonly made in relation to Citizen's Basic Income:

- we shouldn't pay people for doing nothing;
- immigration would go up;
- people wouldn't work;
- we can't afford it;
- if a Citizen's Basic Income scheme abolished means-tested benefits then we wouldn't know to whom we should give passported benefits such as free school meals;
- there are lots of problems that it wouldn't solve;
- it would increase public expenditure;
- the money could be better used on other things;
- and more …

None of the objections listed has a necessary connection to any particular political ideology. Indeed, they can be found across the political spectrum.[1] We could regard this as a difficulty or as an advantage: a difficulty, because the objections have to be answered for parties and individuals attached to a wide variety of different political ideologies; and an advantage because if the objections can be answered then it should be possible to achieve and maintain cross-party agreement to implementing a Citizen's Basic Income scheme.

We shouldn't pay people to do nothing

This usually means: nobody should receive an income from the government if they are not gainfully employed or looking for employment. The simple response to this objection is that we are already paying people to do nothing, and the way in which we do it discourages them from increasing their earned income. A Citizen's Basic Income would pay people to do nothing in such a way that they could experience more of an incentive to earn additional income, learn new skills and spend time caring for others and volunteering in their communities.

But at the heart of the objection lies a valid principle: reciprocity.[2] This is often taken to imply that the citizens of a country have a duty to contribute to society before society can be expected to provide for them. This might once have made sense: but today much employment is short term, new investment often results in a *loss* of employment,[3] and the duty to be gainfully employed is now problematic: for how can there be a duty to be gainfully employed when for many people there is no opportunity, and when often what is available is part-time employment when what is required to lift a family off means-tested benefits is well-paid full-time employment?[4] High marginal deduction rates extract from the worker a high proportion of any additional income earned, compromising the obligation to work for an income.

In this new situation, should we not alter the definition of 'work' to mean 'beneficial activity' so that it covers paid and unpaid work, and particularly caring work in the family and in the community? It is always easier to change one's attitudes when financially and socially secure, and many of those most in need of being able to re-evaluate their own unpaid work are those who take their obligations to their families seriously and yet have the least secure incomes. For them, financial security is both more of a necessity and more difficult to achieve.[5] Belonging to any community entails obligations, but those obligations must be amenable to being met. If an obligation to be gainfully employed is no longer amenable to being sufficiently met for a growing proportion of the population, then the obligation needs to be reframed as a broader moral obligation to contribute to society by paid work, by unpaid work in the community, or by unpaid work caring for others.

Stuart White suggests that

> where institutions governing economic life are otherwise sufficiently just, e.g., in terms of the availability of opportunities for productive participation and the rewards attached to those opportunities, then those who claim the generous share of the social product available to them under these institutions have an obligation to make a decent productive contribution, suitably proportional and fitting for ability and circumstances, to the community in return. I term this the fair-dues conception of reciprocity.[6]

White's arguments for requiring such reciprocity are that self-esteem is a good thing, and that self-esteem depends on reciprocity in social arrangements. Non-reciprocation burdens other people, which is a bad thing, because to expect not to reciprocate is a statement of superiority, to expect others not to reciprocate is a statement of servility, and (a more instrumental argument) a welfare state is more likely to remain politically acceptable if it is founded on reciprocity. Citizenship obligations can be met through paid labour, care work and voluntary community activity, all of which is 'civic labour'; and it is such civic labour that creates the 'civic minimum' of income and healthcare that is the right of every citizen, and is even more of a necessity in the face of growing 'market vulnerability'.[7]

'In a context of otherwise sufficiently fair economic arrangements, everyone should do their bit': but the corollary of this is that if economic arrangements are *not* otherwise fair, then not only is it difficult for a society to sustain citizens' rights, it is equally difficult to sustain citizenship duties.[8]

A further factor is that fulfilling duties should not be the only way to receive resources from society. 'Some resources are properly seen as belonging to a common citizens' inheritance fund, and it is implausible that the individual's entitlement to a share of this fund is entirely dependent on a willingness to work.'[9]

A share of the income that someone in employment earns comes from resources that belong to all of us, so it is not exploitative to tax earnings in order to fund a Citizen's Basic Income;[10] a Citizen's Basic Income calculated on this basis would at least establish one of the necessary bases for just reciprocity because it would provide a secure income floor: a 'civic minimum' on the basis of which a contribution to society can be legitimately expected;[11] and, because a Citizen's Basic Income would make it easier for someone to refuse demeaning or poorly paid employment, and would therefore improve the employment opportunities on offer, it would provide 'opportunity for self-realisation in work': one of the conditions for just reciprocity.[12] White therefore argues for a Citizen's Basic Income of a larger amount than that warranted by the 'common citizens' inheritance fund' on the grounds that

1. Even if basic income is bad for reciprocity, this is outweighed by its positive effects on other concerns of fairness, such as the prevention of market vulnerability.
2. Even if basic income is bad for reciprocity in one way, it is also likely to have positive effects in terms of this same value.[13]

A familiar question might be put like this: is it the welfare state's role to seek to change people's behaviour by applying conditions to the receipt of welfare benefits?[14] A redistributive system based on a Citizen's Basic Income would pose the question differently: given an unconditional income, would people's behaviour change, and, if so, how? Here the answers will stem from empirical study rather than from ideological commitments, although how a philosopher would view the situation would still of course depend on their point of view. Philippe Van Parijs recommends a Citizen's Basic Income on the basis of the 'real freedom' that it would offer, including the freedom to spend one's days surfing:[15] 'real freedom' because a Citizen's Basic Income would offer not only the theoretical right to choose one's way of life, but also the financial security to turn the right into reality.[16] White would prefer to see a bit more reciprocity in the situation – although he is still happy to recommend a Citizen's Basic Income, because while free riding is against the idea of just reciprocity, a small number of people not fulfilling their obligations would be a small price to pay for a secure income floor that would establish one of the main criteria for a *just* reciprocity.[17]

So yes, we should pay people for doing nothing: and we should expect the financial security that this would provide to act as a springboard for enhanced engagement with the employment market, business creation, voluntary work in the community, and caring for others.

Immigration would go up

The assumption often lying behind this objection is that a Citizen's Basic Income would hand out additional money to everyone living in the UK, and that the level of inward migration would therefore rise. The assumption is not necessarily correct. It would of course be possible to implement a Citizen's Basic Income scheme that gave out additional income (see the objection 'We can't afford it' later in this chapter): but equally it would be possible to implement schemes that would simply turn Income Tax Personal Allowances and proportions of means-tested benefits into unconditional incomes of the same or similar value, meaning that net incomes would remain broadly the same. Because of the complexity of the current tax and benefits system, any change will produce gains and losses: but those gains and losses can be kept to a minimum, and the parameters of the scheme can be adjusted to ensure that gains balance losses, so that on average no additional net income will be experienced. There is thus no reason to believe that implementing a Citizen's Basic Income scheme would increase immigration.

Another assumption sometimes lying behind this objection is that economic migrants might receive state benefits rather than contribute to society by earning a living and paying taxes. For many households currently on means-tested benefits, a Citizen's Basic Income would reduce marginal deduction rates, so they would be more likely to seek employment, start businesses, earn a living and pay taxes. And if the unconditional nature of the Citizen's Basic Income might be thought to be a particular attraction to migrants, then the obvious response is that the UK already has an unconditional and nonwithdrawable Child Benefit, payable to anyone with the care of children if they ordinarily reside in the UK, they have a right to be there, and they are physically present in the country,[18] and that Child Benefit is rarely accused of fuelling inward migration.

Also lying behind this objection is the broader question: who should receive a Citizen's Basic Income? Most Citizen's Basic Income schemes assume that 'citizens' or 'legal residents' will receive the unconditional incomes, which means that those terms need to be given clearer definition than is often the case. The first edition of *Money for Everyone* included a thorough discussion of the highly contested concept of citizenship.[19] I shall not repeat that discussion here but will instead take a more pragmatic approach[20] informed by the regulations for Child Benefit. These suggest that the following should receive a Citizen's Basic Income:

- all those with the right to reside in the UK indefinitely (while we are still in the European Union, this includes EU nationals); and
- refugees with a defined number of years of legal residence (usually five years extendable);[21]

in both cases, on condition (a) that they would be defined as resident in the UK by HMRC,[22] and (b) that they have been resident in the UK for an agreed minimum period, which would presumably be somewhere between two and five years.[23]

A national of another country that had implemented a Citizen's Basic Income would be entitled to receive a Citizen's Basic Income on their arrival in the UK on condition that their country gave the same right to UK nationals. This mirrors Child Benefit provisions.

As important as the question 'who should receive a Citizen's Basic Income?' is the question 'Who should *not* receive one?'

The following should probably not receive Citizen's Basic Incomes:

- international students and foreign workers resident on the basis of visas;
- asylum seekers (that is, people who are seeking refugee status but do not yet have it);
- convicted prisoners (prisoners on remand would continue to receive their Citizen's Basic Incomes; and Citizen's Basic Incomes would be paid to ex-prisoners immediately on release).

Whether these suggestions will be experienced as an adequate response to the objection that a Citizen's Basic Income would encourage additional inward migration is of course unknown until there is some realistic prospect of a Citizen's Basic Income scheme being implemented. I suspect that if the general public and policy makers come to recognise a Citizen's Basic Income as a desirable and feasible policy option, then the arguments contained in this chapter will be understood to be an adequate response. If policy makers and the public do not come to recognise a Citizen's Basic Income as a desirable and feasible policy to implement, then the objection will continue to carry weight, and the arguments in this chapter will not be experienced as adequate.

But to return to the question of precisely who should receive a Citizen's Basic Income: one possibility would be to pay a Citizen's Basic Income to anyone on the electoral register (and to under-18s if they would be on the electoral register if they were not under 18). If the current register were to be used then this would clearly pose problems: someone with no address cannot be on the register, so to give a Citizen's Basic Income only to people on the register would leave those without an address still on means-tested benefits rather than in receipt of a Citizen's Basic Income. Of more importance numerically is the current state of the register. Electoral registers are only about 90% accurate when they are at their most accurate after the annual October canvass: but some local registers are only 85% accurate, particularly in the larger urban areas outside London. Under-25s, private sector tenants, and black and minority ethnic (BME) British residents are particularly underrepresented.[24]

It is of course possible that to use the electoral register as the criterion for payment of a Citizen's Basic Income would encourage people to register and would therefore improve democratic participation:[25] but the problem of who should and who should not be on the electoral register would still need to be addressed. Some way would have to be found of including people with no fixed abode; decisions would need to be taken as to whether British citizens permanently abroad should

(a) be on the electoral register, and (b) receive a Citizen's Basic Income; and decisions would need to be taken as to which foreign nationals resident here would be entitled to a Citizen's Basic Income. European Union citizens living here are allowed onto the electoral register and are entitled to a variety of existing benefits, and would presumably receive a Citizen's Basic Income.[26] Whether such rights will continue after the UK leaves the European Union is currently unknown.

A good reason for considering a link between the electoral register and a Citizen's Basic Income is that legislation for a Citizen's Basic Income would need voter support, and to link receipt of a Citizen's Basic Income to the electoral register might achieve this, as it would clearly link the right to a Citizen's Basic Income to the fulfilment of duties (especially to the duty to vote) as well as to the rights of citizenship (especially to the right to vote).[27] By encouraging both paid and unpaid work, and offering increased possibilities for care work, a Citizen's Basic Income would encourage an active citizenship; and to link its payment to the electoral register would emphasise this.

The two approaches to the question as to who should receive a Citizen's Basic Income that we have considered – the link to the electoral register, and the parallel with current Child Benefit regulations – could be considered either separately or together; and one way of combining them would be to determine eligibility for a Citizen's Basic Income via a set of simple rules, and then use receipt of a Citizen's Basic Income as the gateway both to voter registration and to Child Benefit for one's children.

People wouldn't work

The reader will already be able to construct their own response to this objection from material in Chapter 3: but the frequency with which this objection is raised means that it is essential to include a detailed response here.

Far from people being unwilling to work, they would be more likely to do so: more likely to seek paid employment; more likely to keep skills up to date; more likely to seek promotion or a better job; more likely to spend time caring for relatives; and more likely to volunteer in their community. It is today's system that discourages people from seeking employment: and the sanctions regime attached to means-tested benefits makes it even less likely that they will do so.[28] A Citizen's Basic Income would deliver lower marginal deduction rates for many households, particularly those at the lower end of the earnings range, and so would provide a greater employment incentive than people experience today; and it would reduce the budgetary chaos that households experience when someone's employment market status changes, and so would enable households to rearrange their employment patterns if that was what their own and the employment market's needs required. Overall, a Citizen's Basic Income would mean that people would be more likely to seek employment, not less.

The vast majority of people wish to be in employment or self-employment. An important piece of evidence for this is that people with multiple needs still wish to be in employment even if society regards them as people who 'can't work';[29] and another is that workers in the UK believe that other people might need an incentive to seek employment, but that they do not. Because other people are perceived as needing an incentive to seek employment, and 'Working Tax Credit' and 'Universal Credit' are perceived as such incentives, these benefits are experienced as stigmatising.[30] A further reason to think that people would be more likely to seek employment, or to seek additional employment, if they had a Citizen's Basic Income is that some wage levels would rise. Because at the moment low wages do not have to provide the whole of someone's subsistence income, the wage level and the value of the worker's labour to the employer will more nearly match each other than if the wage had to provide the whole of a household's subsistence needs. There is no evidence that increasing 'Working Tax Credit' depresses wages,[31] which suggests that the low wage is not far from the economic value of the worker's labour: an economic value that recognises that paying a sufficient wage to retain the loyalty of workers is of economic benefit to the firm.[32] A Citizen's Basic Income would generate this effect across the entire earnings range, thus extending the free market character of the employment market; and because a Citizen's Basic Income would function as a 'static subsidy' to wages – that is, it would not rise if wages fell – it would provide an added protection relative to means-tested in-work benefits, which function as a 'dynamic subsidy', rising as wages fall and offering less of a disincentive to wage reductions. The quest for a fair wage, far from leading to rejection of an unconditional income, becomes a justification for it.[33]

While 'Tax Credits' and 'Universal Credit' might perform a useful function in matching some wage levels to work's economic value, they still ensure that low wages are perceived as insufficient, they can cause household budgetary chaos when circumstances change, and they are reduced by increases in the worker's or their partner's earnings. A Citizen's Basic Income would solve these problems. It would not be experienced as a top-up for low wages because everybody would receive it; it would not be withdrawn as earnings rose, so it would enable the employment market to function more like a classical market across the entire earnings range, meaning that the economic value of work would be more accurately reflected in the wage rate across the entire earnings range; and the Citizen's Basic Income, and the better functioning employment market, would mean that the less desirable jobs would have to offer higher wages in order to persuade people to do them, and the more desirable jobs would be able to offer lower wages because more people would want them.[34] A particularly interesting development would be that internships would cease to be the preserve of children of wealthier parents, and so could become a source of social mobility rather than of social rigidity. In general, the employment market would have a lot more space in it for individual choice and initiative in relation to the jobs that people might choose to do and the ways in which households might wish to organise their working lives, because not only would a better functioning market enable jobs' desirability and wages to match each other more closely, but it would also enable the hours of employment offered by industry, commerce and service industries to more nearly match the hours of employment that workers might want. A more equal balance of power between employee and employer, an employment market in which negotiation delivered benefits to all parties involved, and an increasing humanisation of workplaces in order to attract employees, would be important consequences.[35]

But do high marginal deduction rates *really* reduce incentives to seek paid employment or to seek additional employment? There is evidence that higher tax rates make people less likely to involve themselves in the employment market, or in earnings-generating activity generally,[36] which means that high marginal deduction rates generated by the deduction of Income Tax and the withdrawal of benefits will have the same effect. A Citizen's Basic Income would reduce these marginal deduction rates for many low-income households, making it more likely that adults without employment would enter the employment market, and that those already in it would seek to increase their earnings. In Denmark, Italy, Portugal and the UK, a Citizen's Basic Income, along with progressive taxation, would offer outcomes better than means-tested and work-tested systems in terms of employment market participation and net income equality; and in Denmark and the UK a Citizen's Basic Income, again with progressive taxation, would offer better outcomes in relation to female employment market participation.[37]

An important source of evidence for the different outcomes generated by unconditional and means-tested benefits is New Zealand, where a Universal Family Benefit was abolished in favour of an income-tested benefit. Research has shown that the new system entrenched families in poverty in ways in which the unconditional benefit did not.[38] In the United States, the earnings rule was abolished for workers above normal retirement age, and the probability of being gainfully employed after retirement age went up.[39] In Canada, when the marginal deduction rates experienced by higher earners decreased, particularly for women in part-time employment, part-time employment rose by 10% among higher-earning women, and not at all among lower-earning women.[40] While employment market participation *is* a complex matter, and is subject to numerous personal, household and employment market factors, the evidence suggests that the lower marginal deduction rates that a Citizen's Basic Income would offer *would* promote greater employment market activity, and that the earnings ranges across which reductions in marginal deduction rates were currently highest would experience the greatest increased participation. This would particularly benefit part-time workers because of the high marginal deduction rates that they currently suffer now, and because a Citizen's Basic Income – even quite a small one[41] – could significantly affect those deduction rates.

Employment market participation research predicts the effect of the falling marginal deduction rates offered by unconditional benefits. It does not tell us the additional effects of the income security that they would offer, nor the reduction of administrative chaos that currently results from changes in employment market status. These changes are bound to have positive effects on employment market participation, suggesting that additional employment market activity will be even more likely with unconditional benefits than the research suggests.

But as a Citizen's Basic Income rose, would there not be pressure in the opposite direction? If someone's subsistence needs were small, then would the provision of a Citizen's Basic Income mean that they would be *less* likely to seek employment because earnings would no longer be the only route to a subsistence income? The answer to that question is this: as things stand now, earnings are not the only route to a subsistence income. Contributory and means-tested benefits are available, and these do make it less likely that someone will enter the employment market because employment will often provide little additional net income and can burden the claimant and their dependents with domestic budgetary insecurity. So in the current circumstances, employment market activity has to be coerced by such 'active labour market' policies as compulsory interviews with public officials, benefit cuts if employment offers are not taken up, and unpaid work to promote 'job readiness'.[42] A Citizen's Basic Income would reduce the disincentives and would therefore make such 'active labour market' policies less necessary. Of course, if a Citizen's Basic Income high enough to live on comfortably were to be implemented, then we would see rather more withdrawal from the employment market. The likelihood is that the incentive-enhancing effect of lower marginal deduction rates and the incentive-reducing effect of the high Citizen's Basic Income would have an ambiguous overall effect:[43] but such an eventuality is sufficiently far off for it not to be of concern to us here.

Motivation is a complex matter. Do some people *choose* not to seek employment? If so: why? Burchardt and Le Grand suggest that there are four 'layers' of factors involved in someone not seeking employment: 1. those factors over which an individual has no control (such as age); 2. those factors over which someone has no control at present (such as educational achievement); 3. those factors that someone can change in the near future, but where high costs of various kinds might be experienced (such as place of residence); and 4. those factors that someone could change easily (such as starting voluntary work). On the basis of their research, Burchardt and Le Grand conclude that 'just 1 in 10 of non-employed men, and a similar proportion of non-employed women, can be unambiguously classified as voluntarily out of work'.[44] Others will of course be on the voluntary–involuntary spectrum: so for one tenth of non-employed workers the question of motivation is pivotal, and for a larger number it remains important.

But is there not evidence that such 'active labour market' policies as benefits sanctions actually work? Definitions are important. Take, for instance, a study that compares 'employment commitment' both to the generosity of benefits and to government expenditure on 'active labour market' policies. Positive correlations are found, which might suggest that a sanctions regime enhances employment commitment. However, the researchers define 'active labour market' policies as 'the effort made by the welfare state to support employment by increasing skills, motivation and abilities among people outside the labour market',[45] and the detailed list does not include benefits sanctions. This research can therefore tell us nothing about the kind of active labour market policies pursued in the UK. But also, as the researchers admit, active labour market expenditure defined as positive support, and the generosity of benefits, are strongly correlated, so 'no conclusion regarding their independent effects can be drawn from this study'.[46] What this interesting study *does* show is that 'the notion that big welfare states are associated with widespread cultures of dependency, or other adverse consequences of poor short-term incentives to work, receives little support':[47] which is a useful conclusion to be able to draw.

At the heart of the UK's 'active labour market' policies lies a contradiction: 'external surveillance and sanctions, and encouragement to internal motivation and effort'.[48] Sanctions destroy motivation,[49] whereas what is required is 'genuine empowerment [that] can only come from freely exercised choice, and ... this ... is the only realistic and socially just way of tackling labour market exclusion'.[50] So which is the most effective employment market motivator: the coercion related to means-tested out-of-work benefits, or the certainty of retaining a substantial proportion of every extra £1 earned? A number of empirical studies have found that benefits sanctions are counterproductive: they disempower the individuals sanctioned and their families, impose long-term health and financial problems, and make it *less* likely that the sanctioned individual will enter employment.[51] This means that as coercion rises, the employment market becomes less efficient, not more: and the overall effect of 'active labour market' policies is inefficiency for the economy and inefficiency for the individual worker and their household.[52] Coercion would be impossible with a Citizen's Basic Income, so both the employment market and the worker would experience greater efficiency.

For supply and demand in the employment market to be more accurately coordinated through the price mechanism would be good for industry,[53] would be good for the efficiency of the economy,[54] and would enable the worker to behave as a genuine participant in a market, and able to refuse employment for which the wage did not sufficiently value the time, skills and activity on offer.[55] Even if this meant that some wages had to rise in order to attract sufficient people to take on the necessary work,[56] the greater efficiency would mean that firms and public sector organisations would make more rational decisions about mechanisation; postholders would have increased expectations of the training and development that an employer might provide, thus reducing the number of poor jobs and increasing the number of good jobs;[57] a Citizen's Basic Income would increase individuals' employment choices, and would enhance their bargaining power in the workplace, which would enhance trades' unions' bargaining power, which in turn would further increase the likelihood that more jobs would be good jobs;[58] the increasing quality of jobs would attract and retain older and more mature workers, benefiting both themselves and their employers;[59] working-age adults would be more likely to find the work that they wanted, and industry and commerce would be more likely to find the workers that they needed; and every citizen would find themselves nearer to the 'democratic republican' ideal of autonomous individuals relating to each other and to institutions from a position of strength rather than from a position of weakness.[60]

It is not irrational to believe that if someone received a Citizen's Basic Income then they might not wish to seek employment: but it is inconsistent to believe this at the same time as recognising that high marginal deduction rates disincentivise employment market participation.[61] If means-tested benefits were to be replaced wholly or in part by a Citizen's Basic Income, then some wages might rise in order to attract workers: but employment market incentives would also improve (without coercion having to be used), and supply and demand in the employment market would more nearly match each other across the entire earnings range. A Citizen's Basic Income would be unambiguously beneficial both for the employment market and for workers.

But as we have seen, it is not just the actual marginal deduction rates that matter. As Tony Atkinson has said, 'it's not just the actual but also the apparent disincentive that has to be avoided'.[62] Household employment decisions can be extremely complex, involving such factors as the particular hours worked, educational or training possibilities or requirements, and the care needs of children and aged relatives. A particularly complex factor is a psychological one that means that families in which the woman is the main breadwinner and the man is out of work are relatively rare:

> There remains a strong normative expectation against female breadwinners. Once the existence of such a taboo is hypothesised, many of the conundrums surrounding no-earner families fall into place. The number of non-working husbands has increased. Women are all but forbidden to work if their husbands have not got jobs, so the wives in these families cannot share in the general increase in employment experienced by women in other domestic situations. This means that the number of no-earner couples must increase. Such a process could entirely explain the apparent growth in within-family polarisation.[63]

In 2005, the Organisation for Economic Co-operation and Development found that a reduction of marginal effective tax rates [marginal deduction rates] by 20% ... implies a rise in the probability of moving from unemployment to employment by nearly 10% ... . The strongest effects are found for the unemployed with a working partner, whose reemployment probability would increase by seven percentage points, from 51% to nearly 58%.[64]

This result corroborates Atkinson and Sutherland's finding that 'the poverty trap tends to be discussed in terms of the effect of the husband earning an extra £1, but the marginal tax rate on the earnings of the wife may be quite different – and may well be more relevant, since the empirical evidence suggests that her decision may be more affected'.[65]

If a Citizen's Basic Income made part-time employment more attractive for both men and women, might this make it more likely that both women and men in no-earner families would seek employment and feel more comfortable about the woman finding employment before the man managed to do so?

The desire to work (with work broadly defined) seems to be innate to our human nature: but it is still true that it needs to be in people's interests to exchange their labour for the wage on offer. First of all, money is an indicator of the value that society places on our work, and we wish to have our contribution properly recognised; and secondly, we work for pay in order to obtain for ourselves and our families the goods and services necessary to the lives that we wish to lead. Because we wish to work, and to exchange our labour for money, there is a market in labour. Unfortunately, in the context of means-tested benefits, the employment market does not work like a free market. Under 'Universal Credit', over one million families with children face marginal deduction rates between 70% and 80%, and currently 900,000 families with children and receiving 'Tax Credits' experience these rates.[66] A Citizen's Basic Income would begin to put this right.[67]

In 1999 J.K. Galbraith suggested that

everybody should be guaranteed a decent basic income. A rich country such as the US can well afford to keep everybody out of poverty. Some, it will be said, will seize upon the income and won't work. So it is now with more limited welfare, as it is called. Let us accept some resort to leisure by the poor as well as by the rich.[68]

While such debates in the fields of philosophy, ethics and political economy might be important, they will mean little if we have not previously answered the question: would a Citizen's Basic Income make people more or less likely to seek employment if they were unemployed, and more or less likely to seek additional employment or additional self-employment if already employed? Further research, and discussions like those offered here, are clearly going to be important to this process, but unfortunately that is not all that will be required. Prejudice remains a problem. However good the evidence that a Citizen's Basic Income would increase rather than reduce work effort, we seem to find it difficult to believe that that could be true. In the previous chapter we discussed the evidence for a Citizen's Basic Income's positive effects on work effort generated by the pilot project in Otjivero, in Namibia. Following the project the Namibian Basic Income Grant Coalition issued a press release:

> Despite the positive results, the Namibian government has still not committed itself to the introduction of a BIG [Basic Income Grant: Citizen's Basic Income] in Namibia. Instead, senior government leaders have raised concerns that the grant would make people lazy and dependent on hand-outs. Such perceptions are rooted in prejudices rather than being based on the evidence provided by Otjivero! We wish to point out that the BIG Coalition arranged for many Namibians, including Members of Parliament (MPs), to visit Otjivero and to witness the developments there first-hand. The honourable MPs were free to assess the impact of the BIG themselves and they were impressed with the results achieved in Otjivero. However, they preferred to express their views in private instead of speaking out publicly in support of a national BIG.[69]

We can't afford it

This objection breaks down into two questions: how large should the Citizen's Basic Income be and how will it be funded? Answers to the two questions will never be entirely separable, of course, because the funding mechanism might entirely or to some extent determine the levels of Citizen's Basic Incomes that would be paid: but for the purposes of this response to the objection I shall express the answers separately.

There are several ways of answering the first question: the amounts of the Citizen's Basic Incomes for each age group could be set to ease the transition, for instance by aligning them with the values of tax allowances that would be abolished; or the amounts could start very low and be slowly increased so that public opinion and affordability could be evaluated before each rise in the amounts; or the amounts could be aligned with a set of Minimum Income Standards[70] designed for the UK.[71]

The second question can also be answered in several different ways.

The Citizen's Basic Incomes could be funded by making changes to the existing tax and benefits system

Reducing or abolishing the Income Tax Personal Allowance, reducing or abolishing the National Insurance Contribution Primary Earnings Threshold, and/or raising the rates at which Income Tax and/or National Insurance Contributions are collected would result in additional Income Tax and/or National Insurance Contributions being collected, and the additional revenue could be used to fund the Citizen's Basic Incomes. There is nothing radical about a Citizen's Basic Income scheme funded in this way because all we are doing is rearranging the way in which we move money around the domestic economy.[72]

The method required to calculate the changes required to fund Citizen's Basic Incomes of specific levels varies with the changes envisaged and the information required.

If all means-tested benefits are going to be abolished, then the national accounts can be employed to calculate the money which that would save, and the additional revenue that would be generated by changes to Income Tax and National Insurance Contribution rates and thresholds, and this could be matched to the cost of the Citizen's Basic Incomes, calculated by multiplying the levels of the Citizen's Basic Incomes by population statistics.[73] This method cannot be used if any means-tested benefits are to be retained because the changes in net earnings brought about by changes in Income Tax and National Insurance Contribution rates and thresholds, and changes to means-tested benefits brought about by changed net earnings and by the payment of Citizen's Basic Incomes, will be different for each household, so the change in the overall cost of means-tested benefits cannot be calculated. The national accounts method also does not deliver a vital piece of information: the number and amounts of losses experienced by low-income households at the point of implementation.[74]

If means-tested benefits are to be retained and recalculated, and if information is required on the levels of losses experienced at the point of implementation, then microsimulation has to be used. This uses a computer program into which is programmed the details of the current tax and benefits scheme. Family Resource Survey (FRS) data, based on surveys of 0.1% of all households in the UK, is then fed through the programme to produce a list of disposable incomes for individuals and households in the sample. These can then be scaled up to the whole population by using the weights included in the FRS data. A new tax and benefits system can then be created in the program by adding new benefits and by changing the regulations, rates and thresholds of existing taxes and benefits, and the program can then be run again to create a new list of disposable incomes for individuals and households. The lists of disposable incomes can then be used to calculate the net cost of a scheme, the numbers of losers at various levels of loss for different disposable or original income deciles, and marginal deduction rates of various kinds. Alongside individuals' and households' disposable incomes, the program also delivers lists of the amounts of different benefits being paid to individuals and households. These can be used to calculate changes in the numbers of households claiming different benefits, the average values of their claims, and the total costs of the different benefits. Microsimulation programs can also deliver inequality and poverty statistics, and therefore the changes in these statistics brought about by changes in the tax and benefits system.[75] The appendix of this book contains a microsimulation evaluation that exhibits the diverse results that can be obtained by using microsimulation.

Now that questions of feasibility are so central to the debate on Citizen's Basic Income, microsimulation has become the essential means for responding to many of the questions that are being asked, and to some significant objections and hesitations being expressed. The results contained in the appendix show that there is at least one Citizen's Basic Income scheme that is affordable. There will be others, but one is sufficient.

Taxing appropriation of the commons could fund Citizen's Basic Incomes

As James Robertson points out, gainful employment is a contribution to society so to tax it seems rather strange, as taxing an activity can discourage it. It would surely be better to tax those things that we wish to discourage, such as fossil fuel usage. Another problem with taxing paid employment is that supply and demand are elastic: that is, to tax paid employment might reduce both demand for it (because it becomes more expensive to hire labour) and the supply of it (because the monetary reward for labour goes down, so we might prefer to use more of our time for other activities). So the result of taxing paid employment is likely to reduce the amount of paid employment, meaning that there will be less of it to tax. Far better, surely, to tax things that do not change in quantity when they are taxed, such as land. It does not matter how much tax is applied to land, there will always be the same amount of it. Taxation of land might reduce land's desirability as an investment option, all taxation needs to be sufficiently intelligent not to compromise the ability to tax, and an agreed and feasible way would need to be found to value land and collect the tax: but the principle remains true, that it is better to tax things that do not reduce in quantity if they are taxed.

In principle, land belongs to nobody, or to all of us.[76] Certain people and organisations have acquired greater rights than others over resources such as land, which is why we tax them: to return some of the resources' value to the population as a whole. This suggests that the revenue raised should be applied in such a way that everyone benefits equally. To pay a Citizen's Basic Income out of taxation raised on common resources would therefore be a most appropriate use of the revenue.[77]

A similar argument could be made in relation to fossil fuels. Like land, fossil fuels buried in the ground belong to all of us. Companies, and sometimes individuals, have acquired the ability to extract and sell fossil fuels. In this case, taxing fossil fuels at a high rate would offer two significant benefits, not one. It would recognise our common ownership of fossil fuels, and the revenue, like a land value tax, could legitimately be applied to paying a Citizen's Basic Income (the Alaska Permanent Fund Dividend operates in a similar way); and at the same time a 'carbon tax' could usefully reduce the amount of fossil fuel extracted and sold, benefiting the climate, the ecosystem and ourselves.[78]

A problem related to carbon taxation that does not apply to a land value tax is that land will not run out, whereas fossil fuels will: and, before they do, we shall need to stop extracting and burning them. This is why the Alaskan oil extraction royalties are being paid into a fund, some of the profits from which are recycled back into the fund so that it retains its value and can continue to pay a dividend in the future. Such 'sovereign wealth funds' exist elsewhere,[79] and could exist in a lot more places.[80] An interesting question is why most of them do not pay out dividends to those countries' populations. One possibility, of course, is that those controlling the funds would rather control the capital and the revenue than pay dividends to others and thus attract demands for greater accountability.[81]

A Financial Transaction Tax

If I buy a holiday, then I pay a consumption tax (Value Added Tax in Europe): but if I buy currency to take on holiday then I will pay a commission to the vendor but I will pay no tax. The fact that currency transactions are costless in this sense has been blamed for the volume of currency transactions undertaken for purely speculative purposes: that is, currencies bought and sold on the expectation of making a profit if the currency bought increases in value relative to the currency used to pay for it. Currency transactions undertaken to facilitate the import or export of goods or services can be of value to the economy and to society, but it can be argued that purely speculative transactions are not. This is why James Tobin recommended a Financial Transaction Tax (a 'Tobin Tax').[82] There are two ways in which such a tax could make economies more rather than less efficient: it would stabilise exchange rates, and therefore make it easier for exporters and importers to plan ahead; and, because economies are already far from efficient, a tax on currency transactions could make them more efficient. Concern has been expressed that a Financial Transaction Tax could drive trading abroad. The UK already taxes purchases of shares in UK companies at 0.5%, and New York levies a similar tax on its stock exchange: but there are still plenty of share transactions in the UK and in New York. If a Financial Transaction Tax were low enough then it would not drive business abroad.

Most of the debate about Financial Transaction Taxes has centred on currency exchange transactions. There is of course no reason why a tax should not be levied on other kinds of financial transactions as well.[83]

A national Financial Transaction Tax, or a similar Financial Activity Tax, could be used to help to fund a national Citizen's Basic Income; a European tax could help to fund a European Citizen's Basic Income; and, in the longer term, a global Financial Transaction Tax could help to fund a global Citizen's Basic Income. A Financial Transaction Tax could therefore help to create a Citizen's Basic Income, with all of its benefits, and at the same time slow down currency speculation and therefore make the economy more efficient.

Consumption taxes

Consumption taxes are regressive because poorer people spend a higher proportion of their incomes on taxed goods than do wealthier people.[84] However, this is only true if we study consumption taxes on their own. A collection of essays on the funding of Citizen's Basic Income in a variety of European countries finds that in many countries consumption taxes would be a viable funding method, and that the total package of Citizen's Basic Income and consumption taxes could redistribute from rich to poor. This means that funding a Citizen's Basic Income using consumption taxes could be both financially and socially feasible.[85]

While at the moment this method of funding a Citizen's Basic Income might not seem particularly significant as an option, it is possible that the ways in which the employment market is changing might make consumption taxes more significant in the future. One of the benefits to industry and commerce of a Citizen's Basic Income would be that the employment market would behave more like a classical market. In some industries this might mean additional employment at low wage rates: but in other industries it could mean unpleasant jobs being declined at their current wage rates. Some of these jobs could be mechanised rather than offered at higher wage rates.[86] We cannot know the extent to which mechanisation will replace unpleasant jobs, nor the extent of additional employment; and neither can we know to what extent mechanisation will in any case replace human labour in the years ahead: but if automation displaces jobs to any great extent, then labour's proportion of the value of production will decline even faster than it does now, and capital investment and company profits will take even larger shares.[87] This suggests that, whether or not a Citizen's Basic Income is implemented, the tax burden might need to shift from personal income to company profits, or to the products now being produced more efficiently and therefore more cheaply. Company profits are increasingly difficult to tax, which suggests that production will need to be taxed directly as consumption taxes, rather than indirectly through wage taxation.

Money creation

Since the recent financial crisis, governments have been creating money, which of course they can: and through this 'quantitative easing' their central banks have been buying government bonds, effectively buying back government debt.[88] An unfortunate effect has been bond price inflation, making investors wealthier. This has done little for employment and economic growth, and has exacerbated inequality.

A more effective way of stimulating economic growth would be to spend the new money into the real economy as payments to members of the public.[89] Because amounts and frequencies might vary, we cannot necessarily call such an idea a proposal for a Citizen's Basic Income, but the effects might not be dissimilar from those of Alaska's Permanent Fund Dividend, which is a varying annual payment.[90] The economy would benefit, poverty would be reduced, social cohesion would be enhanced, and we would be closer to establishing a genuine Citizen's Basic Income.

There is no reason in principle why a national government should not create money up to the value of Gross Domestic Product (GDP)[91] and spend it into the real economy in the form of payments for infrastructure projects and a Citizen's Basic Income.[92] This could reap considerable economic and social rewards.[93]

In some ways, the situation relating to money creation mirrors that facing tax and benefits systems. Both have evolved over time, both exhibit complexities, both are tangled up with a wide variety of other aspects of societies and economies: and genuine reform of both is resisted because the transitions look difficult and the effects of change are difficult to predict. It is precisely these aspects of the two situations that make it so difficult to generate the necessary political will to create the necessary change. Both fields would benefit from wide-ranging consultation exercises. In both cases, the international effects of making the recommended changes would be important matters for discussion, as would be the details of the transitions that would need to be managed between current situations and the future situations envisaged. What is required in both cases is widespread debate, high-quality research and political willingness to make changes if they are in the longer-term interests of society, the economy and the planet.

Further possibilities

Numerous other funding mechanisms have been proposed: the taxation of lifetime gifts to fund a Citizen's Basic Income thought of as a 'social inheritance';[94] tax on rare natural resources (a variant of a land value tax);[95] a Megabyte tax[96] (internet traffic continues to expand exponentially, so such a tax at a very low rate could provide a valuable source of revenue); and Bill Gates' proposal to tax robots:[97] an appealingly direct way to recycle the proportion of the proceeds of production going to capital back into consumption of the goods produced.

A particularly interesting possibility is that a Citizen's Basic Income would improve the population's health,[98] which would reduce expenditure on health services, and therefore provide additional revenue with which to increase the levels of the Citizen's Basic Incomes, which in turn would improve the population's health …

There is clearly a wide variety of possible funding methods. Initially, the obvious way to fund a Citizen's Basic Income would be from within the current tax and benefits system. While this would not provide a subsistence income, and so would not deliver a Citizen's Basic Income that would provide the kind of freedom that some scholars would like to see,[99] it would offer two advantages: it could be clearly affordable; and it would keep the political debate simple, whereas to employ any other funding method would require debate about the desirability and feasibility of Citizen's Basic Income to be conducted in the context of a debate about new forms of taxation, which would be politically problematic. As Andrew Harrop suggests: 'A basic income becomes a more practical proposition if it is conceived, not as vast new spending, but as a process of integrating and rationalising existing entitlements of broadly similar generosity.'[100] But once a small Citizen's Basic Income had been established, there is no reason why additional funding methods might not be attempted.

If a Citizen's Basic Income scheme abolished means-tested benefits then we wouldn't know to whom we should give passported benefits such as free school meals

By passported benefits we mean those benefits to which working-age claimants of certain means-tested benefits are automatically entitled: for instance, free school meals for their children, free prescriptions and free dental treatment.[101]

This definition was occasioned by the UK government's Social Security Advisory Committee's review of passported benefits in the light of the impending transition from 'Tax Credits' and Jobseeker's Allowance to 'Universal Credit'. If a Citizen's Basic Income were to be implemented, then an even more thorough review would clearly be required. The transition to 'Universal Credit' might result in a few households not in receipt of passported benefits receiving them, and some currently in receipt not receiving them: but a Citizen's Basic Income would automatically remove large numbers of households from means-tested benefits (and would make it advantageous, and therefore likely, for other households to abandon means-tested benefits in favour of employment or self-employment), which would mean that far fewer households would be entitled to current passported benefits if the regulations relating to them were to remain as they are.

A small Citizen's Basic Income would require a continuing means-tested safety net, particularly for housing costs, so there would still be a mechanism for testing some of the poorer households for passported benefits if such benefits were regarded as beneficial in their current form:[102] but another approach would be to make the current passported benefits unconditional and therefore universal. So, for instance, school meals could be free for every child. This would be no more of a problem than Child Benefit is now: that is, it would not be a problem, because wealthier families would be paying far more in Income Tax than they would be receiving in the value of school meals. The benefits of universal free school meals could be considerable. No longer would a school's families be divided into those receiving free school means and those not; and universal provision of nutritious school meals would improve child health, and thus the health of the whole population in the future.

Further problems would arise, of course. Schools receive additional funding for children receiving free school meals: so a passported benefit has itself become a passport to other benefits. It would not be difficult to find another way to allocate additional resources to schools facing particular challenges.

There are lots of problems that it wouldn't solve

This is of course entirely true.[103] There will always be some aspects of household budgets that cannot be dealt with by unconditional benefits. Housing costs are different in different parts of the country; fuel costs pose problems similar to those posed by housing costs; and someone with a disability that means that they are unable to earn a living might have housing and care needs that a universal and unconditional benefit would never be able to cover. Perhaps the most important problem that Citizen's Basic Income cannot solve is climate change.

Disability

People living with physical or mental disabilities would, of course, receive a Citizen's Basic Income along with everybody else: but whereas a Citizen's Basic Income would provide additional choices for people in the employment market or able to enter it, such additional choices might not be available to people with disabilities, simply because of those disabilities. In addition, many people living with disabilities have care needs beyond those experienced by people without disabilities.

As things stand, social care needs are assessed by local authorities; the contributory or means-tested Employment and Support Allowance provides a subsistence income to people who cannot earn one; the non-means-tested Disability Living Allowance (for under 65s) – now being replaced by Personal Independence Payments[104] – or Attendance Allowance (for people over 65), is paid to help to fund the care that disabled people need; someone caring for a disabled person can claim means-tested Carer's Allowance; and people with disabilities are increasingly given a local authority budget to enable them to pay for the care that they need. Might it make sense to maintain local provision for payment for care and to roll Attendance Allowance and Disabled Living Allowance/Personal Independence Payment into it?

One immediate benefit of a Citizen's Basic Income is that it would for the first time provide an unconditional income for relatives who choose to care for people with disabilities: an income that should continue to be topped up by payment from the Local Authority budget allocated to the person for whom they care.[105] But this still leaves unresolved the problem that many people with disabilities cannot earn a living, so they need additional income. Any attempt to alter their Citizen's Basic Income in order to achieve this would mean that it would no longer be a Citizen's Basic Income.[106] This means that either an additional unconditional benefit will be required, or an additional conditional benefit.[107]

Whatever route is chosen to provide for the care and subsistence needs of people with disabilities, the goal is clear. Those adults requiring care should have an unconditional and adequate income that enables them to make the kind of choices that the rest of us take for granted. Both they and their carers should be able to relate to each other and the outside world with dignity. A Citizen's Basic Income would play a part in bringing that about.[108]

Housing costs[109]

The UK has traditionally focused on four ways of providing housing support: the provision of social housing at affordable, below-market rents; the regulation of private sector rents; means-tested Housing Benefit; and tax benefits for owner-occupiers.

Housing Benefit is means-tested, is withdrawn at a rate of 65% as earnings rise, and is therefore a major cause of the poverty and unemployment traps into which those with low earnings potential will frequently fall. Housing Benefit is available to those in work and to those out of work, and is now being rolled into 'Universal Credit', and so will still serve those both in and out of employment, so in theory should not prove a disincentive to seeking employment: but the high marginal deduction rate to which it contributes will certainly be a disincentive to taking employment if there is no certainty that net income will rise sufficiently to make the transition financially worthwhile.[110]

This is one of the reasons for questioning the way in which Housing Benefit is calculated and administered. The other is that Housing Benefit either creates an incentive for landlords (including social housing landlords[111]) to maximise rental return from Housing Benefit claimants, and a lack of incentive for Housing Benefit claimants to seek cheaper accommodation, or, as is increasingly the case, Housing Benefit payments are restricted in various ways, forcing families to move out of areas in which they work or in which they have family support: and yet still the amount of Housing Benefit continues to rise, and is now nearly £24 billion per annum.[112]

Until we see a major increase in the number of dwellings being built,[113] and a reduction in the number being sold abroad as investments, dedicated support for housing costs will be needed: which means that a housing benefit of some kind will continue to be needed alongside Citizen's Basic Income. Here we have a choice: either the current means-tested variety, or a flat-rate, individualised housing benefit, adjusted for the level of housing costs in an area. The logic of the latter suggestion is the same as that for a Citizen's Basic Income: that it would be simple to administer, that it would not create market distortions, and that, although the rich might be able to pay for housing without it, it would be no problem for them to receive it because they would be paying more in tax than they would be receiving in universal housing benefit.[114]

In the absence of such a radical solution to the problem of housing costs, we must look for ways of improving the situation for hard-pressed tenants, such as rent controls. A Citizen's Basic Income cannot on its own solve the problem of housing costs, but one thing it could do: because its marginal deduction rate would be zero, for many households it would leave a residual means-tested housing benefit as the only means-tested benefit that they would suffer, providing an incentive to move to cheaper accommodation and to increase earned income in order to escape from means testing.

Fuel poverty

Another problem that a Citizen's Basic Income would not solve is fuel poverty. Poorer people often live in accommodation of poor quality. Insulation might not be adequate, heating systems might not be efficient, and, on larger estates, tenants might have little control over the type, level and cost of heating, and in particular might only have electricity available for heating, which tends to be more expensive than gas. If householders have a coin or key meter then they might not have available to them the cheaper direct debit tariffs. Either fuel bills will be higher than they can afford, or they will turn the heating down or off, meaning that their homes will not be sufficiently warm, and health problems will be the result. A report has estimated that 5 million individuals are affected by fuel poverty.[115]

The only long-term solution is to improve the quality of the entire housing stock: but, in the meantime, ensuring that households can afford sufficient heating to enable them to keep warm must be a priority. A Citizen's Basic Income would not solve this problem, but it would do for fuel poverty what it would do for housing costs: it would give to many households a larger number of options. Households in which no one was employed might seek employment because with a Citizen's Basic Income it would be more worthwhile to do so. Sufficient warmth would therefore become more affordable. Or people already employed might seek higher earnings because it would be more worthwhile to do so; and more people would start their own businesses, because their Citizen's Basic Incomes would give them sufficient financial security to take the risk of coming off means-tested benefits and relying on their own skills and motivation. As we have seen, because a Citizen's Basic Income would provide such additional options, it would be easier for people to move to new accommodation, and this might be better insulated and more efficiently heated.

A Citizen's Basic Income would not, on its own, solve the problem of fuel poverty, just as it would not solve the problem of expensive, inadequate or absent housing: but it would begin to make a difference to the options available to thousands, and perhaps millions, of households, and it would therefore make a contribution to resolving fuel poverty.

Climate change

The current economic system links employment to subsistence income, thus encouraging employment, which in turn correlates with Gross Domestic Product: so for a Citizen's Basic Income to begin to break the link between income and employment might reduce employment, might reduce growth (as measured by GDP[116]), and might offer a 'post-productivist'[117] and 'sustainable post-capitalist world' that takes the danger of climate change seriously and would be characterised by 'social equality, ... human solidarity, ... positive freedom and democratic self-government'.[118] On the other hand, a Citizen's Basic Income could exacerbate climate change by reducing marginal deduction rates, increasing net incomes and increasing consumption, rather suggesting that energy justice and tackling climate change might be conflicting objectives.[119] Or perhaps both tendencies might be in play, in which case what will matter will be the balance between them. An additional causality might be less direct. Fitzpatrick proposes a 'Green policy package' that would 'include not only [a Citizen's Basic Income] but also land and energy taxes, working-time reductions and the expansion of informal exchanges in the third sector', with the Citizen's Basic Income seen not as one of a number of ingredients, but as 'the instrument by which that package is constructed in the first place'.[120] This argument has also been made by the UK's Green Party: 'We cannot expect people still stuck in the poverty trap to think of [saving the planet] as a priority. Creating a fairer society and saving the planet go hand-in-hand'.[121] It is not a disadvantage of Citizen's Basic Income that it does not solve the problem of climate change, but it would be a disadvantage if it were to make the problem worse. It would be useful to find out what the ecological effects of a Citizen's Basic Income might be.[122]

What a Citizen's Basic Income can do

It is of course true that Citizen's Basic Income cannot solve all of the world's problems. It certainly can't solve the UK's housing crisis, nor fuel poverty, nor the problem of disability costs – not all on its own: but the lesson to be learnt from our discussion is that a Citizen's Basic Income could help, and that to apply the same kind of unconditionality to other areas of our social provision could offer immediate advantages.

The important thing is to allocate benefit types on the basis of rational argument. Housing costs vary, and we have some choice over the housing we occupy, so it makes sense to tailor income to actual housing costs and to a family's ability to pay them, and also to construct a system that incentivises a family to achieve housing costs that they can manage on a combination of earnings and unconditional benefits. But subsistence costs are much less amenable to personal choice, and everybody's subsistence costs are similar. It therefore makes sense to pay an unconditional income that makes a substantial contribution to subsistence costs, and to expect people to be able to earn the rest of the income that they need in the employment market, which, in the context of a new benefits structure, would offer them the hours of employment, or the self-employment opportunities, that they require.

The ideal situation would be a Citizen's Basic Income on top of which could be constructed additional benefits for contingencies such as disability and housing costs. As Richard Titmuss has put it: 'In all the main spheres of need, some structure of universalism is an essential prerequisite to selective positive discrimination:' the universal foundation providing a 'sense of community' and providing the basis for a 'welfare society' rather than just a 'welfare state'.[123]

Having recognised that there are things that Citizen's Basic Income cannot do, it is important to remember that the rest of this book is about what it *can* do. It *can* make the employment market, and therefore the economy, more efficient; it *can* create a more cohesive society; it *can* make it more worthwhile for all of us to seek paid employment, to seek self-employment, to seek new skills, and to increase our earned income; and it *can* give to every individual and household more freedom to decide how to organise their relationships, their activity and their time. But one of the problems that a Citizen's Basic Income would not be able to solve really does matter, and that is climate change. Without a solution to that there will be no future for our planet, and for a Citizen's Basic Income to exacerbate climate change would be deeply problematic. This area in particular cries out for further research.

It would increase public expenditure

It would be easy for civil servants to brief against a Citizen's Basic Income. To replace Income Tax Personal Allowances with cash benefits would look as if it would increase public expenditure: and the general public might see it the same way.[124] This objection was actually made by the Treasury when Margaret Thatcher's policy unit proposed a Citizen's Basic Income.[125] It is of course a ridiculous objection, and the making of it does not reflect well on the intellectual powers of civil servants of the time. If revenue foregone by the Treasury through tax allowances is replaced by an income paid out to citizens, and the revenue foregone is equal to the money paid out, then the Treasury will suffer no loss and public expenditure will not have increased. This suggests that we should regard the value of tax allowances as public expenditure. We might then be able to have a more rational discussion about the advantages of a Citizen's Basic Income because we would be regarding tax allowances as a social policy issue alongside cash benefits. As things stand, any proposal to shift income maintenance from tax allowances to cash payments will suffer from a disadvantage, and any proposal to shift policy from cash payments to tax allowances will experience a positive advantage. This is entirely irrational, as Atkinson and Sutherland have pointed out: 'In terms of cash, there is no difference between paying less tax and receiving a benefit, as was recognized when child tax allowance and family allowance were fused into a single child benefit. The integration of income taxation and social security would be the logical development of this process.'[126]

The money could be better used on other things[127]

There is of course an assumption underlying this objection: that is, that money will be spent on Citizen's Basic Incomes. For schemes that fund Citizen's Basic Incomes out of changes to the existing tax and benefits system, no additional public expenditure will be required, so there will be no additional money that could have been diverted to other purposes. Because the majority of illustrative Citizen's Basic Income schemes raise the necessary funds by raising Income Tax and National Insurance Contribution rates, as well as by reducing thresholds, it might look as if such increases could instead be employed to fund other public services. However, those changes are designed to avoid losses to low-income households at the same time as achieving a revenue-neutral Citizen's Basic Income scheme. Within the overall scheme, the increased taxation will be balanced, or almost balanced, by the Citizen's Basic Incomes coming into the household. In the absence of the Citizen's Basic Income, to use the additional taxation to fund public services could leave a lot of households, including low-income households, a great deal worse off: something that the Citizen's Basic Income scheme would not do.

Of course, if additional revenue were to become available, perhaps from a Financial Transaction Tax, or from some other source, then it would be a political decision as to whether to use it to fund a Citizen's Basic Income or some other public provision: but in the short to medium term such additional revenue does not seem a very likely prospect, which means that any Citizen's Basic Income scheme would need to be funded from within the current tax and benefits system, any rise in tax revenue would need to be applied to the Citizen's Basic Incomes, and if it was not then households would be left worse off.

More objections

The objections listed, and to which responses have been offered, are not the only ones.

David Piachaud objects that what matters is establishing goals and then asking how they might be met, rather than starting out from Citizen's Basic Income.[128] Those of us who have administered means-tested benefits, who have long experience of families suffering from their effects, who have understood a Citizen's Basic Income's advantages over means testing, and who have noticed that all of the goals of poverty reduction, inequality reduction, human dignity, employment incentives, employment choice, and administrative simplicity would be well served by a Citizen's Basic Income, have in fact done the work required by this objection. We have tested Citizen's Basic Income, and found it to be both useful and feasible.

John Kay objects that 'either the level of basic income is unacceptably low, or the cost of providing it is unacceptably high':[129] and if a low Citizen's Basic Income were to be accompanied by continuing means-tested benefits then the Citizen's Basic Income would lose its simplicity.[130] Readers will see in the appendix a Citizen's Basic Income scheme with low Citizen's Basic Incomes and continuing means-tested benefits that would reduce poverty, reduce inequality, enhance employment incentives, take a lot of households off means-tested benefits (and thus provide for those households a greater simplicity), reduce the prevalence of stigmatising means testing, and not impose significant losses at the point of implementation.

It might be objected that means-tested benefits provide an automatic stabiliser, pumping additional money into the economy when unemployment rises, whereas a Citizen's Basic Income would not fulfil the same function because the amounts paid would not rise as unemployment rose. First of all, if means-tested benefits remained in place, then those would continue to function as a dynamic stabiliser; and secondly, income taxation would decline and Citizen's Basic Incomes would not, so they would continue to stabilise the economy.

It might be objected that there are Citizen's Basic Income schemes that would impose losses on poor families.[131] There certainly are Citizen's Basic Income schemes that would result in poor people losing large amounts of money at the point of implementation, and as far as we know every revenue-neutral scheme that abolished means-tested benefits would have this unfortunate effect.[132] But there are also schemes that minimise this effect. It would never be possible to eliminate it entirely, because although a Citizen's Basic Income is inherently simple, the current system is not, and whenever changes are made to it some households are bound to suffer net losses, particularly if changes to the system have to deliver the zero net cost required by any reform seeking political feasibility in the current economic climate. So what is essential is to minimise the losses, particularly for poorer households, and also to minimise the number of households suffering losses.

And finally, it might be objected that the rich don't need the money. If money is in short supply then we ought to give it to poor people and not to rich ones. This sounds sensible, but it isn't. In order to give money only to poor people we have to means-test that money: and if you have reached this point in the book then you will be aware that means testing is not a good idea. To give money to everyone is efficient; and it is no problem giving money to everyone, including the rich, if the rich are paying more in tax than they are receiving in Citizen's Basic Incomes. Illustrative schemes can be designed to give more to the rich than to the poor, or, like the one in the appendix, to redistribute slightly from rich to poor. It is true that the rich don't need more money, and there is no reason why they should end up with more money if they are given a Citizen's Basic Income. The poor need money, and a Citizen's Basic Income gives money to the poor in the most efficient way possible. A Citizen's Basic Income can therefore achieve everything that someone is asking for when they suggest that 'the rich don't need it'.

Conclusion

If you have not been persuaded by the arguments in previous chapters, and if you have not found this chapter's responses to objections entirely satisfying, then you might wish to ask the following question: if I were to write a book about means-tested benefits, then would the arguments for means-tested benefits be more persuasive than this book's arguments for Citizen's Basic Income? And would my responses to objections to means-tested benefits be more persuasive than this chapter's responses to objections to Citizen's Basic Income?

There is no benefits system that will solve all of society's problems, so the next questions to ask are these: am I persuaded that implementing a Citizen's Basic Income would offer us an improved benefits system? And are this chapter's responses to objections sufficiently adequate to enable me to remain persuaded of that?

Notes

1 Torry, 2013: 228.
2 Torry, 2013: 192–5; Lawrence and Lawson, 2017: 72.
3 Sherman and Jenkins, 1995: 57; Standing, 2009.
4 Pasma, 2010.
5 Sherman and Jenkins, 1995: 156–7.
6 White, 2003: 59.
7 White, 2003: 59, 99, 131, 132; Shapiro, 2002: 35.
8 White, 2003: 18, 152; De Wispelaere, undated; Phelps, 2001.
9 White, 2006: 13.
10 Birnbaum, 2012.
11 White, 2003: 155–62.
12 White, 2003: 166–8; Birnbaum, 2008.
13 White, 2006: 14.
14 Deacon, 2002.
15 Van Parijs, 1995: 2, 89, 96, 133; Reeve and Williams, 2002.
16 Solow, 2001: xi; Van Parijs, 2001: 3. On the relationship between Citizen's Basic Income and freedom, see Widerquist, Noguera, Vanderborght and De Wispelaere, 2013: 1–37.
17 White, 2003: 168. Piachaud (2016) offers a critique of Van Parijs's 'real freedom' argument, but does not consider White's argument that a Citizen's Basic Income would contribute to the basis for a just reciprocity. On reciprocity, see Widerquist, Noguera, Vanderborght and De Wispelaere, 2013: 79–140; on freedom, see Widerquist, Noguera, Vanderborght and De Wispelaere, 2013: 1–37.
18 www.gov.uk/child-benefit-move-to-uk, 17/05/2017.
19 Torry, 2013: 187–209; Citizen's Income Trust, 2003; cf Clarke, Coll, Dagnino and Neveu, 2014: 49.
20 Fitzpatrick, 2011: xiv, 211.
21 These suggestions were made by a Citizen's Income Trust working group, and are contained in a paper presented to the Citizen's Income Trust's trustees.
22 As far as HMRC is concerned, someone is regarded as having been resident in the UK for tax purposes if either they spent 183 or more days in the UK in the tax year, or their only home was in the UK and they owned, rented or lived in it for at least 91 days in total and they spent at least 30 days there in the tax year Someone is automatically non-resident if either they spent fewer than 16 days in the UK (or 46 days if they had not been classed as a UK resident for the three previous tax years), or they worked abroad full time (averaging at least 35 hours a week) and spent fewer than 91 days in the UK, of which no more than 30 were spent working (https://www.gov.uk/tax-foreign-income/residence, 02/06/2017).
23 The Runnymede Trust defines 'settled here' as living in the UK for five years (Khan and Weekes-Bernard, 2015: 9). 61% of the UK's population thinks that nationals of other European Union countries should live in the UK for three years before they can receive benefits (Parke, Bryson and Curtice, 2014: iv). The maximum length of time that a legally resident family that has moved to the UK has to wait before they can receive Child Benefit is three months (https://www.gov.uk/child-benefit-move-to-uk, 17/05/2017).
24 Electoral Commission, 2010: 2–3; Vince, 2004.
25 Jordan, 1989: 124.

26 There might well be groups of people not currently on the electoral register who ought to receive a Citizen's Basic Income. Members of the House of Lords, and those whose refugee status is still undetermined, would be two such groups.

27 Whether there is a civil liberties dimension to be debated is an open question. At present it is possible to choose not to be on the electoral register, and that decision has no implications for one's income. However, there would be no compulsion to receive a Citizen's Basic Income or to be on the register, and some citizens might make this choice.

28 Welfare Reform Team, 2016.

29 Dean, 2012b: 444.

30 Dean and Mitchell, 2011.

31 Dickens and McKnight, 2008b.

32 Block and Somers, 2003.

33 Van Parijs, 1990a: 16.

34 Meade, 1995: 57; Van Trier, 1995: 343–407.

35 Werner and Goehler, 2010: 139–51.

36 Davis and Henrekson, 2005.

37 Colombino, Locatelli, Narazani and O'Donoghue, 2010; Lo Vuolo, 2015: 35.

38 O'Brien, 2007: 124.

39 Michaeu and van Soest, 2008.

40 Crossley and Jeon, 2007.

41 Parker and Sutherland, 1988.

42 Handler and Babcock, 2006.

43 Gilroy, Heimann and Schopf, 2013.

44 Burchardt and Le Grand, 2002: 24.

45 van der Wel and Halvorsen, 2015: 101.

46 van der Wel and Halvorsen, 2015: 113.

47 van der Wel and Halvorsen, 2015: 116.

48 Carpenter, Freda and Speeden, 2007: 5; cf Millar and Bennett, 2017; Harrison and Sanders, 2014.

49 Welfare Reform Team, 2016: 51.

50 Carpenter, Freda and Speeden, 2007: 5, 6.

51 Welfare Reform Team, Oxford City Council, 2016: 51; Wright and Stewart, 2016; Roberts, Price and Crosby, 2014: 6.

52 Fraser, Gutiérrez and Peña-Casas, 2011: 314.

53 Oubridge, 1990.

54 Van Parijs, 1990b.

55 Offe, 2008; Liebermann, 2012: 93–5.

56 Pech, 2010.

57 Mayhew, 1991.

58 Gourevitch, 2016.

59 Smeaton and White, 2016.

60 Casassas, 2007; Pettit, 2007; Domènech and Raventós, 2007; Pateman, 2007; White, 2007a.

61 Rowlingson, 2009: 145.

62 Atkinson, 1985: 73.

63 Berthoud, 2007: 51.

64 Organisation for Economic Co-operation and Development, 2005: 127.

65 Atkinson and Sutherland, 1988a: 14.

66 Finch, Corlett and Alakeson, 2014: 19.

[67] See the illustrative Citizen's Basic Income scheme in the appendix.
[68] Galbraith, 1999.
[69] Press release, 'The Basic Income Grant (BIG) is Government's Responsibility', Basic Income Grant Coalition, Namibia, 1 March 2012, http://bignam.org/Publications/Press_release_March_2012_to_Government.pdf, 18/05/2017, p 6.
[70] www.jrf.org.uk/report/minimum-income-standard-uk-2016, 18/05/2017; Cribb, Joyce and Phillips, 2012: 95–117; Fitzpatrick, 2011: 7–8, 24–5, 108; Lansley and Mack, 1983; Lansley and Mack, 2015; Miller, 2009b.
[71] Deeming, 2017.
[72] Jameson, 2016: 21–4.
[73] For an example of this method, see Citizen's Income Trust, 2013.
[74] For further difficulties with using the national accounts and other data sources to calculate the revenue that might be raised by making changes to the tax system, see Torry, 2013: 242–7.
[75] For an example of this method, see Citizen's Income Trust, 2017a.
[76] Paine, 1796/2004: 4–7.
[77] Robertson, 1996.
[78] Fitzpatrick, 1999: 201; Cato, 2010.
[79] Lansley, 2016: 41–54.
[80] Widerquist and Howard, 2012b.
[81] Cummine, 2011: 16–17.
[82] Tobin, 1978: 155.
[83] Adam et al, 2011: 151–3, 195–215.
[84] Irvin, Byrne, Murphy, Reed and Ruane, 2009:15; Hobijn and Nussbacher, 2015; Ehrenfreund, 2015.
[85] Dommen-Meade, 2010; Werner and Goehler, 2010: 241–50.
[86] Liebermann, 2012: 93–4.
[87] Piketty, 2014.
[88] www.bankofengland.co.uk/monetarypolicy/pages/qe/default.aspx, 18/05/2017.
[89] Elliott, 2014b; Murphey, 2009; Murphey, 2011: 296.
[90] Zelleke, 2012: 150.
[91] Jackson and Dyson, 2012: 283; Crocker, 2012: 16.
[92] Tideman and Tsang, 2010; Boyle, 2012.
[93] Blyth, Lonergan and Wren-Lewis, 2015; Ryan-Collins, Greenham, Werner and Jackson, 2011; McLeay, Radia and Thomas, 2014.
[94] O'Neill, 2007: 70.
[95] Sullivan and Wetzel, 2007: 16.
[96] Claus Offe, in a presentation on 14 September 2012 at the 14th BIEN Congress.
[97] http://uk.businessinsider.com/bill-gates-robot-tax-brighter-future-2017-3, 18/05/2017.
[98] Forget, 2011.
[99] Widerquist, 2013: 70–71; Van Parijs, 1995.
[100] Harrop, 2016: 136–7.
[101] Social Security Advisory Committee, 2011.
[102] Miller, 2012.
[103] Jordan, 1992: 173; Piachaud, 2016: 10–11; Sage and Diamond, 2017.
[104] www.gov.uk/pip, 18/05/2017.
[105] Leaper, 1986.
[106] Martinelli, 2017a: 15; Martinelli, 2017b: 9–10.
[107] Basic Income Research Group, 1988; Howard and Lawrence, 1996.

[108] Walter, 1989: 131.

[109] Eliot, 2011.

[110] Hills, 2007.

[111] Lowe, 2011: 236.

[112] Department for Work and Pensions, 2016b: 116–17. This figure does not include the amounts paid as the housing element of 'Universal Credit'.

[113] Raynsford, 2016: 37–52.

[114] Torry, 2002.

[115] Hills, 2011: 22.

[116] Fitzpatrick, 1999: 186.

[117] Widerquist, Noguera, Vanderborght and De Wispelaere, 2013: 259–310.

[118] Devine, Pearmain and Purdy, 2009: 65–6. See also Nissen, 1992.

[119] Sovacool, Sidortsov and Jones, 2014: 3.

[120] Fitzpatrick, 1999: 201.

[121] Green Party, 2008.

[122] Remfry and Whalley, 2015: 4.

[123] Titmuss, 1968: 135.

[124] Piachaud, 2016: 17.

[125] Monckton, 1993: 6.

[126] Atkinson and Sutherland, 1988a: 1; Atkinson and Sutherland, 1988b.

[127] Lawrence and Lawson, 2017: 72.

[128] Piachaud, 2016: 19.

[129] Kay, 2017: 72.

[130] Lawrence and Lawson, 2017: 71.

[131] Lawrence and Lawson, 2017: 71–2.

[132] Torry, 2014a; Piachaud, 2016: 15.

ELEVEN

Alternatives to a Citizen's Basic Income

In this chapter we study three proposals with characteristics similar to those of a Citizens' Income: a Negative Income Tax, genuine Tax Credits and a Participation Income.

Tax Credits

In Chapter 2 I described a Tax Credits scheme proposed by the UK's Conservative government in 1972. This was close to a genuine Tax Credits scheme because it allocated a credit that was paid out if there were no earnings, and was withdrawn as earnings rose, up to a break-even point, after which Income Tax was deducted. We noted some disadvantages to this particular scheme: for instance, that workers earning a low weekly income were not included in the scheme, and non-earners were not included either. There is no reason why an alternative Tax Credits scheme should not include every citizen from the date of its implementation, so the particular problems did not relate to the idea of a Tax Credit.

Some disadvantages of the Heath scheme, though, would be experienced by any Tax Credit scheme. For someone employed, the Tax Credit is reduced as earnings rise, so either the Credit has to be administered by an employer (which causes problems as workers move from one employer to another, and also means that the employer needs to know the worker's personal circumstances in order to work out their entitlement), or the Tax Credit has to be paid by a separate government agency which will then need to know the worker's earnings and every change in those earnings (as the Department for Work and Pensions does for 'Universal Credit'). Neither solution would make for easy administration. If the former method were to be employed, then if someone experienced a period of unemployment between two employments, the administration of their Tax Credits would pass from the employer to a government agency and then back again. This would not be a good recipe for seamless administration.

It rather looks as if Tax Credits are designed for a world of long-term full-time employment. The Heath scheme was also designed for a world of stable families. The level of the Tax Credit depended on whether someone was married, so changes in personal circumstances would not only have affected the level of the Tax Credit, but would also have been known to someone's employer. An individual-based Tax Credit scheme would of course be perfectly feasible, and would avoid such problems.

A too-little-noted problem with Tax Credits is the restriction imposed on tax rates by the fact that Tax Credits are managed via a non-cumulative tax system. Our current income tax system is a cumulative one. Each earner is allocated an annual tax allowance so there is an annual amount of income that is not taxed. Each week, or each month, the employer has to work out how much tax to deduct so that by the end of the year the correct amount of tax has been paid, at the correct rates, on the correct amounts of taxable pay (earned income minus the tax allowance, taking into account the thresholds between the different tax rates). Tables are published, and software is available, based on a system of tax codes related to earners' circumstances; and if at the end of the year the correct amount of tax has not been paid, then an adjustment takes place: a tax refund, a tax demand, or next year's tax code is amended so as to recoup unpaid tax during the following year. One of the advantages of a Tax Credit scheme is its non-cumulative tax system. Each week, or each month, the employer can work out tax due, or Tax Credit to be paid out, simply from the Tax Credit withdrawal rate, the tax rate, and the earner's circumstances (for instance, whether married or single, and whether they have dependent children). Only those paying higher-rate tax would require either an end-of-year adjustment or a cumulative scheme designed just for them (so that the higher tax could be collected throughout the year rather than all together at the end). In order to avoid such complexities, income tax would need to be collected at the same rate throughout the earnings range. While this would have the virtue of simplicity, it would severely restrict the government's ability to redistribute income.[1]

A Citizen's Basic Income would be radically simple to operate, it would not impose any additional administrative burden on employers, it would not require administrative changes as employments or relationships changed, and it would leave a government free to develop whatever income tax system it wished. Citizen's Basic Income would be far preferable to Tax Credits: even genuine ones.

Negative Income Tax

An idea often proposed both 50 years ago and today, and a subject of testing in both the United States and Canada, a 'Negative Income Tax' is essentially the same as genuine Tax Credits.[2] It is merely the specification that differs. To specify a Tax Credit scheme, the amount to be paid out if there are no earnings is specified along with a withdrawal rate as earnings rise. For a Negative Income Tax scheme, the threshold is specified along with a tax rate. For earnings below the threshold, the same amount is paid out for earnings of £x below the threshold as would be collected in tax on earnings of £x above the threshold. Negative Income Tax schemes have been suggested with different rates above and below the threshold, just as there are Income Tax schemes with different tax rates for different levels of earnings. The advantage of a low rate of withdrawal below the threshold is that the low-paid would end up with higher net earnings without the break-even point being too high.[3]

As a Negative Income Tax is essentially the same as a Tax Credit scheme, all of the same problems would apply. An additional 'problem' arose during a Negative Income Tax experiment in the US. The particular scheme tested in the US treated the household as the tax unit, and the tax deducted or payments made depended on the combined incomes of married couples.[4] Women tend to earn less than men, so they benefited more than men from the new system, particularly if they left the marriage and established a new claimant unit, because although their previous tax allowance had been useless to them if they earned below the tax threshold, the Negative Income Tax paid out money if their earnings were below the threshold, so their post-tax income was now higher than their gross income. Greater financial independence gave to some women the ability to leave their husbands, whereas their previous financial dependence had prevented them from doing so. Whether we would now regard as a problem the greater freedom that an increase in net income had given to those women I rather doubt: if it is only financial dependence that is holding together a marriage then perhaps it ought to end. If during the experiment the individual had been taken as the tax unit then it would have made no difference financially whether a couple stayed together, except that separation would have resulted in having to maintain two homes rather than one, so the couple would have been more likely to stay together. There can be no clearer example of the necessity of predicting the consequences of scheme design, and in particular of studying the effects of different claimant units, than this particular Negative Income Tax experiment.

In some respects, though, the Negative Income Tax experiments were unambiguously helpful. Even though marginal deduction rates fell and net incomes rose, the experiments found no evidence of employment market withdrawal, and no evidence that labour supply falls if marginal deduction rates fall. Some particularly interesting results were that there was some employment market withdrawal among women with children, suggesting that for some families it had become possible for a parent to spend more time with their children; and that some men took longer than before to accept a new job if they became unemployed, suggesting that they were now more able to seek the right job rather than simply any job. The results suggest that a Citizen's Basic Income would not stop people from wanting to earn an income, that beneficial employment market withdrawal would become more possible, and that there would be a sufficient tax base to enable the payment of a Citizen's Basic Income.

As in the Namibian Citizen's Basic Income pilot project, there were some other interesting outcomes. School attendance and performance rose, nutritional adequacy increased, there was less low birth weight, and home ownership rose. A recent examination of data collected during a similar Negative Income Tax experiment in Canada during the mid-1970s has produced some equally interesting results. Engagement in education beyond the age of 16 rose substantially, as much among members of those households whose net incomes did not rise during the experiment as among those whose incomes did; and a variety of health indicators improved,[5] leading the Canadian Medical Association to recommend that the Canadian government should implement a Citizen's Basic Income.[6] Similar health benefits, particularly for children, were found when casino profits were distributed to a Cherokee community as a Citizen's Basic Income.[7] As with the United States experiments, no primary earner employment market withdrawal occurred during the Canadian experiment, and some secondary earner withdrawal did.[8]

These are all positive and significant results with clear implications for the current debate on the Citizen's Basic Income approach to tax and benefits reform.

As we have seen, a problem faced both by Tax Credit and Negative Income Tax schemes is that they are themselves complex, and that they are complex to administer because they take the household as the tax unit, and because they require the constant adjustment of amounts paid out as circumstances change.[9] This means that if they did not enable the abolition of all other benefits then they would add considerably to the complexity of the tax and benefits system.[10] As we saw with the Heath Government's Tax Credit scheme, a substantial number of people would have been left out of the scheme, and the only benefit to be replaced would have been Family Income Supplement, the in-work means-tested benefit that preceded Family Credit and New Labour's 'Tax Credits'. It is not surprising that a minority on the Parliamentary Select Committee that examined the Tax Credits scheme had hesitations about putting employers and employees through a major change that would not have reduced complexity and might have increased it.[11]

If the administrative complexities of a Negative Income Tax are left out of the discussion then the advantages of a Negative Income Tax can look very like those of a Citizen's Basic Income,[12] which makes it essential to be clear that a Citizen's Basic Income is an unconditional and nonwithdrawable income for every individual, whereas a Negative Income Tax is not – and that a household-based Negative Income Tax only for families containing at least one employable adult[13] is certainly not a Citizen's Basic Income.

A Citizen's Basic Income would, of course, achieve everything that either a Negative Income Tax or a genuine Tax Credits scheme would achieve, and it would do all of it in a far simpler way and at reduced administrative cost.[14] Pech shows that for maximum acceptability a Citizen's Basic Income scheme would need a more progressive tax system and a Negative Income Tax a flatter one,[15] but these effects would be small in relation to the more important aspects of the administrative differences outlined, and in particular the simplicity of a Citizen's Basic Income and the administrative complexity of a Negative Income Tax.

The simplicity of the Citizen's Basic Income is the result of the universal payment being entirely separate from the tax system, enabling the universal payment to remain as simple as possible, and leaving the tax system to deal with revenue collection and the fine detail of income redistribution. A simpler and more efficient system is simply not possible.[16]

Graphical representations of a Citizen's Basic Income and of Tax Credits/Negative Income Tax

Figure 11.1 shows a Citizen's Basic Income's effects on net earnings. Figure 11.2 shows the effect of a Tax Credits scheme or a Negative Income Tax.[17]

Figure 11.1: Graphical representation of a Citizen's Basic Income

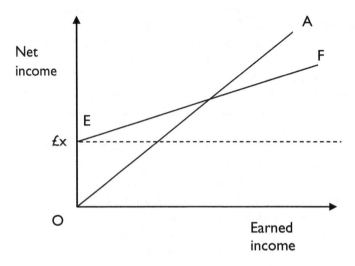

Figure 11.2: Graphical representation of a Negative Income Tax or Tax Credits

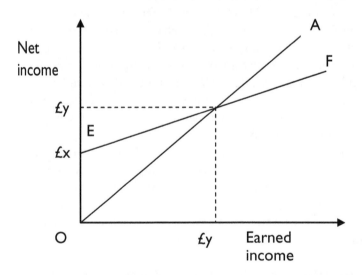

For Tax Credits, if the individual or household has no earnings, then a Tax Credit of £x is paid. As earned income rises, less Tax Credit is paid, until at earned income £y no Tax Credit is received. At this earnings level income tax begins to be paid. The line EF shows net income rising as earned income rises. The slope of the line represents both the tax rate and the rate at which Tax Credits are withdrawn.

If the rates are different then the slopes of EF will be different either side of £y of earned income. The graph looks the same for a Negative Income Tax, the only difference between Tax Credits and Negative Income Tax being a matter of specification and administrative detail.

As we can see, if the rate of withdrawal of Tax Credits is the same as the income tax rate, then Tax Credits have the same effects on net income as a Citizen's Basic Income would have. The difference is one of administration. (There might also be differences created by giving additional Tax Credits to such categories as married men, as in the Heath Government's scheme.)

If, as we can see, Tax Credits or Negative Income Tax have the same income effects as a Citizen's Basic Income, and if, as we can see, costs related to income levels will be the same, then the only difference is administrative. The administration of Tax Credits and of Negative Income Tax would be more complex than the administration of a Citizen's Basic Income. The only potential advantage of Tax Credits or Negative Income Tax over a Citizen's Basic Income would come from higher levels of public acceptability. There could be no inherent advantage.

A Participation Income

Tony Atkinson has recognised, as we have done, that 'it will be difficult to secure political support for a Citizen's Basic Income while it remains unconditional on employment market or other activity'. He suggests that a compromise is required, whereby some kind of participation in society would be required from those who were to receive what would otherwise be an unconditional and nonwithdrawable income: although such 'participation' would be assumed if people would be participating if they were not prevented from doing so by such contingencies as sickness, old age or lack of employment opportunity. The list of possible 'participation' conditions would therefore include employment or self-employment, retirement, absence from work because of sickness or injury, inability to work because of disability, and approved forms of voluntary activity. Students, trainees, those caring for the young, for older people, or for disabled dependents, and those unemployed but available for work, would also be counted as 'participating'.[18] The idea of a 'Participation Income' has an obvious attraction for those for whom reciprocity is an important concept, and for those who think that a Participation Income would quickly become a Citizen's Basic Income.[19] What a Participation Income's proponents fail to recognise is that it would be complex to administer, would require a casework approach, and would hand to junior civil servants the kind of discretion that contributes to means-tested benefits being so demeaning.[20] De Wispelaere and Stirton suggest that 'Participation Income might not be such a great idea after all' because all three of these questions would require an answer:

- What sort of activities qualify as participation?
- How will the system identify those engaging in these activities?
- How do we ensure compliance with such a broad set of requirements?

Every possible answer offered could be contested.

A Participation Income would generate a variety of behavioural responses. Some claimants would seek just enough voluntary labour to enable them to claim the Participation Income; organisations would offer this bare minimum; and administrators would develop their own rules of thumb to enable them to grant the Participation Income whenever possible. De Wispelaere and Stirton call this 'creative compliance',[21] and it would quickly compromise any public acceptability of Participation Income posited on the idea that only genuine participation in society entitles someone to the benefit. More importantly, a Participation Income would turn everyone into a claimant, rather than a citizen receiving a civic minimum. An interesting consequence of the complexity of administering a Participation Income is that it cannot be submitted to microsimulation research because participation conditions cannot be simulated in a computer program. In Atkinson's last book, *Inequality*, it looks as if a Participation Income has been simulated, whereas what has in fact been simulated is a Citizen's Basic Income.[22]

Would arguing for a Participation Income make it more or less likely that we would one day see a Citizen's Basic Income? There are two possibilities. Very few people would not receive the Participation Income,[23] and the administrative burden involved in evaluating who was and who was not participating in society might lead the government to abolish the participation conditions and establish a true Citizen's Basic Income. We might therefore see a Participation Income as a politically acceptable way to establish a Citizen's Basic Income. Another possibility is that the difficulty of establishing and managing a Participation Income would be so onerous (as the implementation of the much more restricted *Revenu Minimum d'Insertion* in France proved to be[24]) that the difficult experience of something described as similar to a Citizen's Basic Income would make it much more difficult to argue for a true Citizen's Basic Income. Similarly, the Royal Society of Arts' proposal for a non-binding 'contribution contract'[25] to accompany their Citizen's Basic Income could too easily turn into a binding contract, generating bureaucratic intrusion throughout the population, making the whole idea of Citizen's Basic Income unpopular.

The temptation to compromise on the definition of a Citizen's Basic Income should be resisted. As Parker has suggested, 'a major public education exercise is necessary before voters are likely to adjust their value systems to the problems of post-industrial societies. Fudging the issues could delay this process.'[26]

Improved National Insurance benefits

In 1994 the Labour Party's Social Justice Commission favoured improved National Insurance benefits.[27] An increase in the value of National Insurance benefits would lift some families receiving them off means-tested benefits and would thus provide many of the advantages that a Citizen's Basic Income would give to them. (This is the method used by the new Single Tier State Pension to lift state pensioners off the means-tested Guarantee Pension Credit.[28]) The downside to the proposal to increase the value of National Insurance benefits is that National Insurance benefits are given for short periods, and that their receipt depends on contribution records. The upside is that benefits that declare themselves to be 'insurance' are psychologically acceptable. We feel that we have paid our premiums, so when we need the benefits we feel that we deserve them. Benefits are 'something for something'.[29] The problem is that this is largely a myth, leading to Ben Gummer MP's suggestion that National Insurance Contributions should be renamed an Earnings Tax.[30] Total National Insurance Contributions paid in do not match total National Insurance benefits paid out. However, if National Insurance benefits were to be somehow extended into paid employment, then they would alleviate the problems that people experience as they move from unemployment to employment and back again; and if payment of out-of-work benefits were to become indefinite, rather than time limited, then there would be households that would find themselves taken off means-tested benefits. This could all be useful.

However, a Citizen's Basic Income would do for more families what enhanced National Insurance benefits would do for some families, and it would do it permanently, whatever their employment market status. It would certainly do more for families than a privatised version of National Insurance benefits.[31] So if National Insurance benefits are considered as a viable way of improving our benefits system, then they should be evaluated both in their own right, as a step towards a Citizen's Basic Income, and as a continuing element alongside both Citizen's Basic Income and means-tested benefits. Within such a context, continuing National Insurance benefits could prove to be both useful and popular.

'National insurance' is the British version of 'social insurance': a term used to describe the social security arrangements in many of the world's nation states. The problem with the 'social insurance' label is that it covers such a wide diversity of schemes. In countries where there was previously no social security system, or where a patchwork of private provision left large numbers of people without financial support when they needed it, a government social insurance scheme can be an acceptable step in the right direction. 'The principle of social insurance appeals partly to the rational self-interest of the individual, assuring them of access to benefits not normally attainable through private means, but also partly to their natural sentiment of solidarity and respect for other human beings.'[32] Some schemes are not far from being Citizen's Basic Incomes: others are a long way from it, because they are time limited, or income tested, or closely related to the number of contributions paid, or otherwise conditional. It is possible that in some countries, improving the social insurance scheme would create outcomes close to those that a Citizen's Basic Income would deliver, but any social insurance scheme with similarities to the scheme in the UK would struggle to achieve that.

Conclusion

Each of the alternative policy proposals discussed in this chapter would have advantages, but, as we have seen, they all have considerable disadvantages when compared to a Citizen's Basic Income, with the disadvantages often being most clear in relation to their administration: an issue at least as important as any other. A further alternative that we might have mentioned would have been a job guarantee, with the government functioning as employer of last resort.[33] Although this looks like a different approach to those discussed in this chapter, the problems would be the same: administration would be complex and expensive; a sanctions regime would result in significant bureaucratic intrusion; expensive supervision would be needed; there would be little incentive on the part of the worker or of the government agency to move a participant into regular employment; individuals would be trapped in a 'minimalist, make-work, low-wage program';[34] and either the artificial jobs created would compromise the efficiency of the employment market, or they would be designed not to do so and would therefore produce little of any value.[35] As with the other alternatives that we have studied, to implement a Citizen's Basic Income would offer many of the advantages of a job guarantee without the disadvantages, and it would only cost more[36] if the Citizen's Basic Income scheme was not revenue neutral.

This is not to suggest that alternative policy proposals are of no value. Take, for example, the National Minimum Wage (in the UK now somewhat erroneously called a 'National Living Wage'). A National Minimum Wage offers many advantages, and few if any disadvantages if carefully designed; and a National Minimum Wage and a Citizen's Basic Income could work very happily alongside each other.[37] If a job guarantee were ever to be implemented, then that too could function very happily alongside a Citizen's Basic Income;[38] free childcare for every child in the UK could be provided at a relatively small additional cost, and would mirror in the childcare field a Citizen's Basic Income in the income maintenance field;[39] and an extension of a variety of public services, whether provided free or on a subsidised basis, could usefully complement a Citizen's Basic Income.[40]

Research on alternatives to a Citizen's Basic Income should continue, and particularly research on those policy options that would complement a Citizen's Basic Income.

Notes

[1] Atkinson, 1973: 70, 76–8, 80. Sheahen, 2012, recommends what looks like an annual version of a Tax Credit.

[2] Tobin, 1966; Friedman, 1968; Story, 2015.

[3] Atkinson, 1985: 51.

[4] Parker, 1989: 153–5.

[5] Forget, 2011.

[6] www.cma.ca/Assets/assets-library/document/en/advocacy/Income-inequality-Brief_en.pdf, 09/06/2017; cf Painter, 2016b.

[7] Akee, Simeonova, Costello and Copeland, 2015: 9.

[8] Widerquist, 2005: 57, 60, 68; Pasma, 2010: 3–4; Widerquist and Sheahan, 2012: 18–22; Forget, 2012: 90–6.

[9] Spicker, 2011:122; Parker, 1989: 138–55; Block, 2001.

[10] Honkanen, 2014.

[11] Spicker, 2011: 122.

[12] Story, 2015.

[13] Sommer, 2016: 83.

[14] Harvey, 2006.

[15] Pech, 2010: 14.

[16] Kesselman and Garfinkel, 1978: 211.

[17] For similar graphs, see Piachaud, 2016: 12.

[18] Atkinson, 1993; Atkinson, 1996.

[19] White, 2003: 170–5; Fitzpatrick, 1999: 101, 111–22.

[20] It is not unusual for academics not to factor in the administrative questions that come naturally to those of us who have administered the benefits system, however long ago our experience of doing so might be.

[21] De Wispelaere and Stirton, 2008.

[22] Atkinson, 2015: 297. For a review of Atkinson, 2015, see http://citizensincome. org/book-reviews/inequality-by-anthony-b-atkinson/, 03/06/2017.

[23] 1.2% of the UK's population would not conform to any of the participation conditions: Torry, 2016a: 138.

[24] Euzéby, 1994.

[25] Painter and Thoung, 2015: 20–1.

[26] Parker, 1994: 9.

[27] Commission on Social Justice, 1994: 227.

[28] www.gov.uk/new-state-pension/what-youll-get; www.gov.uk/pension-credit, 07/10/2017.

[29] Michael Ward, at a seminar 'What was Beatrice Webb thinking and why should we still care?' at the London School of Economics, 12/10/2011. Contributors to the seminar recognised that even though contributory benefits are not genuine insurance benefits, and there are now conditions attached to their receipt, the idea of paying a contribution and being paid a benefit if we need it is still popular.

[30] www.publications.parliament.uk/pa/cm201314/cmhansrd/cm140225/ debtext/140225-0001.htm, 07/06/2017.

[31] Centre for Social Justice, 2016.

[32] Rys, 2010: 116.

[33] Piachaud, 2016: 18.

[34] Tymoigne, 2013: 63.

[35] Gregg, 2009.

[36] Harvey, 2013: 6–9.

[37] Gray, 2014: 13.

[38] Torry, 2016a: 177, 209–14.

[39] Wadsworth, 2016.

[40] Percy, 2016.

TWELVE

A brief summary[1]

What is a Citizen's Basic Income?

A Citizen's Basic Income is an unconditional, automatic and nonwithdrawable regular income for each individual legally resident. (A Citizen's Basic Income is sometimes called a Basic Income or a Citizen's Income.)

- 'Unconditional': A Citizen's Basic Income would vary with age, but there would be no other conditions: so everyone of the same age would receive the same Citizen's Basic Income, whatever their gender, employment status, income, family structure, contribution to society, housing costs, or anything else.
- 'Automatic': Someone's Citizen's Basic Income would be paid weekly or monthly, automatically.
- 'Nonwithdrawable': Citizen's Basic Incomes would not be means-tested. Whether someone's earnings increase, decrease, or stay the same, their Citizen's Basic Income will not change.
- 'Individual': Citizen's Basic Incomes would be paid on an individual basis, and not on the basis of a couple or household.
- 'As a right': Everybody legally resident in the UK would receive a Citizen's Basic Income, subject to a minimum period of legal residency in the UK, and continuing residency for most of the year.

A Citizen's Basic Income scheme would phase out as many allowances against personal income tax as possible, would phase out or reduce many existing means-tested benefits, and would pay a Citizen's Basic Income automatically to every man, woman and child.

The Citizen's Basic Income would

- create a financial platform on which all would be free to build;
- encourage individual freedom and responsibility;
- help to bring about social cohesion;
- reduce perverse incentives that discourage work and savings;
- be affordable within current revenue and expenditure constraints;
- be easy to understand;

- be cheap to administer and easy to automate;
- be without work or any other tests;
- not attract error or fraud;
- not require bureaucratic interference;
- not generate stigma;
- encourage caring and community activity; and
- be implemented all at once for the entire population, or for particular age cohorts and then extended to the rest of the population.

Figure 12.1 shows what a Citizen's Basic Income looks like

Figure 12.1: Graphical representation of a Citizen's Basic Income

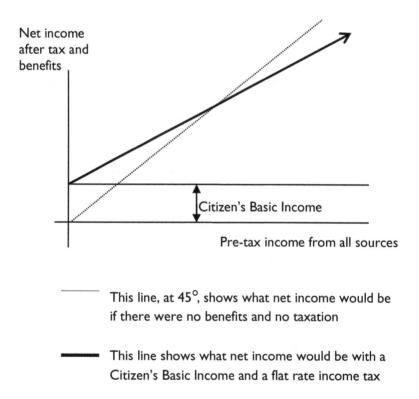

This line, at 45°, shows what net income would be if there were no benefits and no taxation

This line shows what net income would be with a Citizen's Basic Income and a flat rate income tax

Note

[1.] This summary is based on an introductory booklet published by the Citizen's Basic Income Trust in 2017. The complete text, along with calculations for a revenue-neutral Citizen's Basic Income scheme, can be found on the website www.citizensincome.org.

Afterword

Hermione Parker concludes her book *Instead of the Dole* with some words of Barbara Wootton:

> The limits of the possible constantly shift, and those who ignore them are apt to win in the end. Again and again, I have had the satisfaction of seeing the laughable idealism of one generation evolve into the accepted common-place of the next.[1]

In the UK during the 1920s, family allowances were 'seen as an issue for cranks and utopians', and the 1930s were a time of recession and rising unemployment; but by 1946 every family with more than one child was in receipt of Family Allowances.[2]

As this book has shown, a Citizen's Basic Income is no longer just an issue for cranks and utopians. Given the significant advantages that a Citizen's Basic Income would offer to society and to the economy, it is an issue that every policy maker needs to address. It is high time for implementation.

Notes

[1] Wootton, Barbara (1967) *In a World I Never Made*, London: George Allen and Unwin, p. 279, quoted in Parker, 1989: 384.

[2] Levitas, 2012: 450.

Appendix

Introduction[1]

Chapter 8 describes a consultation undertaken by the Institute of Chartered Accountants in England and Wales (ICAEW)[2] that considered four implementation methods for Citizen's Basic Income:

1. A Citizen's Basic Income for every UK citizen, large enough to take every household off means-tested benefits (including Working Tax Credits, Child Tax Credits, and Universal Credit), and to ensure that no household with low earned income would suffer a financial loss at the point of implementation. The scheme would be implemented all in one go.
2. A Citizen's Basic Income for every UK citizen, funded from within the current tax and benefits system by charging National Insurance Contributions on all earnings at 12%, reducing to zero the Income Tax Personal Allowance, and raising Income Tax rates. Current means-tested benefits would be left in place, and each household's means-tested benefits would be recalculated to take into account household members' Citizen's Basic Incomes in the same way as earned income is taken into account. Again, implementation would be all in one go.
3. This scheme would start with an increase in Child Benefit. A Citizen's Basic Income would then be paid to all 16-year-olds, and they would be allowed to keep it as they grew older, with each new cohort of 16-year-olds receiving the same Citizen's Basic Income and being allowed to keep it.
4. Inviting volunteers among the pre-retired, between the age of 60 and the state pension age.[3]

We know that a Citizen's Basic Income scheme that abolished existing means-tested benefits, and that was funded purely by making adjustments to the current Income Tax system, would generate significant losses for low-income households.[4] A Citizen's Basic Income scheme that both abolished existing means-tested benefits and avoided losses for low-income households would need additional funding from outside the current tax and benefits systems. In the foreseeable future such additional funding is unlikely to be forthcoming. In the longer term a Citizen's Basic Income large enough to enable current means-tested benefits to be abolished while not imposing losses on low-income households might be a possibility, but its current infeasibility suggests that further research effort in this direction is unlikely to be immediately useful.

The fourth option, while interesting, is impossible to evaluate for poverty and inequality indices, household gains and losses, and net cost, because it is impossible to know which individuals or households would volunteer.

This leaves options 2 and 3 to evaluate in terms of the Income Tax rate increase required for revenue neutrality; the numbers of households suffering specified losses at the point of implementation; the numbers of low-income households suffering specified losses; the numbers of households taken off means-tested benefits of various kinds, and the numbers brought within striking distance of coming off them; changes in inequality and poverty indices; and redistributions achieved. An additional test is also applied in relation to a question that has become more insistent as the Citizen's Basic Income debate has evolved, and that is the question of employment market behaviour. Would individuals be more or less likely to seek paid employment, or to seek additional earned income, if they were paid a Citizen's Basic Income? Factors often discussed in this context are the marginal effective tax rate (METR: also called the marginal tax rate, the marginal withdrawal rate, or the marginal deduction rate): a measure of the extent to which an employed individual's additional earned income fails to result in additional disposable income; and the participation tax rate (PTR: also a marginal deduction rate): a measure of the extent to which an unemployed individual's new earned income fails to result in additional disposable income. While a wide variety of factors will determine whether an individual seeks paid employment, or seeks additional earned income, if a substantial rise in earned income results in only a small rise in disposable income then further employment market engagement is less likely to be forthcoming. Because the METR and the PTR are factors that can be measured, and other factors cannot be, these particular indicators might sometimes be given more prominence than they deserve: but because they can be measured, and because they are likely to be at least of some significance, this appendix defines and calculates a variety of different METRs and PTRs.

A Citizen's Basic Income could be paid to an entire population, or, as long as it was still a genuine Citizen's Basic Income, to a section of the population: usually to a particular age group. It might be objected that to pay an income to people in a particular age group would be to make the income conditional; and, indeed, that to pay Citizen's Basic

Incomes of different amounts to different age groups, as is generally envisaged, might also be regarded as not legitimate. However, as we saw in the note on terminology at the beginning of this book, there are two kinds of conditionality: 1. those that we cannot affect and about which enquiry does not need to be made; and 2. those that we can affect and about which enquiry does need to be made. An example of the first kind is someone's age. We cannot change our age, and once a benefits system knows someone's date of birth, it never again needs to enquire about their age. Examples of the second kind are household structure, employment status, earned income, and savings. We can affect all of these, and if a benefits system needs to know about them then enquiry has to be made. It is the latter kind of conditionality that generates administrative complexity, incentives and disincentives of various kinds, bureaucratic intrusion, and stigma. This is why the first kind of conditionality is permitted in a Citizen's Basic Income scheme, and the second is not.[5]

There would clearly be a multitude of different ways of adjusting the current tax and benefits system on the implementation of a Citizen's Basic Income, whether the new unconditional incomes were to be for an entire population, or for chosen age cohorts. The guiding principle employed here is that as few changes as possible will be made, consistent with the other aims in view: revenue neutrality, and the avoidance of significant losses, particularly for low-income households. I shall assume that raising Income Tax rates by more than 3 percentage points would be politically infeasible.[6]

The 'all at once' scheme

The Citizen's Basic Income scheme to be tested is constructed as follows:

- Child Benefit is increased by £20 per week for each child.
- National Insurance Contributions (NICs) above the Upper Earnings Limit are raised from 2% to 12%, and the Primary Earnings Threshold is reduced to zero. This has the effect of making NICs payable on all earned income at 12%. (This would appear to be an entirely legitimate change to make. The ethos of a flat rate benefit such as Citizen's Basic Income is consistent with both progressive tax systems and with flat-rate tax systems, but not with a regressive tax system.)[7]
- The Income Tax Personal Allowances are set at zero.

- Citizen's Basic Income levels are set as follows: A Young Person's Citizen's Basic Income (YCBI), for people aged 16 to 24, is set at £50 per week; a Working-Age Adult Citizen's Basic Income (WACBI, or simply CBI), for people aged 25 to 64, is set at £61 per week; [8] and a Citizen's Pension, for everyone aged over 65, is set at £40 per week. The existing National Insurance Basic State Pension is left in place. (In this particular scheme the YCBI is not paid to someone still in full-time education, in recognition of the fact that their main carer is receiving Child Benefit on their behalf.)
- Income Tax rates are adjusted as required in order to achieve revenue neutrality.

It might be suggested that it would be better either to retain Child Benefit as it is and pay a separate small Child Citizen's Basic Income at the same rate for every child, or to abolish Child Benefit and to pay an equal Citizen's Basic Income, and that to continue to pay Child Benefit at different rates for the first and for the second and subsequent children would compromise the principle that everyone of the same age should receive the same level of income. This might be true in theory, but in practice the situation is more complex. Every Citizen's Basic Income scheme envisages that Child Citizen's Basic Incomes will be paid to the main carer, as is Child Benefit: so what is happening in practice is that children receive no Citizen's Basic Incomes while their main carers receive varying amounts in relation to the number of children in their families. This means that to pay different amounts for the first and for the second and subsequent children would simply vary the already varying amounts paid to main carers of children, and that it would preserve sufficient of the unconditionality principle by ensuring that every main carer of the same number of children would receive the same total level of Citizen's Basic Income, made up of their own Citizen's Basic Incomes and those for their children. To enhance the level of Child Benefit is therefore legitimate in practice as well as conforming to our principle of making the smallest number of changes possible.[9]

Net cost, and household gains and losses

This appendix evaluates the effects of the Citizen's Basic Income scheme on household disposable incomes rather than on individuals' disposable incomes. There are good arguments for both approaches. It is individuals who receive income so gain or loss is an individual experience; and within a household, income is not necessarily equitably shared so the amounts that individuals receive might be more relevant than the amount that the household receives. However, we can assume that in most cases income is pooled within households, at least to some extent, so if one member gains and another loses then the household might be better off, and that might be a more significant factor than that one member of the household has suffered a loss in disposable income. Because households are of different sizes, an absolute gain or loss is not particularly relevant. However, percentage gains and losses are relevant, so this is the measure that we use.

Table A.1 summarises the results obtained from microsimulation of the scheme proposed here.[10]

Table A.1: An evaluation of an illustrative Citizen's Basic Income scheme with the working-age adult Citizen's Basic Income set at £61 per week

Citizen's Pension per week (existing state pensions remain in payment)	£40
Working-age adult Citizen's Basic Income per week	£61
Young adult Citizen's Basic Income per week	£50
(Child Benefit is increased by £20 per week)	(£20)
Income Tax rate increase required for strict revenue neutrality	3 %
Income Tax, basic rate (on £0 – 43,000)	23 %
Income Tax, higher rate (on £43,000 – 150,000)	43 %
Income Tax, top rate (on £150,000 –)	48 %
Proportion of households in the lowest original income quintile experiencing losses of over 10% at the point of implementation*	1.6 %
Proportion of households in the lowest original income quintile experiencing losses of over 5% at the point of implementation	2.3 %
Proportion of all households experiencing losses of over 10% at the point of implementation	2.0 %
Proportion of all households experiencing losses of over 5% at the point of implementation	9.3 %
Net cost of scheme	£1.96bn p.a.

* For an explanation of the ordering of households into deciles, see Torry, 2017c

We can conclude that the scheme would be strictly revenue neutral (that is, it could be funded from within the current income tax and benefits system); that the increase in Income Tax rate required would be feasible; and that the scheme would not impose significant numbers of significant losses on low-income households. In theory there should be no losses for low-income households because current means-tested benefits would still be in place and would be recalculated to take account of households' Citizen's Basic Incomes and changes in net incomes.

Further research on the detail of the Family Resources Survey data would be required to discover the particular household circumstances that generate losses. Losses for higher-income households will be due to increased Income Tax and National Insurance Contribution rates on higher earnings.

We can conclude that the scheme would be financially feasible.

Changes to means-tested benefits claims brought about by the scheme

Tables A.2 and A.3 give the results of calculations based on microsimulation of the current scheme and of the Citizen's Basic Income scheme.

Table A.2: Percentage of households claiming means-tested social security benefits for the existing scheme in 2016 and for the Citizen's Basic Income Scheme

	The existing scheme in 2016	The Citizen's Basic Income scheme	% reduction
Percentage of households claiming out-of-work benefits (Income Support, Income-related Jobseeker's Allowance, Income-related Employment Support Allowance)	13.2%	11.0%	16.7%
Percentage of households claiming more than £100 per month in out-of-work benefits (defined as above)	13.0%	5.2%	60%
Percentage of households claiming in-work benefits (Working Tax Credits and Child Tax Credits)	14.0%	11.7%	16.4%
Percentage of households claiming more than £100 per month in in-work benefits (defined as above)	12.8%	10.7%	16.4%
Percentage of households claiming Pension Credit	6.8%	6.2%	8.8%
Percentage of households claiming more than £50 per month in Pension Credit	5.8%	4.9%	15.5%
Percentage of households claiming Housing Benefit	16.2%	16.3%	- 0.6% (an increase)
Percentage of households claiming more than £100 per month in Housing Benefit	15.3%	15.2%	0.7%
Percentage of households claiming Council Tax Benefit	19.3%	17.5%	9.3%
Percentage of households claiming more than £50 per month in Council Tax Benefit	14.5%	13.0%	10.3%

Note: The Family Resources Survey data employed by EUROMOD G4.0+ is uprated 2013/14 data, and so is based on data collected before Universal Credit began to be rolled out and before Council Tax Benefit was localised (De Agostini, 2017: 56, 65, 69, 72-4).

Table A.3: Percentage reductions in total costs of means-tested benefits, and percentage reductions in average value of household claims, on the implementation of the Citizen's Basic Income scheme

	Reduction in total cost	Reduction in average value of claim
Out-of-work benefits (Income Support, Income-related Jobseeker's Allowance, Income-related Employment Support Allowance)	74.4%	65.6%
In-work benefits (Working Tax Credits and Child Tax Credits)	21.6%	6.3%
Pension Credit	35.5%	29.0%
Housing Benefit	3.3%	-3.9% (an increase)
Council Tax Reduction (see note for table A.2)	10.8%	1.8%

These results show that the effects of the Citizen's Basic Income scheme would be as follows:

- It would reduce by 16.7% the number of households claiming the out-of-work benefits Income Support, Income-related Jobseekers' Allowance and Income-related Employment Support Allowance; would reduce the total cost of these benefits by 74.4%; would reduce by 65.6% the average amount of these benefits received by households claiming them; and would reduce by 60% the number of households receiving more than £100 per month of these benefits.
- It would reduce by 16.4% the number of households claiming in-work benefits Working Tax Credits and Child Tax Credits; would reduce by 21.6% the total cost; would reduce by 6.3% the average amount of benefits received by households claiming them; and would reduce by 16.4% the number of households receiving more than £100 per month in these out-of-work benefits.
- It would not alter by very much the number of claims for Housing Benefit, nor their average value, and so would not alter the total cost of Housing Benefit. This suggests that a Citizen's Basic Income scheme of this type – that is, a strictly revenue-neutral scheme that did not impose appreciable losses on low-income households at the point of implementation – would not help to solve the problem of housing costs; and it would be difficult to see how any affordable Citizen's Basic Income scheme would able to do so. A solution based on housing supply will need to be found.
- It would reduce by more than one third the total cost of Pension Credit, and the average value of household claims would fall by more

than a quarter. The number of claims for Pension Credit would fall by 8.8%, so the reduction in total cost is due mainly to the reduction in the average value of claims. (The current transition from Basic State Pension to a Single Tier State Pension (STP) will change this picture by removing most elderly households from Pension Credit. Once roll-out of the STP has been achieved, it will be relatively simple to abandon the National Insurance record conditionality and turn the STP into a Citizen's Pension.)

(In 2013 Council Tax Benefit was still centrally regulated, and the uprating of the 2013 FRS (Family Resources Survey) data employed by EUROMOD G4.0+ continues to assume this situation. Under the government's localisation agenda, Council Tax Benefit's replacement, Council Tax Reduction, is now locally regulated as well as locally administered. This means that every borough in the country can now invent its own regulations, and, in particular, its own taper rate. It will be far from easy to include Council Tax Support in future tax and benefits simulations. EUROMOD G4.0+ assumes that Council Tax Support is still regulated as it was in 2013.[11])

The poverty, inequality and redistributional effects of the Citizen's Basic Income scheme

Table A.4 shows the changes that the illustrative Citizen's Basic Income scheme would bring about in relation to poverty and inequality.

Table A.4: Changes in poverty and inequality indices brought about by the Citizen's Basic Income scheme

	The current tax and benefits scheme in 2016	The Citizen's Basic Income scheme	Percentage change in the indices
Inequality			
Disposable income Gini coefficient	0.3038	0.2704	11.0%
Poverty headcount rates			
Total population in poverty	14.84%	11.80%	18.1%
Children in poverty	15.72%	10.43%	33.7%
Working-age adults in poverty	14.69%	11.70%	20.4%
Economically active working-age adults in poverty	5.74%	4.34%	24.4%
Elderly people in poverty	14.26%	13.90%	2.52%

Note: Poverty is defined as household incomes below 60% of median household income (De Agostini, 2017: 67-9).

We can conclude that

- the Citizen's Basic Income scheme would deliver a significant reduction in inequality;
- more significantly, child poverty would fall by a third, and working-age poverty would also fall.

Table A.5 and Figure A.1 show the aggregate redistribution that would occur if the Citizen's Basic Income scheme were to be implemented.[12]

Table A.5: The redistributional effect of the illustrative Citizen's Basic Income scheme

Disposable income decile	1	2	3	4	5	6	7	8	9	10
% increase in mean disposable income	20.1	8.4	6.6	5.7	6.4	3.5	2.7	0	-2.3	-5.9

Figure A.1: The redistributional effect of the illustrative Citizen's Basic Income scheme

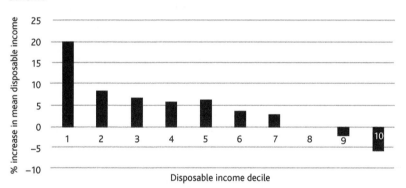

The table and graph show that the scheme would achieve manageable and useful redistribution from rich to poor, with those households in disposable income deciles 2 to 5 – the 'squeezed middle'[13] – benefiting from the transition as well as the poorest households.

Marginal effective tax rates

The METR measures the extent to which additional earned income does not result in additional disposable income. If y is the earned income before an increase, y' is earned income after an increase, d is disposable income before the increase in earned income, and d' is disposable income after the increase, then the METR is given by

$(1 - ((d' - d)/(y' - y))) \times 100$. So if an additional £200 in earnings results in an additional £150 of disposable income, the METR is 25%.

Until 2003 the Department for Work and Pensions published in printed form a set of graphs and tables that showed the METRs experienced by a range of household types across a wide range of earnings at £10 intervals.[14] The tables then went online for a couple of years before publication ceased. It would be enormously valuable to the research community for the calculation and publication of the tables to resume. This appendix is not the place for an attempt at such a major exercise. Instead, it offers sufficient information to enable us to draw some tentative conclusions about possible employment market effects.

Here I shall take two different approaches.

Marginal effective tax rates, method 1

EUROMOD's 'MTR' add-on calculates METRs for all individuals who are earning an income. The add-on increases by 3% the earned income of each working-age adult in the household in turn and calculates the increase in the household disposable income that this generates. If y is an individual's original earned income, d the original household disposable income, and d' the final household disposable income, then the METR is given by $(1 - ((d' - d)/0.03y)) \times 100$.[15]

This method assumes that in every household every individual adult has complete knowledge of the household's financial resources, that all household members possess equal power in relation to household resources, and that each individual's motivation is a function of household disposable income.

Marginal effective tax rates and participation tax rates, method 2

A second method increases the earned income of every individual 16 years old and above by £200 per month, and calculates the change in that individual's disposable income. This method therefore generates results for individuals already in employment, and also for individuals not in employment. For someone not in employment who enters employment, the ratio between the change in disposable income and the new earned income is the PTR; and for someone already in employment, the ratio between the change in disposable income and the change in earned income is the METR. A high PTR represents an 'unemployment trap' and a high METR a 'poverty trap'. In relation both to individuals initially in employment and to those not, a household's benefits income is assumed to be received by the individual to which the payment is made rather than by the household as a whole; and the earnings of all adults in the household are increased at the same time (as opposed to method 1, which increases each earned income in turn). The calculation is the same for both the PTR and the METR: If d is the individual's original disposable income and d' is their final disposable income, then the PTR/METR is given by $(1 - ((d' - d)/200)) \times 100$. £200 per month represents something between half a day a week and a day a week of additional employed hours at the National Living Wage, and so represents the kind of real-world employment market decision with which many individuals might be faced.

This method does not assume equal knowledge or sharing of a household's financial resources within the household, but it does assume that each individual's motivation is a function of the payments that they personally receive. So if one member of a couple receives Working Tax Credits payments on behalf of the household, then they and not their partner will be assumed to be influenced by any decrease in that payment; and if the other member receives Child Benefit, then they and not their partner will be influenced by that.

The reality in relation to household members' knowledge and sharing of household resources will generally lie somewhere between the two methods' assumptions for each household, with, I suspect, very few households at either end of the spectrum.[16]

A set of results for the current tax and benefits scheme and for the illustrative Citizen's Basic Income scheme are given in Tables A.6, A.7a and A.7b.

Method 1 studies only households in which at least one adult has earned income. As we have already seen, some households containing gainfully employed individuals will escape from Working Tax Credits (although not necessarily from Housing Benefit), but others will experience raised Income Tax rates, and some will experience higher NICs. While there will be fewer households on extremely high METRs, the number with METRs over 70% will rise by approximately 2%, and similarly for METRs over 80% and over 90%. Average METRs rise by approximately 6.5%, and the medians by approximately 3%.

Method 2 captures the effect of increases in earned income for both themselves and their partner on the payments made to the individual in the household who receives benefits payments (in-work benefits payments in the case of METRs, and out-of-work benefits payments in the case of PTRs). As we can see from the tables, the problem of high METRs and PTRs is somewhat reduced.

The lower medians for the current system result from positive Income Tax Personal Allowances (so that low earnings are not taxed) and from an individual's additional earnings reducing benefits payments made to another household member and not payments made to themselves. In the context of a Citizen's Basic Income scheme, all earnings are taxed, raising the medians.

Table A.6: Results for method 1: average marginal effective tax rates and numbers of marginal effective tax rates at various levels for households containing gainfully employed working-age adults, both for the current tax and benefits system and for the illustrative Citizen's Basic Income scheme, when individuals' earned incomes rise by 3%

Marginal effective tax rates	Percentage of individuals experiencing these METRs with the current tax and benefits system	Percentage of individuals experiencing these METRs with the illustrative Citizen's Basic Income scheme
Over 100%	0.26%	0.18%
Over 90%	2.93%	5.14%
Over 80%	3.90%	5.60%
Over 70%	10.96%	12.60%
Median METR	34.80%	37.57%
Mean METR	38.68%	45.18%

Table A.7a: Results for method 2: proportions of initially waged individuals over the age of 16 experiencing various marginal effective tax rates, both for the current tax and benefits system and for the illustrative Citizen's Basic Income scheme, when all adults' earned incomes are raised by £200 per month

Marginal Effective Tax Rates	Percentage of individuals experiencing these METRs with the current tax and benefits system	Percentage of individuals experiencing these METRs with the illustrative Citizen's Basic Income scheme
Over 100%	3.94%	3.13%
Over 90%	4.75%	4.60%
Over 80%	5.41%	5.36%
Over 70%	6.95%	7.79%
Median METR	33.83%	36.6%

Note: Averages (means) have not been calculated.

Table A.7b: Results for method 2: Proportions of initially unwaged individuals over the age of 16 experiencing various participation tax rates, both for the current tax and benefits system and for the illustrative Citizen's Basic Income scheme, when all adults' earned incomes are raised by £200 per month

Participation Tax Rates	Percentage of individuals experiencing these PTRs with the current tax and benefits system	Percentage of individuals experiencing these PTRs with the illustrative Citizen's Basic Income scheme
Over 100%	7.02%	6.14%
Over 90%	7.74%	6.73%
Over 80%	11.20%	9.14%
Over 70%	15.56%	11.88%
Median PTR	32.00%	35.00%

A feasible and useful Citizen's Basic Income scheme

Because the only changes required in order to implement this scheme would be

- payment of the Citizen's Basic Incomes for every individual above the age of 16, calculated purely in relation to the age of each individual (with perhaps a transitional arrangement for individuals between their 16th and 19th birthdays and still in full-time education),
- increases in the rates of Child Benefit,
- changes to Income Tax and National Insurance Contribution rates and thresholds, and
- easy-to-achieve recalculations in existing means-tested benefits claims,

the entire scheme could be implemented very quickly.

This simple scheme would offer improved poverty and inequality indicators; it would provide additional employment market incentives to the extent that changes in both earned income and benefits payments made to the individual influence employment market behaviour; it would remove large numbers of households from a variety of means-tested benefits; it would reduce means-tested benefit claim values and the total costs of means-tested benefits; it would avoid significant numbers of losses at the point of implementation; and it would require almost no additional public expenditure.

This simple illustrative scheme could be both feasible and useful.

A gradual roll-out, one age cohort at a time

The second of the implementation methods discussed by the ICAEW at its consultation envisages the Citizen's Basic Income being rolled out one age cohort at a time: a suggestion now also being made by the OECD.[17] First, Child Benefit could be enhanced. The second stage could be a Citizen's Basic Income paid to everyone aged 16, 17 and 18. Then every new cohort of 16-year-olds could receive a Citizen's Basic Income. (We shall test this third stage when 21-year-olds are receiving Citizen's Basic Incomes.)

Alongside the results that have already been achieved for a scheme that would cover the entire population, results for the first seven years of a gradual roll-out will offer some confidence that a Citizen's Basic Income scheme could be successfully rolled out and would have beneficial outcomes.

Stages of the gradual roll-out

Stage 1: Child Benefit would be increased by £20 for every child, the increase being paid for by raising NICs above the Upper Earnings Limit to 12% and by raising Income Tax rates to the extent required for revenue neutrality, understood here as a net cost for the scheme of between −£2bn and +£2bn per annum.

Stage 2: all of the characteristics of stage 1 would be retained, except that Child Benefit would be equalised at £40.70 for every child in order to achieve a smoother transition at age 16 for all children and their families. A Citizen's Basic Income of £45 per week[18] would be paid to everyone aged 16, 17 and 18. This would be paid for by reducing their Income Tax Personal Allowance to zero (by applying a Basic Rate (BR) tax code) and by restricting Child Benefit to under 16s. If necessary, the Income Tax Basic Rate would be adjusted to ensure revenue neutrality.

Stage 3: Citizen's Basic Incomes would be paid to further one-year cohorts by the simple expedient of allowing everyone who already has one to keep it and paying Citizen's Basic Incomes to everyone aged 16 and setting their Income Tax Personal Allowances to zero. Whereas the first three one-year age cohorts of 16, 17 and 18 year olds would have to receive their new Citizen's Basic Incomes at the same time in order to enable Child Benefit to be restricted to under-16s, subsequent one-year cohorts could be added one year at a time. This stage will be tested after three years have been added, that is, when Citizen's Basic Incomes are being paid to 21-year-olds.

Results will be given for all three stages, and results already obtained for the complete Citizen's Basic Income scheme described at the beginning of this appendix will be repeated for comparison.

Net cost and losses at the point of implementation for the stages of the roll-out and for the complete scheme

Tables A.8a and A.8b show the characteristics of the stages of the gradual roll-out, the additional tax rates required, and the extent of household losses at the point of implementation.

We can conclude that at no stage during the gradual roll-out would there be major problems with net cost or with household losses at the point of implementation.

Changes in the numbers of households claiming means-tested benefits, and in the numbers of households within striking distance of coming off them, during the roll-out and for the complete scheme

Table A.9 gives the proportions of households claiming various means-tested benefits for the existing scheme, for the stages of the gradual roll-out, and for the complete scheme. No table is included for changes to the average amounts of means-tested benefit claims or changes in the total costs of means-tested benefits because all such changes are negligible.

The numbers of means-tested benefits claimants, and the number within striking distance of coming off them, are moving slowly downwards in the direction of the results discovered for the complete scheme. There is every reason to expect these downward trends to continue throughout the roll-out.

Reductions in total costs of benefits and in average value of claim will be small by the end of the third stage so these have not been calculated.

Table A.8a: An evaluation of the three-stage roll-out and the complete Citizen's Basic Income scheme

	Stage 1	Stage 2	Stage 3	Complete scheme
Citizen's Pension per week (existing state pensions remain in payment)	n/a	n/a	n/a	£40
Working-age adult Citizen's Basic Income per week	n/a	n/a	n/a	£61
Young adult Citizen's Basic Income per week	n/a	£45	£45	£50
Child Benefit increased. Figures are given for first and for second and subsequent children	£40.70 / £33.70	£40.70 / £40.70	£40.70 / £40.70	£40.70 / £33.70
Income Tax rate increase relative to current rates required for strict revenue neutrality	1%	1%	1%	3%
Income Tax, basic rate	21%	21%	21%	23%
Income Tax, higher rate	41%	41%	41%	43%
Income Tax, top rate	46%	46%	46%	48%

Notes: In relation to the gradual roll-out, the young adult's Citizen's Basic Income is paid to everyone of the relevant age, and Child Benefit is restricted to under 16s. In relation to the complete scheme, a different approach was taken: the Young Person's Citizen's Basic Income was not paid to anyone still in full time education because their carer was already receiving the enhanced Child Benefit on their behalf. A phased transition from the second to the first option might be the most appropriate approach.

For Child Benefit payable as part of the complete scheme to be equalised at £40.70 per week for every child would require an additional £2bn or so. See Torry, 2017c for the calculation.

The additions to Income Tax rates are relative to current rates. No additions would be required for stages 2 or 3 in order to achieve revenue neutrality.

During the early stages of the gradual roll-out the threshold above which the higher rate of Income Tax is paid can be left where it is at £32,000. As the roll-out progresses it will need to be raised to £43,000 to ensure that the basic rate is paid on the same amount of earned income as in the current tax system.

Table A.8b: An evaluation of the three-stage roll-out and the complete Citizen's Basic Income scheme (continued)

	Stage 1	Stage 2	Stage 3	Complete scheme
Proportion of households in the lowest original income quintile experiencing losses of over 10% at the point of implementation (see note attached to table 1 on the ordering of households)	0.2%	0.2%	0%	1.6%
Proportion of households in the lowest original income quintile experiencing losses of over 5% at the point of implementation	0.4%	0.3%	0%	2.3%
Proportion of all households experiencing losses of over 10% at the point of implementation	1.1%	0.6%	0.05%	2.0%
Proportion of all households experiencing losses of over 5% at the point of implementation	3.8%	1.3%	0.16%	9.3%
Net cost of scheme	-£0.82bn (i.e. a saving of £0.82bn p.a.	-£1.76bn (i.e. a saving of £1.76bn p.a.	£1.45bn	£1.96bn p.a.

Notes: The figures given for household losses at stages 2 and 3 give losses relative to the previous stage because this is how losses would be experienced. Losses given for the complete scheme are relative to the current system because that is how losses would be experienced if the complete scheme were to be implemented all in one go. The net costs for stages 2 and 3 are each net costs relative to the previous stage. The cumulative saving at the end of stage 3 would be £1.13bn p.a.. The net cost for the complete scheme is relative to the current system.

Table A.9: Percentages of households claiming means-tested social security benefits for the existing scheme in 2016, during the gradual roll-out, and for the complete scheme

	Current system	Stage 1	Stage 2	Stage 3	Complete scheme
Percentage of households claiming out-of-work benefits (Income Support, Income-related Jobseeker's Allowance, Income-related Employment Support Allowance)	13.2%	13.2%	13.2%	13.1%	11.0%
Percentage of households claiming more than £100 per month in out-of-work benefits (defined as above)	13.0%	13.0%	12.5%	11.7%	5.2%
Percentage of households claiming in-work benefits (Working Tax Credits and Child Tax Credits)	14.0%	14.0%	13.8%	13.8%	11.7%
Percentage of households claiming more than £100 per month in in-work benefits (defined as above)	12.8%	12.8%	12.6%	12.6%	10.7%
Percentage of households claiming Pension Credit	6.8%	6.8%	6.8%	6.8%	6.2%
Percentage of households claiming more than £50 per month in Pension Credit	5.8%	5.8%	5.8%	5.8%	4.9%
Percentage of households claiming Housing Benefit	16.2%	16.2%	16.2%	16.2%	16.3%
Percentage of households claiming more than £100 per month in Housing Benefit	15.3%	15.3%	15.2%	15.2%	15.2%
Percentage of households claiming Council Tax Reduction	19.3%	19.3%	19.2%	19.2%	17.5%
Percentage of households claiming more than £50 per month in Council Tax Reduction	14.5%	14.5%	14.5%	14.5%	13.0%

Notes: See notes attached to table A.2 for information about the Universal Credit roll-out and the localisation of Council Tax Benefit, now Council Tax Reduction.

Poverty and inequality indices for the roll-out and the complete scheme

Table A.10 shows inequality and poverty indices for the various stages of the roll-out and also for the complete Citizen's Basic Income scheme.

Table A.10: Poverty and inequality indices for the stages of the roll-out and for the complete scheme

	Current system	Stage 1	Stage 2	Stage 3	The complete scheme
Inequality					
Disposable income Gini coefficient	0.3038	0.3038	0.283	0.2818	0.2704
Poverty headcount rates					
Total population in poverty	14.84%	13.99%	14.11%	13.98%	11.80%
Children in poverty	15.72%	12.44%	12.40%	12.34%	10.43%
Working-age adults in poverty	14.69%	14.24%	14.41%	14.13%	11.70%
Economically active working age adults in poverty	5.74%	5.49%	5.55%	5.38%	4.34%
Elderly people in poverty	14.26%	15.08%	15.26%	15.54%	13.90%

Notes: Poverty is defined as household incomes below 60% of median household income (De Agostini, 2017: 67-9).

Stage 1 leaves inequality where it is, whereas stages 2 and 3 start a gradual reduction towards the significantly lower level reached by the complete scheme.

Similarly, poverty levels fall in the direction of the lower levels achieved by the complete scheme, with an increase in Child Benefit offering a particularly useful reduction in child poverty.[19] The one anomaly is the figures for elderly poverty. The small increase in measured poverty delivered by EUROMOD's SumStat tool at stage 1 will be partly a result of the 1% increase in Income Tax rates, as that is the only factor that could affect elderly individuals. A study of microsimulation results shows that no elderly person's disposable income falls by more than 1.7%, and all losses over 1% are experienced by individuals with disposable incomes of over £3,000 per month, so losses related to the change in the Income Tax rates cannot be the only reason for the increase in this poverty index. At stages 2 and 3 there are no new factors that could affect elderly individuals' incomes. It would appear that the way in which SumStat chooses poverty lines is part of the reason for the apparent increase in elderly poverty. The complete scheme, as we have already recognised, would deliver significant reductions in all of the poverty indices.

Redistribution during the roll-out

I have already reported, in figure A.1, on the redistribution achieved by the complete scheme. The following tables and figures report on redistributions achieved during the gradual roll-out.

Table A.11: Redistribution achieved by stage 1 relative to the current tax and benefits system

Disposable income decile	1	2	3	4	5	6	7	8	9	10
% increase in mean disposable income	2.9	3.6	3.3	5.0	4.3	3.3	2.0	0.4	-0.6	-4.5

Figure A.2: Redistribution achieved by stage 1 relative to the current tax and benefits system

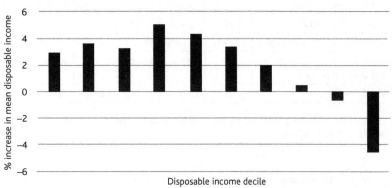

Table A.12: The cumulative distribution achieved by the time stage 3 of the roll-out is reached, relative to the current tax and benefits system

Disposable income decile	1	2	3	4	5	6	7	8	9	10
% increase in mean disposable income	4.0	4.3	3.6	6.2	4.8	4.8	3.1	1.6	0.0	-6.0

Figure A.3: The cumulative distribution achieved by the time stage 3 of the roll-out is reached, relative to the current tax and benefits system

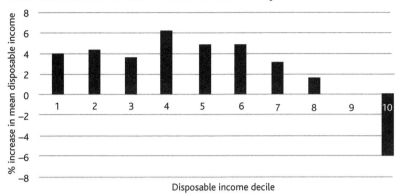

Disposable income decile

For comparison, I repeat here the redistribution achieved by the complete scheme:

Table A.13: The redistributional effect of the illustrative Citizen's Basic Income scheme

Disposable income decile	1	2	3	4	5	6	7	8	9	10
% increase in mean disposable income	20.1	8.4	6.6	5.7	6.4	3.5	2.7	0	-2.3	-5.9

Figure A.4: The redistribution achieved by the complete scheme

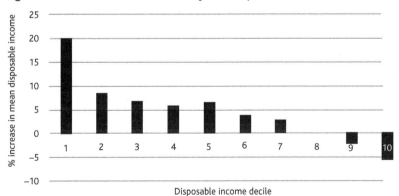

Disposable income decile

As we can see from the graphs, much of the redistributional work is done by the enhancement of Child Benefit levels. Stages 2 and 3 achieve only minor changes, but changes would continue to accumulate during the roll-out as Citizen's Basic Incomes were paid to the entire age range. The mean loss for the highest decile should be manageable, particularly if a gradual roll-out is implemented.

Conclusion

This appendix has evaluated a Citizen's Basic Income scheme in the UK implemented all in one go, and has also evaluated three stages of a gradual roll-out of a similar scheme.

In order for the gradual roll-out to reach the complete scheme, a Citizen's Pension would need to be implemented (and at the same time Income Tax Personal Allowances for those over state retirement age would be reduced to zero); Citizen's Basic Incomes would need to be paid to every new cohort of 16-year-olds until every working-age adult between the ages of 22 and state retirement age had a Citizen's Basic Income; the NICs Primary Earnings Threshold would need to be slowly reduced to zero; the threshold above which higher-rate Income Tax is paid would need to be raised, and Income Tax rates would need to be slowly raised to 3 percentage points above current levels. No 16-year-old would receive an Income Tax Personal Allowance, so by the time every working-age adult had a Citizen's Basic Income, all Income Tax Personal Allowances would have been set to zero.

The evaluations contained in this appendix suggest that it would be administratively and financially feasible to implement a Citizen's Basic Income in either of the two ways envisaged, and that whichever route was chosen, useful effects in terms of poverty reduction, inequality reduction, METR reductions (in relation to the individual's experience, but not necessarily the household's), and escape from means testing could be confidently predicted. In relation to the complete scheme, and in relation to each of the stages of the gradual roll-out, redistribution from rich to poor can be predicted, with manageable reductions for the better off, and significant average percentage increases for those in the lowest disposable income deciles. Whether in relation to the implementation of the complete scheme, or in relation to each of the stages of the gradual roll-out, the number of household losses at the point of implementation would be insignificant for households in the lowest original income quintile, and relatively insignificant for all households.

Now that the Citizen's Basic Income debate is increasingly interested in feasibility and implementation, it would be useful for more microsimulation research of this kind to be undertaken on a wide variety of illustrative schemes; and it would also be useful for 'typical household' research of the kind that used to inform the Department for

Work and Pensions Tax Benefit Model Tables to be carried out.[20] Lists of METRs for a wide variety of household types across wide earnings ranges, using both of the methods employed in this appendix, for the current tax and benefits system and for a variety of illustrative Citizen's Basic Income schemes, would make an important contribution to a debate that both needs and seeks this kind of analysis.

Notes

[1] This appendix is based on Torry, 2017c. Readers should consult the working paper for a full description of the method and of the research results. An error was made in the working paper in relation to METRs and PTRs. This appendix contains corrected figures.

[2] Torry, 2016e; http://citizensincome.org/news/icaew-report-on-implementing-citizens-income/, 03/06/2017.

[3] Torry, 2016e: 6.

[4] Torry, 2014a.

[5] Torry, 2017a; Torry, 2017b.

[6] Hirsch, 2015: 25–28.

[7] Atkinson, 1995.

[8] For the calculation, see Torry, 2017c.

[9] A similar approach is taken by Painter and Thoung, 2015.

[10] For the method, see Torry, 2017c.

[11] For further information, see De Agostini, 2017: 39.

[12] For the purposes of this exercise households are ranked by total equivalised disposable incomes (See De Agostini, 2017: 67 for further information).

[13] Parker, 2013.

[14] Department for Work and Pensions, 2003.

[15] Torry, 2017c repeats the exercise for 20% increases in earned income. The results are very little different from those for 3%.

[16] Lott, 2017.

[17] OECD, 2017: 8.

[18] For the calculation, see Torry, 2017c.

[19] Piachaud, 2016: 3.

[20] Department for Work and Pensions, 2003. An example of a particular household type at just one earnings level can be found in an introductory booklet published by the Citizen's Basic Income Trust in 2017. The complete text can be found on the website www.citizensincome.org.

Bibliography

Basic Income Research Group and Citizen's Income Trust publications are all available to download via the Trust's website at http://citizensincome.org/ publications/.

Abel-Smith, Brian and Peter Townsend (1965) *The poor and the poorest: A new analysis of the Ministry of Labour's Family Expenditure Surveys of 1953–54 and 1960*, London: Bell

Adam, Stuart et al (eds) (2010) *Dimensions of tax design: The Mirrlees Review*, Oxford: Oxford University Press for the Institute for Fiscal Studies

Adam, Stuart et al (eds) (2011) *Tax by design: The Mirrlees Review*, Oxford: Oxford University Press

Adam, Stuart, Mike Brewer and Andrew Shephard (2006) *The poverty trade-off: Work incentives and income redistribution in Britain*, Bristol: Policy Press/York: Joseph Rowntree Foundation

Adam, Stuart, James Browne, Carl Emmerson, Andrew Hood, Paul Johnson, Robert Joyce, Helen Miller, David Phillips, Thomas Pope and Barra Roantree (2015) *Taxes and benefits: The parties' plans*, London: Institute for Fiscal Studies, http://www.ifs.org.uk/publications/7733, 26/06/2017

Addabbo, Tindara, Marie-Pierre Arrizabalaga, Cristina Borderias and Alastair Owens (eds) (2010) *Gender inequalities, households and the production of well-being in modern Europe*, Aldershot: Ashgate

Adelman, Laura, Sue Middleton and Karl Ashworth (1999) *Intra-household distribution of poverty and social exclusion: Evidence from the 1999 PSE Survey of Britain*, Working paper no 23, Loughborough: Centre for Research in Social Policy

Adler, Michael, Colin Bell, Joachin Clasen and Adrian Sinfield (eds) (1991) *The Sociology of Social Security*, Edinburgh: Edinburgh University Press

Akee, Randall, Emilia Simeonova, E. Jane Costello, William Copeland (2015) *How does household income affect child personality traits and behaviors*, Cambridge, MA: National Bureau of Economic Research, http://www.nber.org/papers/w21562.pdf, 10/06/2017

Albi, Emilio and Jorge Martinez-Vazquez (eds) (2011) *The Elgar guide to tax systems*, Cheltenham: Edward Elgar

Alm, James (ed.) (2011) *The economics of taxation*, The International Library of Critical Writings in Economics 251, Cheltenham: Edward Elgar

Alstott, Anne L. (2001) 'Good for Women', in Joshua Cohen and Joel Rogers (eds) *What's wrong with a free lunch?* Boston, MA: Beacon Press, pp 75–9

Altman, Sam (2016) *Basic Income*, California: Y Combinator, https://blog.ycombinator.com/basic-income/

Andersson, Jan Otto (2001) 'Why does Basic Income thrill the Finns, but not the Swedes?' *Citizen's Income Newsletter*, issue 2 for 2001: 2–4

Anglund, Sandra M. (1999) 'American core values and policy problem definition', in Stuart S. Nagel (ed.) *The policy process*, New York: Nova Science Publishers, pp 147–63

Arneson, Richard J. (2002) 'Why justice requires transfers to offset income and wealth inequalities', in Ellen Frankel Paul, Fred D. Miller Jr. and Jeffrey Paul (eds) *Should differences in income and wealth matter?* Cambridge: Cambridge University Press, pp 172–200

Arntz, Melanie, Terry Gregory and Ulrich Zierahn (2016) *The risk of automation for jobs in OECD countries: A comparative analysis*, Paris: OECD Publishing, www.oecd-ilibrary.org/social-issues-migration-health/the-risk-of-automation-for-jobs-in-oecd-countries_5jlz9h56dvq7-en

Ashdown, Paddy (1990) 'Breaking the poverty trap: A Basic Income', *BIRG Bulletin*, no 10, Autumn/Winter 1990: 5–6

Ashdown, Paddy (1992) 'What the politicians say', *BIRG Bulletin*, no 14, February 1992: 4–6a

Atkinson, A.B. (1969) *Poverty in Britain and the reform of social security*, Cambridge: Cambridge University Press

Atkinson, A.B. (1973) *The Tax Credit scheme and the redistribution of income*, London: Institute for Fiscal Studies

Atkinson, A.B. (1984) *The costs of social dividend and tax credit schemes*, Tax, Incentives and the Distribution of Income paper no 63, London: London School of Economics

Atkinson, A.B. (1985) *Income maintenance and social insurance: A survey*, Welfare State Programme, paper no 5, London: London School of Economics

Atkinson, A.B. (1989a) *Basic Income schemes and the lessons from public economics*, Tax, Incentives and the Distribution of Income paper no 136, London: London School of Economics

Atkinson, A.B. (1989b) *Poverty and social security*, London: Harvester/Wheatsheaf

Atkinson, Tony (1993) 'Participation Income', *Citizen's Income Bulletin*, no 16, July 1993: 7–11

Atkinson, A.B. (1995) *Public economics in action: The Basic Income/Flat Tax proposal*, Oxford: Clarendon Press

Atkinson, A.B. (1996) 'The case for a Participation Income', *The Political Quarterly*, 67(1): 67–70

Atkinson, Tony (2011) 'The case for universal child benefit', in Alan Walker, Adrian Sinfield and Carol Walker (eds) *Fighting poverty, inequality and injustice: A manifesto inspired by Peter Townsend*, Cambridge: Polity Press, pp 79–90

Atkinson, Anthony B. (2015) *Inequality: What can be done?* Cambridge, MA: Harvard University Press

Atkinson, A.B. and Gunnar Viby Mogensen (eds) (1993) *Welfare and work incentives*, Oxford: Oxford University Press

Atkinson, A.B. and H. Sutherland (1984) *A Tax Credit scheme and families in work*, Tax, Incentives and the Distribution of Income no 54, London: London School of Economics

Atkinson, A.B. and Holly Sutherland (1988a) *Integrating incomes taxation and social security: Analysis of a Partial Basic Income*, Tax, Incentives and the Distribution of Income paper no 123, London: London School of Economics

Atkinson, Tony and Holly Sutherland (1988b) 'Analysis of a Partial Basic Income', *BIRG Bulletin*, no 8, Autumn 1988: 12–14

Auerbach, Paul (2016) *Socialist optimism: An alternative political economy for the twenty-first century*, Basingstoke: Palgrave Macmillan

Avery, Michael D. (1963) *Industry in South-east London (Bermondsey and Southwark)* thesis submitted for M.A. degree, University of London

Avram, Silvia (2015) *Benefit losses loom larger than taxes: The effects of framing and loss aversion on behavioural responses to taxes and benefits*, Colchester: Institute for Social and Economic Research, www.iser. essex.ac.uk/research/publications/working-papers/iser/2015-17.pdf

Bahle, Thomas, Vanessa Hubl and Michaela Pfeifer (2011) *The last safety net: A handbook of minimum income protection in Europe*, Bristol: Policy Press

Baillie, Richard (2011) 'An examination of the public discourse on benefit claimants in the media', *Journal of Poverty and Social Justice*, 19(1): 67–70

Baker, John (1995) 'Basic Income in Ireland: Recent developments', *Citizen's Income Bulletin*, no 20, July 1995: 10–11

Baker, John (2008) 'All things considered, should feminists embrace Basic Income?', *Basic Income Studies*, 3(3): 1–8

Bambrick, Laura (2006) 'Wollstonecraft's dilemma: Is a Citizen's Income the answer?' *Citizen's Income Newsletter*, issue 2 for 2006: 3–10

Banting, Keith G. (1979) *Poverty, politics and policy: Britain in the 1960s*, London: Macmillan

Barkai, Haim (1998) *The evolution of Israel's social security system*, Aldershot: Ashgate

Barnes, Peter (2014) *With liberty and dividends for all: How to save our middle class when jobs don't pay enough*, Oakland, CA: Berret-Koehler Publishers

Barr, Nicholas (1987) *The economics of the Welfare State*, London: Weidenfeld and Nicholson

Barr, Nicholas and Fiona Coulter (1991) 'Social security: Solution of problem', in John Hills (ed.) *The state of welfare: The Welfare State in Britain since 1974*, Oxford: Clarendon Press, pp 274–337

Barrientos, Armando (2011) 'Conditions in antipoverty programmes', *Journal of Poverty and Social Justice*, 19(1): 15–26

Barrientos, Armando and Sony Pellissery (2011) 'The road to global citizenship?' in Armando Barrientos, Benjamin Davy, Ulrike Davy, Hartley Dean, Harvey M. Jacobs, Lutz Leisering and Sony Pellissery (2011) *A road to global social citizenship?* Financial Assistance, Land Policy, and Global Social Rights Working Paper No 10, pp 6–14, www.tinyurl.com/3n9jh5h

Basic Income Grant Coalition (2009) *Making the difference: The BIG in Namibia: Basic Income Grant Pilot Project, Assessment Report*, Namibia: NGO Forum, www.bignam.org/Publications/BIG_Assessment_report_08b.pdf

Basic Income Research Group (1986) 'Basic Incomes and elderly people', *BIRG Bulletin*, no 6, Autumn 1986: 5–10

Basic Income Research Group (1988) 'Implications of Basic Income for people with disabilities', *BIRG Bulletin*, no 7, Spring 1988: 10–19

Bauman, Zygmunt (2000) *Liquid modernity*, Cambridge: Polity Press

Baumberg, Ben (2016) 'The stigma of claiming benefits: A quantitative study', *Journal of Social Policy*, 45(2): 181–99

Baumberg, Ben, Kate Bell and Declan Gaffney, with Rachel Deacon, Clancy Hood and Daniel Sage (2013) *Benefits stigma in Britain*, Canterbury: University of Kent/Elizabeth Finn Care, www.turn2us.org.uk/About-Us/Research-and-Insights/Benefits-Stigma-in-Britain

Beaumont, Jen (2011) *Households and families: Social trends 41*, London: Office for National Statistics, www.ons.gov.uk/ons/rel/social-trends-rd/social-trends/social-trends-41/social-trends-41---household-and-families.pdf

Béland, Daniel and Klaus Petersen (eds) (2014) *Analysing social policy concepts and language: Comparative and transnational perspectives*, Bristol: Policy Press

Belfield, Chris, Jonathan Cribb, Andrew Hood and Robert Joyce (2015) *Living standards, poverty and inequality in the UK: 2015*, London: Institute for Fiscal Studies, www.ifs.org.uk/publications/7878

Belfield, Chris, Jonathan Cribb, Andrew Hood and Robert Joyce (2016) *Living standards, poverty and inequality in the UK: 2016*, London: Institute for Fiscal Studies, www.ifs.org.uk/publications/8371

Bennett, Fran (1988) 'Alternatives to Basic Income: A personal view', *BIRG Bulletin*, no 7, Spring 1988: 8–10

Bennett, Fran and Holly Sutherland (2011) *The importance of independent income: Understanding the role of non-means-tested earnings replacement benefits*, ISER working paper no 2011-09, Colchester: Institute for Social and Economic Research, University of Essex

Bennett, Fran, Mike Brewer and Jonathan Shaw (2009) *Understanding the compliance costs of benefits and Tax Credits*, London: Institute for Fiscal Studies

Berg, Gary A. (2010) *Low-income students and the perpetuation of inequality*, Aldershot: Ashgate

Bergh, Andreas, Therese Bilsson and Daniel Waldenström (2016) *Sick of inequality? An introduction to the relationship between inequality and health*, Cheltenham: Edward Elgar

Berthoud, Richard (2007) *Work-rich and work-poor*, Bristol: Policy Press

Beveridge, Sir William (1942) *Social insurance and allied services*, Cmd 6404, London: Her Majesty's Stationery Office

BIRG youth group (1985) 'Basic Incomes and young people', *BIRG Bulletin*, no 4, Autumn 1985: 8–11

Birnbaum, Simon (2008) *Just distribution: Rawlsian liberalism and the politics of Basic Income*, Stockholm Studies in Politics 122, Stockholm: Stockholm University

Birnbaum, Simon (2012), *Basic Income reconsidered: Social justice, liberalism, and the demands of equality*, New York: Palgrave Macmillan

Birnbaum, Simon and Jürgen De Wispelaere (2016) 'Basic Income in the capitalist economy: The mirage of "exit" from employment', *Basic Income Studies*, 11(1): 61–74

Blair, Tony (2001) speech, 23 May 2001: www.guardian.co.uk/politics/2001/may/23/labour.tonyblair

Blaschke, Ronald (2012) *From the idea of a Basic Income to the political movement in Europe: Development and questions*, Berlin: Rosa Luxemburg Foundation, tr. Katharina Messinger

Blauner, Robert (1964) *Alienation and freedom: The factory worker and his industry*, Chicago: University of Chicago Press

Blix, Mårten (2017) *Digitalization, immigration and the Welfare State*, Cheltenham: Edward Elgar

Block, Fred (2001) 'Why pay Bill Gates?' in Joshua Cohen and Joel Rogers (eds) *What's wrong with a free lunch?* Boston, MA: Beacon Press, pp 85–9

Block, Fred and Margaret Somers (2003) 'In the shadow of Speenhamland: Social policy and old Poor Law', *Politics and Society*, 31(2): 283–323

Blyth, Mark, Eric Lonergan and Simon Wren-Lewis (2015) 'Now the Bank of England needs to deliver QE for the people', *The Guardian*, 21 May 2015, www.theguardian.com/business/economics-blog/2015/may/21/now-the-bank-of-england-needs-to-deliver-qe-for-the-people

Bochel, Hugh (2011) 'Conservative approaches to social policy since 1997', in Hugh Bochel (ed.) *The Conservative Party and social policy*, Bristol: Policy Press, pp 1–22

Bochel, Hugh and Andrew Defty (2007) *Welfare policy under New Labour*, Bristol: Policy Press

Booker, H.A. (1946) 'Lady Rhys Williams' Proposals for the Amalgamation of Direct Taxation with Social Insurance', *The Economic Journal*, 56: 230–43

Booth, Robert (2017) 'Uber granted right to appeal against ruling on UK drivers' rights', *The Guardian*, 19 April 2017, www.theguardian.com/technology/2017/apr/19/uber-appeal-uk-employment-ruling-drivers-working-rights

Born, Theo Barry, Sabrina Bushe, Tom MacInnes and Adam Tinson (2015) *Managing the challenges of localised Council Tax Support*, Rickmansworth: New Policy Institute

Boyle, Conall (2012) 'Funding Citizen's Income from money creation: The message of James Robertson's *Future Money*', *Citizen's Income Newsletter*, issue 3 for 2012: 5–7

Braverman, Harry (1974) *Labor and monopoly capital*, New York: Monthly Review Press

Bregman, Rutger (2017) *Utopia for Realists: And how we can get there*, London: Bloomsbury

Brittan, Samuel (1995) 'Basic Income and the Welfare State', in Samuel Brittan, *Capitalism with a human face*, Aldershot: Edward Elgar, reprinted in Karl Widerquist, José A. Noguera, Yannick Vanderborght and Jürgen De Wispelaere (eds) (2013) *Basic Income: An anthology of contemporary research*, Chichester: Wiley Blackwell, pp 339–45

Brittan, Samuel (2001) 'An attraction for Gladstonian liberals', *Citizen's Income Newsletter*, issue 1 for 2001: 2

Brittan, Samuel and Steven Webb (1990) *Beyond the Welfare State: An examination of Basic Incomes in a market economy*, Aberdeen: Aberdeen University Press

Britto, Tatiana and Fábio Veras Soares (2011) *Bolsa Família and the Citizen's Basic Income: A misstep*, Working paper no 77, Brasilia: International Policy Centre for Inclusive Growth, https://pdfs.semanticscholar.org/f0e3/eb0740042e627622b761e06038334c05138f.pdf

Brown, Joan (1988) *Child Benefit: Investing in the future*, London: Child Poverty Action Group

Bryan, James B. (2005) 'Targeted programs v. the Basic Income Guarantee: an examination of the efficiency costs of different forms of redistribution', *The Journal of Socioeconomics*, 34(1): 39–47

Brynjolfsson, Erik and Andrew McAfee (2014) *The second machine age: Work, progress, and prosperity in a time of brilliant technologies*, New York: W. W. Norton & Company

Burchardt, Tania and Julian Le Grand (2002) *Constraint and opportunity: Identifying voluntary non-employment*, CASE paper 55, London: Centre for Analysis of Social Exclusion, London School of Economics

Burchardt, Tania and Polly Vizard (2007) *Developing a capabilities list: Final recommendations of the Equalities Review Steering Group on Measurement*, CASE paper no 121, London: Centre for Analysis of Social Exclusion, London School of Economics

Callender, Rosheen (1989) 'Basic Income in Ireland: The debate so far', *BIRG Bulletin*, no 9, Spring/Summer 1989: 10–13

Caputo, Richard (ed.) (2012) *Basic Income Guarantee and politics: International experiences and perspectives on the viability of Income Guarantee*, New York: Palgrave Macmillan

Carpenter, Mick, Belinda Freda and Stuart Speeden (eds) (2007) *Beyond the workfare state*, Bristol: Policy Press

Casassas, David (2007) 'Basic Income and the republican ideal: Rethinking material independence in contemporary societies', *Basic Income Studies*, 2(2): 1–7

Casassas, David (2016) 'Economic sovereignty as the democratization of work: The role of Basic Income', *Basic Income Studies*, 11(1): 1–15

Casassas, David and Sandra González Bailón (2007) 'Corporate watch, consumer responsibility, and economic democracy: Forms of political action in the orbit of a Citizen's Income', *Citizen's Income Newsletter*, issue 3 for 2007: 8–12

Casassas, David, Daniel Raventós and Julie Wark (2010) 'The right to existence in developing countries: Basic Income in East Timor', *Basic Income Studies*, 5(1): 1–14

Cato, Molly Scott (2010) *Green economics: An introduction to theory, policy and practice*, Abingdon: Earthscan

Centre for Social Justice (2016) *Reforming contributory benefits*, London: Centre for Social Justice, www.centreforsocialjustice.org.uk/library/reforming-contributory-benefits

Centre for the Modern Family (2011) *Family: Helping to understand the modern British family*, Edinburgh: Scottish Widows, Centre for the Modern Family

Citizen's Income Trust (2000) 'Alaska Permanent Fund', *Citizen's Income Newsletter*, issue 3 for 2000: 6–7

Citizen's Income Trust (2003) 'Citizenship and a Citizen's Income', *Citizen's Income Newsletter*, issue 3 for 2003: 3–10

Citizen's Income Trust (2007) 'Both the House of Commons and the House of Lords support a Citizen's Income approach to the reform of tax and benefits', *Citizen's Income Newsletter*, issue 2 for 2007: 1–2

Citizen's Income Trust (2010) 'Review: *Governance of Welfare State reform: A cross national and cross sectoral comparison of policy and politics*, by Irene Dingeldey and Heinz Rothgang', *Citizen's Income Newsletter*, issue 2 for 2010: 9–10

Citizen's Income Trust (2011) 'The Citizen's Income Trust's response to the Department for Work and Pensions' consultation paper *A State Pension for the 21st Century*, April 2011, Cm. 8053', *Citizen's Income Newsletter*, issue 3 for 2011: 1–6

Citizen's Income Trust (2013) *Citizen's Income: A brief introduction*, London: Citizen's Income Trust, http://citizensincome.org/wp-content/uploads/2016/03/Booklet-2013.pdf

Citizen's Income Trust (2016) 'Referenda', *Citizen's Income Newsletter*, issue 3 for 2016: 2–3

Citizen's Income Trust (2017a) *Citizen's Basic Income: A brief introduction*, London: Citizen's Income Trust

Citizen's Income Trust (2017b) 'The state of the debate', *Citizen's Income Newsletter*, issue 1 for 2017: 1–2

Citizen's Income Trust (2017c) 'Rebalancing the mix', *Citizen's Income Newsletter*, issue 2 for 2017: 1

Citizen's Income Trust (2017d) 'Framing Citizen's Income', *Citizen's Income Newsletter*, issue 2 for 2017: 1–2

Clark, Charles M.A. (2002) *The Basic Income Guarantee: Ensuring progress and prosperity in the 21st century*, Dublin: The Liffey Press

Clarke, John (2017) *Progressive dreams meet neoliberal realities*, Toronto: Socialist Project, http://www.socialistproject.ca/bullet/1350.php#continue

Clarke, John, Kathleen Coll, Evelina Dagnino and Catherine Neveu (2014) *Disputing citizenship*, Bristol: Policy Press

Coats, David (2012) 'Labour market myths and realities', in Ed Wallis (ed.) *New Forms of Work*, a Fabian Policy Report, London: Fabian Society, pp 2–3

Cobham, Alex (2014) 'Unconditional: The limits of evidence', *Citizen's Income Newsletter*, issue 3 for 2014: 8–10

Coêlho, Denilson Bandeira (2012) 'Brazil: Basic Income – A new model of innovation diffusion', in Matthew C. Murray and Carole Pateman (eds) *Basic Income worldwide: Horizons of reform*, New York: Palgrave Macmillan, pp 59–80

Collard, David (1978) *Altruism and economy: A study in non-selfish economics*, Oxford: Martin Robertson

Colombino, Ugo, Marilena Locatelli, Edlira Narazani and Cathal O'Donoghue (2010) 'Alternative Basic Income mechanisms: An evaluation exercise with a microeconometric model', *Basic Income Studies*, 5(1): 1–31

Commission on Social Justice (1994) *Social justice: Strategies for national renewal*, London: Vintage

Conservative Party (2017) *Forward, together: Our plan for a stronger Britain and a prosperous future*, London: The Conservative and Unionist Party

Coote, Anna, Jane Franklin and Andrew Simms (2010) *21 Hours: Why a shorter working week can help us all to flourish in the 21st century*, London: New Economics Foundation, www.neweconomics.org/blog/entry/10-reasons-for-a-shorter-working-week

Cory, Giselle (2013) *All work and no pay: Second earners' work incentives and childcare costs under Universal Credit*, London: Resolution Foundation

Costabili, Lilia (ed.) (2008) *Institutions for social well-being: Alternatives for Europe*, Basingstoke: Palgrave Macmillan

Craig, David, with Richard Brooks (2006) *Plundering the public sector*, London: Constable

Crawford, Rowena, Soumaya Keynes and Gemma Tetlow (2014) *From me to you? How the UK state pension system redistributes*, London: Institute for Fiscal Studies, https://www.ifs.org.uk/publications/7326

Creedy, John (1998) *Pensions and population ageing*, Cheltenham: Edward Elgar

Creedy, John and Richard Disney (1985) *Social insurance in transition*, Oxford: Clarendon Press

Cribb, Jonathan, Robert Joyce and David Phillips (2012) *Living standards, poverty and inequality in the UK: 2012*, London: The Institute for Fiscal Studies

Crocker, Geoff (2012) 'Why austerity is the wrong answer to debt: A call for a new paradigm', *Citizen's Income Newsletter*, issue 3 for 2012: 13–16

Crossley, Thomas F. and Sung-Hee Jeon (2007) 'Joint taxation and the labour supply of married women: Evidence from the Canadian tax reform of 1988', *Fiscal Studies*, 28(3): 343–65

Cummine, Angela (2011) 'Overcoming dividend skepticism: Why the world's sovereign wealth funds are not paying Basic Income dividends', *Basic Income Studies*, 6(1): 1–18

Cunliffe, John and Guido Erreygers (eds) (2004) *The origins of universal grants: An anthology of historical writings on Basic Capital and Basic Income*, Basingstoke: Palgrave Macmillan

Curchin, Katherine (2017) 'Using behavioural insights to argue for a stronger social safety net: Beyond libertarian paternalism', *Journal of Social Policy*, 46(2): 231–49

Cusworth, Linda (2009) *The impact of parental employment: Young people, well-being and educational achievement*, Aldershot: Ashgate

Darton, David, Donald Hirsch, and Jason Strelitz (2003) *Tackling disadvantage: a 20-year enterprise: A working paper for the Joseph Rowntree Foundation's Centenary Conference, December 2004*, York: Joseph Rowntree Foundation

Davala, Sarath, Renana Jhabvala, Soumya Kapoor Mehta and Guy Standing (2015) *Basic Income: A transformative policy for India*, London: Bloomsbury

Davis, Karen, Kristof Stremikis, David Squires and Cathy Schoen (2014) *Mirror, mirror on the wall: How the performance of the U.S. health care system compares internationally*, New York: The Commonwealth Fund, www.commonwealthfund.org/~/media/files/publications/fund-report/2014/jun/1755_davis_mirror_mirror_2014.pdf

Davis, Steven J. and Magnus Henrekson (2005) 'Tax effects on work activity, industry mix and shadow economy size: Evidence from rich-country comparisons', in Ramon Gomez-Salvador, Ana Lamo, Barbara Petrongolo, Melanie Ward and Etienne Wasmer (eds) *Labour supply and incentives to work in Europe*, Cheltenham: Edward Elgar, pp 44–104

De Agostini, Paola (2017) *EUROMOD country report United Kingdom 2013–2016*, Colchester: Institute for Social and Economic Research, www.euromod.ac.uk/sites/default/files/country-reports/year7/Y7_CR_UK_Final.pdf

De Wispelaere, Jürgen (undated) *Universal Basic Income: Reciprocity and the right to non-exclusion*, London: Citizen's Income Trust

De Wispelaere, Jürgen (2016) 'Basic Income in our time: Improving political prospects through policy learning?' *Journal of Social Policy*, 45(4): 617–34

De Wispelaere, Jürgen and José Antonio Noguera (2012) 'On the political feasibility of Universal Basic Income: An analytic framework', in Richard Caputo (ed.) *Basic Income Guarantee and politics: International experiences and perspectives on the viability of Income Guarantee*, New York: Palgrave Macmillan, pp 17–38

De Wispelaere, Jürgen and Lindsay Stirton (2005) 'The many faces of Universal Basic Income', *Citizen's Income Newsletter*, issue 1 for 2005: 1–8

De Wispelaere, Jurgen and Lindsay Stirton (2008) 'Why Participation Income might not be such a great idea after all', *Citizen's Income Newsletter*, issue 3 for 2008: 3–8

De Wispelaere, Jürgen and Lindsay Stirton (2011) 'The administrative efficiency of Basic Income', *Policy and Politics*, 39(1): 115–32

De Wispelaere, Jürgen and Lindsay Stirton (2012) 'A disarmingly simple idea? Practical bottlenecks in implementing a Universal Basic Income', *International Social Security Review*, 65(2): 103–21

Deacon, Alan (2002) *Perspectives on welfare: Ideas, ideologies and policy debates*, Maidenhead: Open University Press/McGraw-Hill

Deacon, Alan and Jonathan Bradshaw (1983) *Reserved for the poor: The means test in British social policy*, Oxford: Blackwell

Deacon, Bob (2013) *Global social policy in the making: The foundations of the social protection floor*, Bristol: Policy Press

Dean, Hartley (2010) *Understanding human need*, Bristol: Policy Press

Dean, Hartley (2012a) 'The ethical deficit of the UK's proposed Universal Credit: Pimping the Precariat?' *Political Quarterly*, 83(2): 353–9

Dean, Hartley (2012b) 'Re-conceptualising Welfare-to-Work for people with multiple problems and needs', *Journal of Social Policy*, 32(3): 441–59

Dean, Hartley and Margaret Melrose (1999) *Poverty, riches and social citizenship*, Basingstoke: Macmillan

Dean, Hartley and Gerry Mitchell (2011) *Wage top-ups and work incentives: The implications of the UK's Working Tax Credit scheme: A preliminary report*, London: London School of Economics

Dean, Hartley and Lucinda Platt (2016) *Social advantage and disadvantage*, Oxford: Oxford University Press

Deeming, Christopher (2017) 'Defining Minimum Income (and Living) Standards in Europe: Methodological issues and policy debates', *Social Policy and Society*, 16(1): 33–48

Department for Work and Pensions (2003) *Tax benefit model tables, April 2003*, London: Department for Work and Pensions Information Centre, Information and Analysis Directorate

Department for Work and Pensions (2010) *21st century welfare*, Cm. 7913, London: The Stationery Office

Department for Work and Pensions (2011) *A state pension for the 21st century*, Cm. 8053, London: The Stationery Office

Department for Work and Pensions (2016a) *Fraud and error in the benefit system: 2015–16 final estimates*, London: Department for Work and Pensions, www.gov.uk/government/uploads/system/uploads/attachment_data/file/575407/fraud-and-error-stats-release-2015-16-final-estimates.pdf

Department for Work and Pensions (2016b) *Annual report and accounts 2015–16*, London: Department for Work and Pensions, www.gov.uk/government/uploads/system/uploads/attachment_data/file/534933/dwp-annual-report-and-accounts-2015-2016.pdf

Department of Health and Social Security (1985) *Reform of Social Security: Programme for change*, Cm. 9517, London: Her Majesty's Stationery Office

Devine, Pat, Andrew Pearmain and David Purdy (eds) (2009) *Feelbad Britain: How to make it better*, London: Lawrence and Wishart

Dickens, Richard and Abigail McKnight (2008a) *Changes in earnings inequality and mobility in Great Britain 1978/9–2005/6*, CASE paper no 132, London: Centre for Analysis of Social Exclusion, London School of Economics

Dickens, Richard and Abigail McKnight (2008b) *The impact of policy change on job retention and advancement*, CASE paper no 134, London: Centre for Analysis of Social Exclusion, London School of Economics

Dingeldey, Irene (2009) 'Changing forms of governance as welfare state restructuring: Activating labour market policies in Denmark, the UK and Germany', in Irene Dingeldey and Heinz Rothgang (eds) *Governance of welfare state reform: A cross national and cross sectoral comparison of policy and politics*, Cheltenham: Edward Elgar, pp 69–93

Domènech, Antoni and Daniel Raventós (2007) 'Property and republican freedom: An institutional approach to Basic Income', *Basic Income Studies*, 2(2): 1–8

Dommen-Meade, Bridget (ed.) (2010) *Le financement d'un revenu de base inconditionnel*, Zürich: Seismo, for BIEN-Suisse

Donnison, David (1982) *The politics of poverty*, Oxford: Martin Robertson

Doogan, Kevin (2009) *The transformation of work*, Cambridge: Polity Press

Dore, Ronald (2001) 'Dignity and deprivation', in Joshua Cohen and Joel Rogers (eds) *What's wrong with a free lunch?* Boston, MA: Beacon Press, pp 80–84

Dorling, Daniel (2010) *Injustice: Why social inequality persists*, Bristol: Policy Press

Dorling, Danny (2012) *The no-nonsense guide to equality*, London: New Internationalist

Dorling, Danny (2017) *The equality effect: Improving life for everyone*, Oxford: New Internationalist Publications

Douillard, Austin (2017) 'New study published on results of Basic Income pilot in Kenya', *Basic Income News*, Brussels: BIEN, http://basicincome.org/news/2017/03/us-kenya-new-study-published-results-basic-income-pilot-kenya/

Edmiston, Daniel (2017) 'Review article: Welfare, austerity and social citizenship in the UK', *Social Policy and Society*, 16(2): 261–70

Edmiston, Daniel, Ruth Patrick and Kayleigh Garthwaite (2017) 'Introduction: Austerity, welfare and social citizenship', *Social Policy and Society*, 16(2): 253–9

Ehrenfreund, Ernst (2015) 'Where the poor and rich really spend their money', *The Washington Post*, www.washingtonpost.com/news/wonk/wp/2015/04/14/where-the-poor-and-rich-spend-really-spend-their-money

Eichhorst, Werner and Paul Marx (eds) (2015) *Non-standard employment in post-industrial labour markets: An occupational perspective*, Cheltenham: Edward Elgar

Electoral Commission (2010) *The completeness and accuracy of electoral registers in Great Britain*, London: The Electoral Commission

Elgarte, Julieta M. (2008) 'Basic Income and the gendered division of labour', *Basic Income Studies*, 3(3): 1–7

Eliot, Jake (2011) 'Where does housing fit in?' *Citizen's Income Newsletter*, issue 2 for 2011: 14–16

Elliott, Larry (2014a) 'Would a Citizen's Income be better than our benefits system?' *The Guardian*, 10 August 2014, www.theguardian.com/business/2014/aug/10/tax-benefits-citizens-income-self-employment

Elliott, Larry (2014b) 'Quantitative easing: Giving cash to the public would have been more effective', *The Guardian*, 29 October 2014, www.theguardian.com/business/economics-blog/2014/oct/29/quantitative-easing-policy-stimulus-janet-yellen-ecb

Elliott, Larry (2017) 'Robots to replace 1 in 3 UK jobs over next 20 years, warns IPPR', *The Guardian*, 15 April 2017, www.theguardian.com/technology/2017/apr/15/uk-government-urged-help-low-skilled-workers-replaced-robots

Ellison, Marion (ed.) (2011) *Reinventing social solidarity across Europe*, Bristol: Policy Press

Emmerson, Carl, Paul Johnson and Helen Miller (2013) *The IFS Green Budget: February 2013*, London: Institute for Fiscal Studies, www.ifs.org.uk/publications/6562

Emmerson, Carl, Paul Johnson and Helen Miller (2014) *The IFS Green Budget: February 2014*, London: Institute for Fiscal Studies, www.ifs.org.uk/budgets/gb2014/gb2014.pdf

Esam, Peter and Richard Berthoud (1991) *Independent benefits for men and women*, London: Policy Studies Institute

Esping-Andersen, Gøsta (1990) *The three worlds of welfare capitalism*, Cambridge: Polity Press

Esping-Andersen, Gøsta (1994) 'Equality and work in the post-industrial life-cycle', in David Miliband (ed.) *Reinventing the Left*, Cambridge: Polity Press, pp 167–85

Esping-Andersen, Gøsta (1996) 'Positive sum solutions in a world of trade-offs?' in Gøsta Esping-Andersen (ed.) *Welfare states in transition: National adaptations*, London: Sage, pp 256–67

Euzéby, Chantal (1994) 'From "insertion" income to "existence" income', *Citizen's Income Bulletin*, no 17, January 1994: 14–18

Evans, Martin and Jill Eyre (2004) *The opportunities of a lifetime: Model lifetime analysis of current British social policy*, Bristol: Policy Press

Evans, Martin and Susan Harkness (2010) 'The impact of the tax and benefit system on second earners', *Journal of Poverty and Social Justice*, 18(1): 35–51

Evans, Martin and Lewis Williams (2009) *A generation of change, a lifetime of difference? Social policy in Britain since 1979*, Bristol: Policy Press

Eyal, Nir (2010) 'Near-universal Basic Income', *Basic Income Studies*, 5(1): 1–26

Fahey, Tony (2010) *Poverty and the two concepts of relative deprivation*, University College Dublin Working Paper, WP10/1, Dublin: University College Dublin

Farnsworth, Kevin (2012) *Social versus corporate welfare: Competing needs and interests within the Welfare State*, Basingstoke: Palgrave Macmillan

Field, Frank and Andrew Forsey (2016) *Fixing broken Britain? An audit of working-age welfare reform since 2010*, London: Civitas, www.civitas.org.uk/publications/fixing-broken-britain-an-audit-of-working-age-welfare-reform-since-2010/

Finch, David (2016) *Making the most of UC: Final report of the Resolution Foundation review of Universal Credit*, London: Resolution Foundation, http://www.resolutionfoundation.org/app/uploads/2015/06/UC-FINAL-REPORT1.pdf

Finch, David, Adam Corlett and Vidhya Alakeson (2014) *Universal Credit: A policy under review*, London: Resolution Foundation, www.resolutionfoundation.org/app/uploads/2014/09/Universal-Credit-A-policy-under-review1.pdf

FitzGerald, Garret (1997) 'Basic Income system has merit for Ireland', *Citizen's Income Bulletin*, no 24, July 1997: 4–6

Fitzpatrick, Tony (1999) *Freedom and security: An introduction to the Basic Income debate*, Basingstoke: Macmillan

Fitzpatrick, Tony (2011) *Welfare theory: An introduction to the theoretical debates in social policy*, 2nd edition, Basingstoke: Palgrave Macmillan

Floridi, Luciano (2014) *The fourth revolution: How the infosphere is reshaping human reality*, Oxford: Oxford University Press

Forget, Evelyn (2011) 'The town with no poverty: The health effects of a Canadian guaranteed annual income field experiment', *Canadian Public Policy*, 37(3): 283–305

Forget, Evelyn L. (2012), 'Canada: The case for Basic Income', in Matthew C. Murray and Carole Pateman (eds) *Basic Income worldwide: Horizons of reform*, New York: Palgrave Macmillan, pp 81–101

Fraser, Neil, Rodolfo Gutiérrez and Ramón Peña-Casas (2011) *Working poverty in Europe: A comparative approach*, Basingstoke: Palgrave Macmillan

French, J.R.P., Jr., and B.H. Raven (1959) 'The bases of social power', in D. Cartwright (ed.) *Studies in Social Power*, Ann Arbor, MI: Institute for Social Research, pp 150–67, reprinted in D.S. Pugh (1984) *Organization Theory: Selected Readings*, 2nd edition, Harmondsworth: Penguin, pp 150–67

Friedman, Milton (1968) 'The case for a Negative Income Tax: A view from the Right', in J.H. Bunzel (ed.) *Issues in American public policy*, Englewood Cliffs, NJ: Prentice Hall, pp 111–120, reprinted in Karl Widerquist, José A. Noguera, Yannick Vanderborght and Jürgen De Wispelaere (eds) (2013) *Basic Income: An anthology of contemporary research*, Chichester: Wiley Blackwell, pp 11–16

Galbraith, J.K. (1999) speech given on 29 June 1999, and quoted in the *Citizen's Income Newsletter*, issue 3, Autumn 1999: 7

Galbraith, James K. (2002) 'The importance of being sufficiently equal', in Ellen Frankel Paul, Fred D. Miller Jr. and Jeffrey Paul (eds) *Should differences in income and wealth matter?* Cambridge: Cambridge University Press, pp 201–224

Gamble, Andrew (2016) *Can the Welfare State survive?* Cambridge: Polity Press

Garcia, Marito and Charity M.T. Moore (2012) *The cash dividend: The rise of cash transfer programs in Sub-Saharan Africa*, Washington DC: The World Bank

Garthwaite, Kayleigh (2017) '"I feel I'm giving something back to society": Constructing the "active citizen" and responsibilising foodbank use', *Social Policy and Society*, 16(2): 283–92

Gasparini, Leonardo and Guillermo Cruces (2010) 'Las Asignaciones por Hijo en Argentina' ['Child benefits in Argentina'], *Económica*, La Plata, 61: 105–146

George, Vic and Paul Wilding (1984) *The impact of social policy*, London: Routledge and Kegan Paul

Gerlinger, Thomas (2009) 'Competitive transformation and the state regulation of health insurance systems: Germany, Switzerland and the Netherlands compared', in Irene Dingeldey and Heinz Rothgang (eds), *Governance of welfare state reform: A cross national and cross sectoral comparison of policy and politics*, Cheltenham: Edward Elgar, pp 145–75

Gheaus, Anca (2008) 'Basic Income, gender justice and the costs of gender-symmetrical lifestyles', *Basic Income Studies*, 3(3): 1–8

Gilroy, Bernard Michael, Anastasia Heimann and Mark Schopf (2013) 'Basic Income and labour supply: The German case', *Basic Income Studies*, 8(1): 43–70

Gingrich, Jane (2014) 'Structuring the vote: Welfare institutions and value-based vote choices', in Staffan Kumlin and Isabelle Stadelmann-Steffen (eds) *How welfare states shape the democratic public: Policy feedback, participation, voting, and attitudes*, Cheltenham: Edward Elgar, pp 93–112

Ginn, Jay (1993) 'Pension penalties: The gendered division of occupational welfare', *Work, Employment & Society*, 7(1): 47–70

Ginn, Jay (1996) 'Citizens' pensions and women', *Citizen's Income Bulletin*, no 21, February 1996: 10–12

Ginn, Jay (2003) *Gender, pensions and the lifecourse*, Bristol: Policy Press

Ginn, Jay (2015) 'How close is the new state Single Tier Pension (STP) to a Citizen's Pension?' *Citizen's Income Newsletter*, issue 2 for 2015: 3–4

Ginn, Jay (2016) 'Citizen's Pension in the Netherlands', *Citizen's Income Newsletter*, issue 1 for 2016: 3–4

Godwin, Michael and Colin Lawson (2009) 'The Working Tax Credit and Child Tax Credit 2003–08: A critical analysis', *Journal of Poverty and Social Justice*, 17(1): 3–14

Goffman, Erving (1990) *Stigma: Notes on the management of spoiled identity*, London: Penguin

Goldsmith, Scott (2012) 'The economic and social impacts of the Permanent Fund Dividend on Alaska', in Karl Widerquist and Michael W. Howard (eds) *Alaska's Permanent Fund Dividend*, New York: Palgrave Macmillan, pp 49–64

Goodin, Robert E. (2001) 'Something for nothing?' in Joshua Cohen and Joel Rogers, *What's wrong with a free lunch?* Boston, MA: Beacon Press, pp 90–97

Goos, Maarten and Alan Manning (2007) 'Lousy and lovely jobs: The rising polarization of work in Britain', *Review of Economics and Statistics*, 89(1): 118–33

Gourevitch, Alex (2016) 'The limits of a Basic Income: Means and ends of workplace democracy', *Basic Income Studies*, 11(1): 17–28

Gray, Anne (2014) 'Is Citizen's Income the answer to workfare', *Citizen's Income Newsletter*, issue 2 for 2014: 8–13

Gray, Anne (2017) 'Behavioural effects of a Citizen's Income on wages, job security and labour supply', *Citizen's Income Newsletter*, issue 2 for 2017: 4–11

Green Party (2008) *Policy: Citizen's Income: an end to the poverty trap*, London: Green Party

Gregg, Paul (2009) *Job Guarantee: Evidence and design*, Bristol: University of Bristol, www.bristol.ac.uk/media-library/sites/cmpo/migrated/documents/jobguarantee.pdf

Griffiths, Rita (2017) 'No love on the dole: The influence of the UK means-tested welfare system on partnering and family structure', *Journal of Social Policy*, 46(3): 543–61

Groot, Loek (2004) *Basic Income, unemployment and compensatory justice*, Dordrecht: Kluwer Academic Publishers

Groot, Loek (2005) 'Towards a European Basic Income experiment', *Citizen's Income Newsletter*, issue 2 for 2005: 2–7

Groot, Loek (2006) 'Reasons for launching a Basic Income experiment', *Basic Income Studies*, 1(2): 1–7

Haagh, Louise (2011) 'Basic Income, social democracy and control over time', *Policy and Politics*, 39(1): 43–66

Haagh, Louise (2015) 'Alternative social states and the Basic Income debate: Institutions, inequality and human development', *Basic Income Studies*, 10(1): 45–81

Haarman, Claudia and Dirk Haarmann (2007) 'From survival to decent employment: Basic Income security in Namibia', *Basic Income Studies*, 2(1): 1–7

Haarmann, Claudia and Dirk Haarmann (2012) 'Namibia: Seeing the sun rise – The realities and hopes of the Basic Income Grant Pilot Project', in Matthew C. Murray and Carole Pateman (eds) *Basic Income worldwide: Horizons of reform*, New York: Palgrave Macmillan, pp 33–58

Hakim, Catherine (2003) *Models of the family in modern society: Ideals and realities*, Aldershot: Ashgate

Hammond, Jay S. (1994) *Tales of Alaska's Bush Rat Governor*, Kenmore, WA: Epicenter Press

Handler, Joel F. (2005) 'Myth and ceremony in welfare: Rights, contracts, and client satisfaction', *The Journal of Socioeconomics*, 34(1): 101–24

Handler, Joel and Amanda Babcock (2006) 'The failure of workfare: Another reason for a Basic Income Guarantee', *Basic Income Studies*, 1(1): 1–22

Handy, Charles (1990) 'The third age', *BIRG Bulletin*, no 11, July 1990: 3–4

Hanley, Teresa (2009) *Engaging public support for eradicating UK poverty*, York: Joseph Rowntree Foundation, www.jrf.org.uk/report/ engaging-public-support-eradicating-uk-poverty

Harris, J. (1981) 'Some aspects of social policy in Britain during the Second World War', in W. J. Mommsen (ed.) *The emergence of the Welfare State in Britain and Germany, 1850–1950*, London: Croom Helm, pp 247–62

Harrison, Malcolm and Teela Sanders (eds) (2014) *Social policies and social control: New perspectives on the 'not-so-big' society*, Bristol: Policy Press

Harrop, Andrew (2012) *The coalition and universalism*, London: The Fabian Society, http://www.fabians.org.uk/publications/ publications-news/the-coalition-and-universalism/

Harrop, Andrew (2016) *For us all: Redesigning social security for the 2020s*, London: Fabian Society

Harvey, Philip (2006) 'The relative costs of a Universal Basic Income and a Negative Income Tax', *Basic Income Studies*, 1(2): 1–24

Harvey, Philip (2013) 'More for less: The job guarantee strategy', *Basic Income Studies*, 7(2): 3–18

Hawkins, Tim (2011) 'A perspective from Shanghai', *Citizen's Income Newsletter*, issue 3 for 2011: 5–16

Her Majesty's Government (1972) *Proposals for a Tax-Credit system*, Cmnd 5116, London: Her Majesty's Stationery Office

Her Majesty's Revenue and Customs (2016) *Annual report and accounts 2015–16*, London: Her Majesty's Stationery Office, www.gov.uk/government/uploads/system/uploads/attachment_data/file/539608/HMRC_Annual_Report_and_Accounts_2015-16-web.pdf

Herzog, Lisa (2016) 'Basic Income and the ideal of epistemic equality', *Basic Income Studies*, 16(1): 29–38

Hill, Michael (1990) *Social security policy in Britain*, Aldershot: Edward Elgar

Hill, Michael (2009) *The public policy process*, 5th edition, Harlow: Pearson/Longman

Hills, John (2007) *Ends and means: The future roles of social housing in England*, London: Centre for Analysis of Social Exclusion, London School of Economics and Political Science

Hills, John (2011) *Fuel poverty: The problem and its measurement*, The interim report of the Fuel Poverty Review, London: Centre for Analysis of Social Exclusion, London School of Economics

Hills, John (2014) *Good times, bad times: The welfare myth of them and us*, Bristol: Policy Press

Hills, John, Julian Le Grand and David Piachaud (eds) (2002) *Understanding social exclusion*, Oxford: Oxford University Press

Hindriks, Jean and Gareth D. Myles (2006) *Intermediate public economics*, Cambridge, MA: The MIT Press

Hinrichs, Karl and Matteo Jessoula (2012) 'Flexible today, secure tomorrow?' in Karl Hinrichs and Matteo Jessoula (eds) *Labour market flexibility and pension reforms: Flexible today, secure tomorrow?* Basingstoke: Palgrave Macmillan, pp 233–50

Hippe, Thorsten (2009) 'Vanishing variety? The regulation of funded pension schemes in comparative perspective', in Irene Dingeldey and Heinz Rothgang (eds) *Governance of welfare state reform: A cross national and cross sectoral comparison of policy and politics*, Cheltenham: Edward Elgar, pp 43–68

Hirsch, Donald (2015) *Could a 'Citizen's Income' work?* York: Joseph Rowntree Foundation, www.jrf.org.uk/publications/could-citizens-income-work

Hirsch, Donald and Laura Valadez (2014) *Wages, taxes and top-ups: The changing role of the state in helping families make ends meet*, York: Joseph Rowntree Foundation, www.jrf.org.uk/report/wages-taxes-and-top-ups-changing-role-state-helping-working-families-make-ends-meet

Hobijn, Bart and Alexander Nussbacher (2015) *The stimulative effect of redistribution*, San Francisco: Federal Reserve Bank of San Francisco, www.frbsf.org/economic-research/publications/economic-letter/2015/june/income-redistribution-policy-economic-stimulus/

Honkanen, Pertti (2014) 'Basic Income and Negative Income Tax: A comparison with a simulation model', *Basic Income Studies*, 9(1/2): 119–35

Honorati, Maddalena, Ugo Gentilini and Ruslan G. Yemtsov (2015) *The state of social safety nets 2015*, Washington DC: The World Bank, http://documents.worldbank.org/curated/en/415491467994645020/The-state-of-social-safety-nets-2015

Horton, Tim and James Gregory (2009) *The solidarity society: Why we can afford to end poverty, and how to do it with public support*, London: The Fabian Society

House of Commons Select Committee on Tax-Credit (1973) *Report and proceedings of the committee*, Session 1972–73, Volume I, London: Her Majesty's Stationery Office, 341–I

House of Commons Treasury and Civil Service Committee Sub-Committee (1982) *The structure of personal income taxation and income support: Minutes of evidence*, HC 331–ix, London: Her Majesty's Stationery Office

House of Commons Treasury and Civil Service Committee (1983) *Enquiry into the structure of personal income taxation and Income Support*, Third Special Report, Session 1982–3

House of Commons Work and Pensions Committee (2007) *Benefit simplification*, The Seventh Report of Session 2006–7, HC 463, vol 2, London: The Stationery Office, www.publications.parliament.uk/pa/cm200607/cmselect/cmworpen/463/463ii.pdf

House of Commons Work and Pensions Committee (2010) *Decision making and appeals in the benefits system*, HC313, p 44, www.publications.parliament.uk/pa/cm200910/cmselect/cmworpen/313/313.pdf

House of Commons Work and Pensions Committee (2014) *Universal Credit implementation: Monitoring DWP's performance in 2012–13*, London: House of Commons Work and Pensions Committee, https://www.publications.parliament.uk/pa/cm201314/cmselect/cmworpen/1209/120902.htm

Howard, Marilyn and Tim Lawrence (1996) 'Private provision – public concern: Meeting the needs of people with disabilities', *Citizen's Income Bulletin*, no 22, July 1996: 9–11

Huber, Evelyne (1996) 'Options for social policy in Latin America: Neoliberal versus social democratic models', in Gøsta Esping-Andersen (ed.) *Welfare states in transition: National adaptations*, London: Sage, pp 141–91

Hughes, John (2007) *The end of work: Theological critiques of capitalism*, Oxford: Blackwell

Hughes, Matthew (ed.) (2010) *Social trends*, no 40, London: Palgrave Macmillan, for the Office for National Statistics, www.ons.gov.uk/ons/rel/social-trends-rd/social-trends/social-trends-40/index.html

Humpage, Louise (2015) *Policy change, public attitudes and social citizenship: Does neoliberalism matter?* Bristol: Policy Press

Huws, Ursula (1997) *Flexibility and security: Towards a new European balance*, London: Citizen's Income Trust

Huws, Ursula (2016) 'The way we work is changing, but the Welfare State hasn't kept pace with the times', *Citizen's Income Newsletter*, issue 3 for 2016: 3–4

Hyggen, Christer (2006) 'Risks and resources: Social capital among social assistance recipients in Norway', *Social Policy and Administration*, 40(5): 493–508

Institute for Fiscal Studies (2011) *Fiscal Studies*, 32(3)

International Labour Office (2013) *Social security for all: Building social protection floors and comprehensive social security systems*, Geneva: International Labour Office, www.social-protection.org/gimi/gess/RessShowRessource.do?ressourceId=34188

International Social Security Association (2014) *Megatrends and social security – Climate change and natural resource scarcity*, Geneva: International Social Security Association, http://socialprotection-humanrights.org/resource/megatrends-and-social-security-climate-change-and-natural-resource-scarcity/

Irvin, George, Dave Byrne, Richard Murphy, Howard Reed and Sally Ruane (2009) *In place of cuts: Tax reform to build a fairer society*, London: Compass

Jackson, Andrew and Ben Dyson (2012) *Modernising money: Why our monetary system is broken, and how it can be fixed*, London: Positive Money

Jacobs, Lawrence R. and Robert Y. Shapiro (1999) 'The media reporting and distorting of public opinion towards entitlements', in Stuart S. Nagel (ed.) *The policy process*, New York: Nova Science Publishers, pp 135–45

James, Sean and Chris Curry (2010) *A Foundation Pension: A PPI evaluation of NAPF* [National Association of Pension Funds] *proposals*, London: Pensions Policy Institute

James, William (2012) *The varieties of religious experience: A study in human nature*, Oxford: Oxford University Press, first published 1902

Jameson, Robert (2016) *The case for a Basic Income*, Robert Jameson/Amazon

Jin, Wenchao, Robert Joyce, David Phillips and Luke Sibieta (2011) *Poverty and inequality in the UK: 2011*, London: Institute for Fiscal Studies

Jones, Hayley (2016) 'More education, better jobs? A critical review of CCTs and Brazil's *Bolsa Família* programme for long-term poverty reduction', *Social Policy and Society*, 15(3): 465–78

Jones, Owen (ed.) (2012), *Why inequality matters*, London: Centre for Labour and Social Studies

Jordan, Bill (1989) *The common good. Citizenship, morality and self-interest*, Oxford: Basil Blackwell

Jordan, Bill (1992) 'Basic Income and the common good', in Philippe Van Parijs (ed.) *Arguing for Basic Income: Ethical foundations for a radical reform*, London: Verso, pp 155–77

Jordan, Bill (1998) *The new politics of welfare*, London: Sage

Jordan, Bill (2008) *Welfare and well-being: Social value in public policy*, Bristol: Policy Press

Jordan, Bill (2010) 'Basic Income and social value', *Basic Income Studies*, 5(2): 1–19

Jordan, Bill (2011) 'The perils of Basic Income: ambiguous opportunities for the implementation of a utopian proposal', *Policy and Politics*, 39(1): 101–14

Jordan, Bill (2012) 'The low road to Basic Income? Tax-benefit integration in the UK', *Journal of Social Policy*, 41(1): 1–17

Jordan, Bill with Simon James (1990) 'The poverty trap: Poor people's accounts', *BIRG Bulletin*, no 11, July 1990: 5–7

Jordan, Bill, Phil Agulnik, Duncan Burbidge and Stuart Duffin (2000) *Stumbling towards Basic Incomes: The prospects for tax-benefit integration*, London: Citizen's Income Trust

Jordan, Bill, Simon James, Helen Kay and Marcus Redley (1992) *Trapped in poverty? Labour-market decisions in low-income households*, London: Routledge

Judge, Lindsay (2014) 'Credit where it's due', *Fabian Review*, Autumn 2014, 126(3): 5

Judge, Lindsay (2015) *Round the clock: In-work poverty and the 'hours question'*, London: Child Poverty Action Group, http://cpag.org.uk/sites/default/files/CPAG_Round_the_clock.pdf

Kangas, Olli (2016) 'The Finnish basic income experiment – "a foolish and outrageously expensive travesty"?' *Tutkimusblogi*, Helsinki: Kela, http://blogi.kansanelakelaitos.fi/arkisto/3316

Kansaneläkelaitos Kela/Social Insurance Institution of Finland Kela (2016) 'From idea to experiment. Report on Universal Basic Income experiment in Finland', https://helda.helsinki.fi/handle/10138/167728?locale-attribute=en

Kay, John (2017) 'The basics of Basic Income', *Intereconomics*, 52(2): 69–74

Keeble, David (1978) 'Industrial decline in the inner city and conurbation', *Transactions of the Institute of British Geographers*, New Series, 3(1): 101–14

Keohane, Nigel and Ryan Shorthouse (2012) *Sink or Swim? The impact of the Universal Credit*, London: Social Market Foundation

Kesselman, J.R. and I. Garfinkel (1978) 'Professor Friedman meet Lady Rhys-Williams: NIT v. CI', *Journal of Public Economics*, 10: 179–216

Khan, Omar and Debbie Weekes-Bernard (2015) *This is still about us*, London: Runnymede Trust

Kirnan, Kathleen and Malcolm Wicks (1990) *Family change and future policy*, York: Joseph Rowntree Memorial Trust/Family Policy Studies Centre

Köhler, Peter A. and Hans F. Zacher (1982) *The evolution of social insurance 1881–1981: Studies of Germany, France, Great Britain, Austria and Switzerland*, London: Frances Pinter

Koistinen, Pertti and Johanna Perkiö (2014) 'Good and bad times of social innovations: The case of Universal Basic Income in Finland', *Basic Income Studies*, 9(1/2): 25–57

Kuitto, Kati (2016) *Post-communist welfare states in European context: Patterns of welfare policies in Central and Eastern Europe*, Cheltenham: Edward Elgar

Kumlin, Staffan and Isabelle Stadelmann-Steffen (eds) (2014) *How welfare states shape the democratic public: Policy feedback, participation, voting, and attitudes*, Cheltenham: Edward Elgar

Land, Hilary (1975) 'The introduction of Family Allowances: An act of historic justice?' in Phoebe Hall, Hilary Land, Roy Parker and Adrian Webb (1975) *Change, choice and conflict in social policy*, London: Heinemann, pp 157–230

Lansley, Stewart (2011a) 'From inequality to instability: Why sustainable capitalism depends on a more equal society', *Fabian Review*, Winter 2011: 12–14

Lansley, Stewart (2011b) *The cost of inequality: Three decades of the super-rich and the economy*, London: Gibson Square

Lansley, Stewart (2016) *A sharing economy: How social wealth funds can reduce inequality and help balance the books*, Bristol: Policy Press

Lansley, Stewart and Joanna Mack (1983) *Breadline Britain*, London: London Weekend Television

Lansley, Stewart and Joanna Mack (2015) *Breadline Britain: The rise of mass poverty*, London: Oneworld Publications

Larsen, Christian Albrekt (2006) *The institutional logic of welfare attitudes*, Aldershot: Ashgate

Lawrence, Mathew (2017) 'Chart of the week: Probability of automation by occupation', London: IPPR, www.commissiononeconomicjustice. org/single-post/2017/03/27/CHART-OF-THE-WEEK-PROBABILITY-OF-AUTOMATION-BY-OCCUPATION

Lawrence, Mathew and Neal Lawson (2017) 'Basic Income: A debate', *Renewal*, 24(4): 69–79

Leaper, R.A.B. (1986) 'Cash and caring', *BIRG Bulletin*, no 5, Spring 1986: 20–22

Lee, Joe (1997) 'Social security in the computer age', *Citizen's Income Bulletin*, no 24, July 1997: 7–8

Lemieux, Pierre (2014) *Who needs jobs? Spreading poverty or increasing welfare*, New York: Palgrave Macmillan

Levitas, Ruth (2012) 'Utopia calling: Eradicating child poverty in the United Kingdom and beyond', in Alberto Minujin and Shailen Nandy (eds) *Global child poverty and well-being: Measurement, concepts, policy and action*, Bristol: Policy Press, pp 449–73

Levy, Horacio, Manos Matsaganis and Holly Sutherland (2014) *Simulating the costs and benefits of a Europe-wide Basic Income scheme for children*, New York: UNICEF, https://www.unicef.org/socialpolicy/files/CPI_Manos_January_2014.pdf

Lewis, Paul (1986) 'A Basic Income for youth', *BIRG Bulletin*, no 6, Autumn 1986: 3–5

Liebermann, Sascha (2012) 'Germany: Far, though close – Problems and prospects of BI in Germany', in Richard Caputo (ed.) *Basic Income Guarantee and politics: International experiences and perspectives on the viability of Income Guarantee*, New York: Palgrave Macmillan, pp 83–106

Lister, Ruth (1997) *Citizenship: Feminist perspectives*, Basingstoke: Macmillan

Lister, Ruth (2004) *Poverty*, Cambridge: Polity Press

Lott, Yvonne (2017) 'When my money becomes our money: Changes in couples' money management', *Social Policy and Society*, 16(2): 199–218

Lo Vuolo, Rubén M. (2015) 'Piketty's *Capital*, his critics and Basic Income', *Basic Income Studies*, 10(1): 29–43

Lowe, Stuart (2011) *The housing debate*, Bristol: Policy Press

Lund, Francie (2011) 'A step in the wrong direction: linking the South Africa Child Support Grant to school attendance', *Journal of Poverty and Social Justice*, 19(1): 5–14

Lundvall, Bengt-Åke and Edward Lorenz (2012) 'From the Lisbon Strategy to EUROPE 2020', in Nathalie Morel, Bruno Palier and Joakim Palme (eds) *Towards a social investment Welfare state? Ideas, policies and challenges*, Bristol: Policy Press, pp 333–51

Lynes, Tony (2011) 'From Unemployment Insurance to Assistance in interwar Britain', *Journal of Poverty and Social Justice*, 19(3): 221–33

Macnicol, John (1980) *The movement for Family Allowances, 1918–1945: A study in social policy development*, London: Heinemann

McFarland, Kate (2017a) 'The Netherlands: Social assistance experiments under review', *Basic Income News*, Brussels: BIEN, http://basicincome.org/news/2017/05/netherlands-social-assistance-experiments-review/

McFarland, Kate (2017b) 'Glasgow, Scotland: Basic Income pilot feasibility study approved by City Council', *Basic Income News*, Brussels: BIEN, http://basicincome.org/news/2017/02/glasgow-scotland-basic-income-pilot-feasibility-study-approved-city-council/

McFarland, Kate (2017c) 'Citizen's Basic Income Network Scotland meeting in Kelty, Fife', *Basic Income News*, Brussels: BIEN, http://basicincome.org/news/2017/02/video-citizens-basic-income-network-scotland-meeting-in-kelty-fife/

McGann, Michael, Helen Kimberley, Dina Bowman and Simon Biggs (2016) 'The netherworld between work and retirement', *Social Policy and Society*, 15(4): 625–36

McGinnity, Frances (2004) *Welfare for the unemployed in Britain and Germany: Who benefits?*, Cheltenham: Edward Elgar

McKay, Ailsa (2005) *The future of social security policy: Women, work and a Citizen's Basic Income*, London: Routledge

McKay, Ailsa and Willie Sullivan (2014) *In place of anxiety: Social security for the common weal*, Biggar: The Reid Foundation, www.compassonline.org.uk/wp-content/uploads/2014/03/InPlaceOfAnxiety.pdf

McKay, Stephen (2010) 'Where do we stand on inequality? Reflections on recent research and its implications', *Journal of Poverty and Social Justice*, 18(1): 19–33

McKay, Stephen and Karen Rowlingson (2008) 'Social security and welfare reform', in Martin Powell (ed.) *Modernising the Welfare State*, Bristol: Policy Press, pp 53–71

McKnight, Abigail, Magali Duque and Mark Rucci (2016) *Creating more equal societies: What works? Evidence review*, Brussels: European Commission, http://ec.europa.eu/social/main.jsp?catId=738&langId=en&pubId=7903&type=2&furtherPubs=yes

McLaughlin, Eithne (1994) *Flexibility in work and benefits*, London: IPPR/Commission on Social Justice

McLeay, Michael, Amar Radia and Ryland Thomas (2014) 'Money creation in the modern economy', *Quarterly Bulletin*, 1st quarter, 2014, London: Bank of England, www.bankofengland.co.uk/publications/Documents/quarterlybulletin/2014/qb14q1prereleasemoneycreation.pdf

McManus, Anne (1997) 'Is Basic Income the answer? Some findings from Ireland', *Citizen's Income Bulletin*, no 23, February 1997: 4–6

Maitland, Alison and Peter Thomson (2014) *Future work: Changing organizational culture for the new world of work*, 2nd edition, Basingstoke: Palgrave Macmillan

Manyika, James (2017) 'What's now and next in analytics, AI, and automation', New York: McKinsey Global Institute, www.mckinsey.com/global-themes/digital-disruption/whats-now-and-next-in-analytics-ai-and-automation?cid=soc-web

Marchal, Sarah, Ive Marx and Natascha van Mechelen (2014) 'The great wake-up call? Social citizenship and minimum income provisions in Europe in times of crisis', *Journal of Social Policy*, 43(2): 247–67

Marshall, T.H. (1981) *The right to welfare and other essays*, London: Heinemann

Martin, J.E. and J.M. Seaman (1974) 'The fate of the London factory: Twenty years of change', *Town and Country Planning*, 43: 492–5

Martin, Josh (2016) 'Universal Credit to Basic Income: A politically feasible transition?' *Basic Income Studies*, 11(2): 97–131

Martinelli, Luke (2017a) *The fiscal and distributional implications of alternative universal Basic Income schemes in the UK*, Bath: Institute for Policy Research, www.bath.ac.uk/ipr/policy-briefs/working-papers/the-fiscal-and-distributional-implications-of-alternative-universal-basic-income-schemes-in-the-uk.html

Martinelli, Luke (2017b) *Exploring the distributional and work incentive effects of plausible illustrative Basic Income schemes*, Bath: Institute for Policy Research, www.bath.ac.uk/ipr/publications/reports/work-incentive-effects-on-basic-income.html

Martinelli, Luke (2017c) 'Exposing a fragile coalition: The state of the Basic Income debate', *Citizen's Income Newsletter*, issue 1 for 2017: 3–5

Mason, Paul (2015) *Postcapitalism: A guide to our future*, London: Allen Lane/Penguin

Matsaganis, Manos and Chrysa Leventi (2011) 'Pathways to a Universal Basic Pension in Greece', *Basic Income Studies*, 6(1): 1–20

Mau, Steffen and Benjamin Veghte (eds) (2007) *Social justice, legitimacy and the Welfare State*, Aldershot: Ashgate

Mayes, David G. and Anna Michalski (2013) *The changing welfare state in Europe: The implications for democracy*, Cheltenham: Edward Elgar

Mayhew, Kevin (1991) 'Basic Income as a lever for economic efficiency', *BIRG Bulletin*, no 12, February 1991: 10–12

Mayhew, Kevin (1995) 'Basic Income and economic efficiency', *Citizen's Income Bulletin*, no 19, February 1995: 13–15

Mays, Jennifer, Greg Marston and John Tomlinson (eds) (2016) *Basic Income in Australia and New Zealand: Perspectives from the neoliberal frontier*, New York: Palgrave Macmillan

Meade, J.E. (1978) *The structure and reform of direct taxation*, Report of a committee chaired by Professor J.E. Meade, London: George Allen and Unwin, for the Institute for Fiscal Studies

Meade, J.E. (1995) *Full employment regained? An agathotopian dream*, University of Cambridge Department of Applied Economics, Occasional Paper no 61, Cambridge: Cambridge University Press

Michaeu, Pierre-Carl and Arthur van Soest (2008) 'How did the elimination of the US earnings test above the normal retirement age affect labour supply expectations', *Fiscal Studies*, 29(2): 197–231

Midtgaard, Søren F. (2008) 'Rawlsian stability and Basic Income', *Basic Income Studies*, 3(2): 1–17

Millar, Jane and Fran Bennett (2017) 'Universal Credit: Assumptions, contradictions and virtual reality', *Social Policy and Society*, 16(2): 169–82

Miller, Anne (2003) 'The Irish situation', *Citizen's Income Newsletter*, issue 2 for 2003: 1–5

Miller, Anne (2009a) 'Citizen's Income and administration', *Citizen's Income Newsletter*, issue 2 for 2009: 6–8

Miller, Anne (2009b) 'Minimum Income Standards: A challenge for Citizen's Income', *Citizen's Income Newsletter*, issue 3 for 2009: 6–14

Miller, Anne (2012) 'Passported benefits and a Citizen's Income', *Citizen's Income Newsletter*, issue 1 for 2012: 1–4

Miller, Annie (2016) 'A Citizen's Basic Income and its implications', in Jim Campbell and Morag Gillespie (eds) *Feminist economics and public policy*, Abingdon: Routledge, pp 164–76

Miller, Annie (forthcoming) *A Basic Income handbook*, Edinburgh: Luath Press

Milner, E. Mabel and Dennis Milner (1918/2004) 'Scheme for a State Bonus', in John Cunliffe and Guido Erreygers (eds) (2004) *The origins of universal grants: An anthology of historical writings on Basic Capital and Basic Income*, Basingstoke: Palgrave Macmillan, pp. 121–33

Monckton, Christopher (1993) 'Universal Benefit', *Citizen's Income Bulletin*, no 16, July 1993: 4–6

Morel, Nathalie, Bruno Palier and Joakim Palme (eds) (2012) *Towards a social investment Welfare State? Ideas, policies and challenges*, Bristol: Policy Press

Morgan, Patricia (1995) *Farewell to the family? Public policy and family breakdown in Britain and the USA*, London: Institute of Economic Affairs

Morley, Robert E. (1985) 'Out of touch: The Flower reforms of social security', *BIRG Bulletin*, no 4, Autumn 1985: 3–4

Morris, C.N. (1982) 'The structure of personal income taxation and income support', *Fiscal Studies*, 3(3): 210–18

Moscovici, Serge (1980) 'Toward a theory of conversion behavior', in Leonard Berkowitz (ed.) *Advances in experimental social psychology*, vol 13, New York: Academic Press, pp 209–39

Mowshowitz, Abbe (1994) 'Virtual organization: A vision of management in the information age', *The Information Society*, 10(4): 267–88

Mullan, Phil (2017) *Creative destruction: How to start an economic renaissance*, Bristol: Policy Press

Mullarney, Maire (1999) 'The rights of children – a justification of Basic Income, hitherto unremarked', *BIRG Bulletin*, no 12, February 1991: 30–2

Mulligan, Roisin (2013) 'Universal Basic Income and recognition theory – A tangible step towards an ideal', *Basic Income Studies*, 8(2): 153–72

Murphey, Dwight (2009) 'A "Classical Liberal" rethinks the market system: Invitation to an intellectual odyssey', *The Journal of Social, Political, and Economic Studies*, 34(3): 347–55

Murphey, Dwight (2011) 'Capitalism's deepening crisis: The imperative of monetary reconstruction', *The Journal of Social, Political, and Economic Studies*, 36(3): 277–300

Murphy, Richard and Howard Reed (2013) *Financing the social state: Towards a full employment economy*, London: Centre for Labour and Social Studies

Murray, Matthew C. and Carole Pateman (2012) *Basic Income worldwide: Horizons of reform*, Basingstoke: Palgrave Macmillan

National Audit Office (2011) *Means testing*, Report by the Comptroller General, HC 1464, Session 2010–2012, London: The Stationery Office

National Audit Office (2013) *Universal Credit: Early progress*, London: National Audit Office, www.nao.org.uk/report/universal-credit-early-progress-2/

National Audit Office (2016a) *HM Revenue & Customs 2015–16 accounts*, Report by the Comptroller and Auditor General, London: National Audit Office, www.nao.org.uk/wp-content/uploads/2016/07/HMRC-Annual-Report-and-Accounts-2015-16.pdf

National Audit Office (2016b) *Department for Work and Pensions 2015–16 accounts: Report by the Comptroller and Auditor General: Fraud and error in benefit expenditure*, London: National Audit Office, www.nao.org.uk/wp-content/uploads/2016/07/DWP-CAG-Report-2015-16.pdf

National Records of Scotland (2016) *Births, deaths and other vital events: Preliminary figures for 2015 released*, Edinburgh: National Records of Scotland, www.nrscotland.gov.uk/news/2016/births-deaths-and-other-vital-events-preliminary-figures-for-2015-released

Nissen, Sylke (1992) 'The jobs dilemma: Ecological versus economic issues', *BIRG Bulletin*, no 14: 9–11

Noguera, José and Jürgen D. De Wispelaere (2006) 'A plea for the use of laboratory experiments in Basic Income research', *Basic Income Studies*, 1(2): 1–8

Noteboom, Bart (1987) 'Basic Income as a basis for small business', *International Small Business Journal*, 5(3): 10–18, reprinted in Karl Widerquist, José A. Noguera, Yannick Vanderborght and Jürgen De Wispelaere (eds) (2013) *Basic Income: An anthology of contemporary research*, Chichester: Wiley Blackwell, pp 211–15

O'Brien, Michael (2007) *Poverty, policy and the state*, Bristol: Policy Press

O'Brien, J. Patrick and Dennis O. Olson (1991) 'The Alaska Permanent Fund and Dividend Distribution Program', *BIRG Bulletin*, no 12, February 1991: 3–6

O'Connell, Alison (2004a) *Citizen's Pension: An introduction*, London: Pensions Policy Institute

O'Connell, Alison (2004b) *Citizen's Pension: Lessons from New Zealand*, London: Pensions Policy Institute

O'Hara, Mary (2014) *Austerity bites: A journey to the sharp end of cuts in the UK*, Bristol: Policy Press

O'Malley, Chris (1989) 'Proposal for a Basic Income in the Republic of Ireland', *BIRG Bulletin*, no 9, Spring/Summer 1989: 13–16

O'Neill, Martin (2007) 'Death and taxes', *Renewal*, 15(4): 70

O'Reilly, Jacqueline (2008) 'Can a Basic Income lead to a more gender equal society?', *Basic Income Studies*, 3(3): 1–7

OECD (2017) *Basic Income as a policy option: Can it add up?* Paris: OECD Publishing, www.oecd.org/employment/emp/Basic-Income-Policy-Option-2017.pdf

Offe, Claus (2008) 'Basic Income and the labor contract', *Basic Income Studies*, 3(1): 1–30

Offe, Claus (2014) 'Berlin, Germany: Basic Income experimentation at the micro level', *Basic Income News*, Brussels: BIEN, http://basicincome.org/news/2014/10/berlin-germany-basic-income-experimentalism-at-the-micro-level/

Office for National Statistics (2010) *2010 Annual survey of hours and earnings*, London: Office for National Statistics, www.ons.gov.uk/ons/rel/ashe/annual-survey-of-hours-and-earnings/2010-results/index.html

Office for National Statistics (2014) *Households and household composition in England and Wales: 2001–2011*, London: Office for National Statistics, www.ons.gov.uk/peoplepopulationandcommunity/birthsdeathsandmarriages/families/articles/householdsandhouseholdcompositioninenglandandwales/2014-05-29

Office for National Statistics (2016) *Annual survey of hours and earnings: 2016 provisional results*, London: Office for National Statistics, www.ons.gov.uk/employmentandlabourmarket/peopleinwork/earningsandworkinghours/bulletins/annualsurveyofhoursandearnings/2016provisionalresults

Office for National Statistics (2017a) *Labour market: Apr 2017*, London: Office for National Statistics, www.ons.gov.uk/employmentandlabourmarket/peopleinwork/employmentandemployeetypes/bulletins/uklabourmarket/apr2017#main-points-for-the-three-months-to-february-2017

Office for National Statistics (2017b) *People in employment on a zero-hours contract: Mar 2017*, London: Office for National Statistics, www.ons.gov.uk/employmentandlabourmarket/peopleinwork/earningsandworkinghours/articles/contractsthatdonotguaranteeaminimumnumberofhours/latest

Office for National Statistics (2017c) *Statistical Bulletin: Marriages in England and Wales, 2014*, London: Office for National Statistics, www.ons.gov.uk/peoplepopulationandcommunity/birthsdeathsandmarriages/marriagecohabitationandcivilpartnerships/bulletins/marriagesinenglandandwalesprovisional/2014

Organisation for Economic Co-operation and Development (2005) *Employment outlook, 2005*, Paris: Organisation for Economic Co-operation and Development

Orton, Ian (2009) 'The Citizen's Income and child labour: Two ships passing at night', *Citizen's Income Newsletter*, issue 1 for 2009: 6–9

Orton, Ian (2011) 'The International Labour Organisation's analysis of social transfers worldwide augurs well for a Citizen's Income in the context of middle and low-income countries', *Citizen's Income Newsletter*, issue 2 for 2011: 4–8

Osborn, Steve (2011) 'People, places and poverty: Getting away from the neighbourhood', in Barry Knight (ed.) *A minority view: What Beatrice Webb would say now*, London: Alliance Publishing Trust, pp 70–84

Osterkamp, Rigmar (2013) 'The Basic Income Grant Pilot Project in Namibia: A critical assessment', *Basic Income Studies*, 8(1): 71–90

Oubridge, Victor (1990) 'Basic Income and industrial development: An employer's viewpoint', *BIRG Bulletin*, no 11, July 1990: 28–30

Owen, Sue and Martin Mogridge (1986) 'The costs of working', *BIRG Bulletin*, no 6, Autumn 1986: 21–24

Padfield, Deborah (2011) 'The human cost of flexible labour', *Citizen's Income Newsletter*, no 1 for 2012: 15–16, first published on the Open Democracy website, 24 October 2011, www.opendemocracy.net/ourkingdom/deborah-padfield/human-cost-of-flexible-labour

Page, Robert (2015) *Clear blue water? The Conservative Party and the Welfare State since 1940*, Bristol: Policy Press

Pahl, Jan (1983) 'The allocation of money and structuring of inequality within marriage', *Sociological Review*, 31(2): 237–62

Pahl, Jan (1986) 'Social security, taxation and family financial arrangements', *BIRG Bulletin*, no 5, Spring 1986: 2–4

Paine, Thomas (1796) 'Agrarian justice', reprinted in John Cunliffe and Guido Erreygers (eds) (2004) *The origins of universal grants: An anthology of historical writings on Basic Capital and Basic Income*, Basingstoke: Palgrave Macmillan, pp 3–16

Painter, Anthony (2016a) 'Confronting "insecurity cubed"', in Yvette Cooper (ed.) *Changing work: Progressive ideas for the modern world of work*, London: Fabian Society, pp 71–6

Painter, Anthony (2016b) 'Behavioural effects of a Citizen's Income on wages, job security and labour supply', *British Medical Journal*, http://www.bmj.com/content/355/bmj.i6473

Painter, Anthony and Chris Thoung (2015) *Report: Creative citizen, creative state – The principled and pragmatic case for a Universal Basic Income*, London: Royal Society of Arts, www.thersa.org/discover/publications-and-articles/reports/basic-income

Papadopoulos, Theodorus and Ricardo Velázquez Leyer (2016a) 'Introduction: Assessing the effects of conditional cash transfers in Latin American societies in the early twenty-first century', *Social Policy and Society*, 15(3): 417–20

Papadopoulos, Theodorus and Ricardo Velázquez Leyer (2016b) 'Two decades of social investment in Latin America: Outcomes, shortcomings and achievements of conditional cash transfers', *Social Policy and Society*, 15(3): 435–49

Parke, Alison, Caroline Bryson and John Curtice (eds) (2014) *British social attitudes 31*, London: NatCen Social Research

Parker, Hermione (1988) 'Are Basic Incomes feasible?' *BIRG Bulletin*, no 7, Spring 1988: 5–7

Parker, Hermione (1989) *Instead of the dole: An enquiry into integration of the tax and benefit systems*, London: Routledge

Parker, Hermione (1991) 'Terminology', *BIRG Bulletin*, no 12, February 1991: 6–9

Parker, Hermione (ed.) (1993) *Citizen's Income and women*, London: Citizen's Income Trust

Parker, Hermione (1994) 'Citizen's Income', *Citizen's Income Bulletin*, no 17, January 1994: 4–12

Parker, Hermione (1995) *Taxes, benefits and family life: The seven deadly traps,* London: Institute of Economic Affairs

Parker, Hermione and Andrew Dilnot (1988) 'Administration of integrated tax/benefit systems', *BIRG Bulletin*, no 8, Autumn 1988: 6–10

Parker, Hermione and Holly Sutherland (1988) 'How to get rid of the poverty trap: Basic Income plus national minimum wage', *Citizen's Income Bulletin*, no 25, February 1988: 11–14

Parker, Hermione and Holly Sutherland (1991) 'Child Benefit, Child Tax Allowances and Basic Incomes: A comparative study', *BIRG Bulletin*, no 13, August 1991: 6–13

Parker, Hermione and Holly Sutherland (1994) 'Basic Income 1994: Redistributive effects of Transitional BIs', *Citizen's Income Bulletin*, no 18, July 1994: 3–8

Parker, Hermione and Holly Sutherland (1995) 'Why a £20 CI is better than lowering income tax to 20%', *Citizen's Income Bulletin*, no 19, February 1995: 15–18

Parker, Hermione and Holly Sutherland (1996) 'Earnings top-up or Basic Income and a minimum wage', *Citizen's Income Bulletin*, no 21, February 1996: 5–8

Parker, Hermione and Holly Sutherland (no date) *Child Tax Allowances? A comparison of child benefit, child tax reliefs, and Basic Incomes as instruments of family policy*, London: Suntory-Toyota International Centre for Economics and Related Disciplines, London School of Economics and Political Science

Parker, Sophia (ed.) (2013) *The squeezed middle: The pressure on ordinary workers in America and Britain*, Bristol: Policy Press

Pasma, Chandra (2010) 'Working through the work disincentive', *Basic Income Studies*, 5(2): 1–20

Pasquali, Francesca (2012) *Virtuous imbalance: Political philosophy between desirability and feasibility*, Farnham: Ashgate

Pateman, Carole (2007) 'Why Republicanism?' *Basic Income Studies*, 2(2): 1–6

Patrick, Ruth (2017a) 'Wither social citizenship? Lived experiences of citizenship in/exclusion for recipients of out-of-work benefits', *Social Policy and Society*, 16(2): 293–304

Patrick, Ruth (2017b) *For whose benefit? The everyday realities of welfare reform*, Bristol: Policy Press

Pech, Wesley (2010) 'Behavioral economics and the Basic Income Guarantee', *Basic Income Studies*, 5(2): 1–17

Pensions Policy Institute (2013a) *The impact of the Government's Single Tier State Pension reform*, London: Pensions Policy Institute, www.pensionspolicyinstitute.org.uk/publications/reports/ppi-single-tier-series-the-impact-of-the-governments-single-tier-state-pension-reform

Pensions Policy Institute (2013b) *Managing the transition between the current system and the single-tier pension*, London: Pensions Policy Institute, www.pensionspolicyinstitute.org.uk/publications/reports/ppi-single-tier-series-the-impact-of-the-governments-single-tier-state-pension-reform

Percy, Andrew (2016) 'The role of public services in Citizen's Income', *Citizen's Income Newsletter*, issue 1 for 2016: 19–20

Perkiö, Johanna (2012) 'The struggle over interpretation: Basic Income in the Finnish public discussion in 2006–2012', paper delivered at the BIEN Congress in Munich, 14–16 September 2012, http://www.basicincome.org/bien/pdf/munich2012/perkio.pdf

Peters, Hans and Axel Marks (2006) 'Lottery games as a tool for empirical Basic Income research', *Basic Income Studies*, 1(2): 1–7

Pettit, Philip (2007) 'A Republican right to Basic Income?', *Basic Income Studies*, 2(2): 1–8

Phelps, Edmund S. (2001) 'Subsidize wages', in Joshua Cohen and Joel Rogers (eds) *What's wrong with a free lunch?* Boston, MA: Beacon Press, pp 51–9

Piachaud, David (2016) *Citizen's Income: Rights and wrongs*, London: Centre for the Analysis of Social Exclusion, London School of Economics, http://sticerd.lse.ac.uk/dps/case/cp/casepaper200.pdf

Pickard, Bertram (1919) *A reasonable revolution, being a discussion of the State Bonus scheme – a proposal for a national minimum income*, reprinted in John Cunliffe and Guido Erreygers (eds) (2004) *The origins of universal grants: An anthology of historical writings on Basic Capital and Basic Income*, Basingstoke: Palgrave Macmillan, pp 134–40

Piketty, Thomas (2014) *Capital in the twenty-first century*, Cambridge, MA: The Belknap Press of the Harvard University Press

Piven, Frances Fox (1994) 'Comment: Economic imperatives and social reform', in David Miliband (ed.) *Reinventing the Left*, Cambridge: Polity Press, pp 186–91

Powell, Martin (ed.) (2008) *Modernising the Welfare State*, Bristol: Policy Press

Prady, Stephanie L., Karen Bloor, Jonathan Bradshaw, Helena Tunstall, Emily S. Petherick and Kate E. Pickett (2016) 'Does administrative data reflect individual experience? Comparing an index of poverty with individually collected data on financial well-being in a multi-ethnic community', *Social Policy and Society*, 15(4): 513–35

Pressman, Steven (2005) 'Income Guarantee and the equity-efficiency tradeoff', *The Journal of Socioeconomics*, 34(1): 83–100

Purdy, David (1988) *Social power and the labour market*, Basingstoke: Macmillan

Purdy, David (2007) 'Is Basic Income viable?' *Basic Income Studies*, 2(2): 1–26

Rathbone, Eleanor (1924/1986) *The disinherited family*, Bristol: Falling Wall Press

Rathbone, Eleanor (1949) *Family Allowances: A new edition of* The disinherited family, London: Allen and Unwin

Raynsford, Nick (2016) *Substance not spin: An insider's view of success and failure in government*, Bristol: Policy Press

Reed, Howard and Stewart Lansley (2016) *Universal Basic Income: An idea whose time has come?* London: Compass

Reeve, Andrew and Andrew Williams (eds) (2002) *Real Libertarianism assessed: Political theory after Van Parijs*, London: Palgrave Macmillan

Reeves, Aaron and Rachel Loopstra (2017) '"Set up to fail"? How welfare conditionality undermines citizenship for vulnerable groups', *Social Policy and Society*, 16(2): 327–38

Rein, Martin and Winfried Schmähl (2004) *Rethinking the Welfare State*, Cheltenham: Edward Elgar

Remfry, Penny and Alison Whalley (2015) 'A Green Party perspective', *Citizen's Income Newsletter*, issue 2 for 2015: 4–5

Rhys Williams, Brandon (1989) *Stepping stones to independence* (edited by Hermione Parker), Aberdeen: Aberdeen University Press, for the One Nation Group of Conservative MPs

Rhys Williams, Juliet (1943) *Something to look forward to*, London: MacDonald and Co.

Rhys Williams, Juliet (1953) *Taxation and incentives*, London: William Hodge and Co.

Richardson, J.J. (1969) *The policy-making process*, London: Routledge and Kegan Paul

Richardson, Jeremy (1999) 'Interest group, multi-arena politics and policy change', in Stuart S. Nagel (ed.) *The policy process*, New York: Nova Science Publishers, pp 65–99

Ritzer, George (2000) *The McDonaldization of society*, Thousand Oaks, CA: Pine Forge Press

Ritzer, George (2010) *McDonaldization: The Reader*, 3rd edition, Thousand Oaks, California: Pine Forge Press

Roberts, Ellie, Luke Price and Liam Crosby (2014) *Just about surviving: A qualitative study on the cumulative impact of Welfare reform in the London Borough of Newham*, London: Community Links, http://www.community-links.org/uploads/documents/Just_About_Surviving.pdf

Roberts, Keith (1982) *Automation, unemployment and the distribution of income*, Maastricht: European Centre for Work and Society

Robertson, James (1988) 'If any would not work, neither should he eat', *BIRG Bulletin*, no 8, Autumn 1988: 23–5

Robertson, James (1996) 'Towards a new social compact: Citizen's Income and radical tax reform', *The Political Quarterly*, 67(1): 54–8

Roca, Emilio (2010) (no title), in *Asignación Universal por Hijo*, Buenos Aires: Asociación Argentina de Politicas Sociales, pp 17–20

Rodger, John J. (2012) '"Regulating the poor": Observations on the "structural coupling" of welfare, criminal justice and the voluntary sector in a "Big Society"', *Social Policy and Administration*, 46(4): 413–31

Roebroek, Joop M. and Erik Hogenboom (1990) 'Basic Income: Alternative benefit or new paradigm?' *BIRG Bulletin*, no 11, July 1990: 8–11

Room, Graham (2011) *Complexity, institutions and public policy: Agile decision-making in a turbulent world*, Cheltenham: Edward Elgar

Rose, Dave and Charles Wohlforth (2008) *Saving for the future: My life and the Alaska Permanent Fund*, Kenmore, WA: Epicenter Press

Rosner, Peter G. (2003) *The economics of social policy*, Cheltenham: Edward Elgar

Rowlingson, Karen (2009) '"From cradle to grave": Social security and the lifecourse', in Jane Millar (ed.) *Understanding Social Security*, 2nd edition, Bristol: Policy Press, pp 133–50

Rowlingson, Karen (2011) *Does income inequality cause health and social problems*, York: Joseph Rowntree Foundation

Runciman, W.G. (1966) *Relative deprivation and social justice: A study of attitudes to social inequality in twentieth-century England*, London: Routledge and Kegan Paul

Ryan-Collins, Josh, Tony Greenham, Richard Werner and Andrew Jackson (2011) *Where does money come from? A guide to the UK monetary and banking system*, London: New Economics Foundation

Rys, Vladimir (2010) *Reinventing social security worldwide*, Bristol: Policy Press

Sage, Daniel and Patrick Diamond (2017) *Europe's new social reality: The case against Universal Basic Income*, Policy Network, http://www.policy-network.net/publications/6190/Europes-New-Social-Reality-the-Case-Against-Universal-Basic-Income

Sainsbury, Diane (1996) *Gender, equality, and welfare states,* Cambridge: Cambridge University Press

Salehi-Isfahani, Djavad (2014) *Iran's subsidy reform: From promise to disappointment*, Policy Perspective no. 13, Egypt: Economic Research Forum, https://erf.org.eg/wp-content/uploads/2015/12/PP13_2014.pdf

Salter, T.A. (1990) 'Pensions, taxes and welfare', *BIRG Bulletin*, no 10, Autumn/Winter 1990: 17–20

Salter, Tony (1997) 'Being realistic about pensions reform', *Citizen's Income Bulletin*, no 24, July 1997: 9–11

Salter, Tony, Andrew Bryans, Colin Redman and Martin Hewitt (2009) *100 years of State Pension: Learning from the past*, London: Institute of Actuaries

Sargant, William (1976) *Battle for the mind: A physiology of conversion and brain-washing*, London: Heinemann

Searle, Beverley A. (2008) *Well-being: In search of a good life*, Bristol: Policy Press

Sedwick, Robert C. (1974) *Interaction: Interpersonal relationships in organisations*, Englewood Cliffs, NJ: Prentice Hall

Sen, Amartya (2009) *The idea of justice*, London: Allen Lane

Shapiro, Daniel (2002) 'Egalitarianism and welfare-state redistribution', in Ellen Frankel Paul, Fred D. Miller Jr. and Jeffrey Paul (eds) *Should differences in income and wealth matter?* Cambridge: Cambridge University Press, pp 1–35

Sheahen, Allan (2012) *Basic Income Guarantee: Your right to economic security*, New York: Palgrave Macmillan

Sherman, Barrie and Phil Jenkins (1995) *Licensed to work*, London: Cassell

Shildrick, Tracy, Robert MacDonald, Colin Webster and Kayleigh Garthwaite (2012) *Poverty and insecurity: Life in low-pay, no-pay Britain*, Bristol: Policy Press

Silva, Francesco, Marco Ponti, Andres Balzarotti and Ronald Dore (1995) 'Welfare and efficiency in a non-work society', *Citizen's Income Bulletin*, no 20, July 1995: 4–6

Sinclair, Stephen (2016) *Introduction to social policy analysis: Illuminating welfare*, Bristol: Policy Press

Skidelsky, Robert and Edward Skidelsky (2012) *How much is enough? The love of money, and the case for the good life*, London: Allen Lane/Penguin Books

Sloman, Peter (2016) 'Beveridge's rival: Juliet Rhys-Williams and the campaign for tax-benefit integration, 1942–1955', *Citizen's Income Newsletter*, issue 3 for 2016: 4–6

Smeaton, Deborah and Micahel White (2016) 'The growing discontents of older British employees: Extended working life at risk from quality of working life', *Social Policy and Society*, 15(3): 369–85

Smith, David (1992) 'Communicating Basic Income', *BIRG Bulletin*, no 14: 7–9

Smith, Douglas (1985) 'Going, going ... gone: The vanishing rights of young people to supplementary benefit', *BIRG Bulletin*, no 3, Spring 1985: 16

Smith, M.J. (1993) 'Policy networks', *Pressure, Power and Policy*, Hemel Hempstead: Harvester Wheatsheaf, pp 56–65, reprinted in Michael Hill (ed.) (1997) *The policy process: A reader*, 2nd edition, Hemel Hempstead: Prentice Hall/Harvester Wheatsheaf, pp 76–86

D.V.L. Smith and Associates (1991) *Basic Income: A research report*, prepared for Age Concern England, London: D.V.L. Smith and Associates

Smithies, Rachel (2007) 'Making a case for flat tax credits: Income fluctuations among low-income families', *Journal of Poverty and Social Justice*, 15(1): 3–16

Social Security Advisory Committee (2011), press release, 15 June 2011, 'Public Consultation: Passported Benefits under Universal Credit – review and advice', www.gov.uk/government/news/public-consultation-passported-benefits-under-universal-credit-review-and-advice

Solow, Robert M. (2001) 'Foreword', in Joshua Cohen and Joel Rogers (eds) *What's wrong with a free lunch?* Boston, MA: Beacon Press, pp ix–xvi

Sommeiller, Estelle, Mark Price and Ellis Wazeter (2016) *Income inequality in the U.S. by state, metropolitan area, and county*, Washington DC: Economic Policy Institute, www.epi.org/publication/income-inequality-in-the-us/

Sommer, Maximilian (2016) *A feasible Basic Income scheme for Germany: Effects on labour supply, poverty, and income inequality*, Ingolstadt: Springer

Sovacool, Benjamin K., Roman V. Sidortsov and Benjamin R. Jones (2014) *Energy security, equality, and justice*, London: Routledge

Spence, Alison (2011) *Labour market: Social trends 41*, London: Office for National Statistics, www.ons.gov.uk/ons/rel/social-trends-rd/social-trends/social-trends-41/social-trends-41---labour-market.pdf

Spence, Thomas (1797) 'The rights of infants', reprinted in John Cunliffe and Guido Erreygers (eds) (2004) *The origins of universal grants: An anthology of historical writings on Basic Capital and Basic Income*, Basingstoke: Palgrave Macmillan, pp 81–91

Spicker, Paul (2000) *The Welfare State: A general theory*, London: Sage

Spicker, Paul (2005) 'Five types of complexity', *Benefits*, 13(1): 5–9

Spicker, Paul (2007) *The idea of poverty*, Bristol: Policy Press

Spicker, Paul (2011) *How social security works: An introduction to benefits in Britain*, Bristol: Policy Press

Spicker, Paul (2013) *Reclaiming individualism: Perspectives on public policy*, Bristol: Policy Press

Spicker, Paul (2014) *Social policy: Theory and practice*, Bristol: Policy Press

Spicker, Paul (2017) *What's wrong with social security benefits?* Bristol: Policy Press

Srnicek, Nick and Alex Williams (2015) *Inventing the future: Postcapitalism and a world without work*, London: Verso

Standing, Guy (1996) 'Social protection in Central and Eastern Europe: A tale of slipping anchors and torn safety nets', in Gøsta Esping-Andersen (ed.) *Welfare states in transition: National adaptations*, London: Sage, pp 225–55

Standing, Guy (1999) *Global labour flexibility: Seeking distributive justice*, Basingstoke: Macmillan

Standing, Guy (2002) *Beyond the new paternalism: Basic security as equality*, London: Verso

Standing, Guy (ed.) (2004) *Economic security for a better world*, Geneva: International Labour Organisation

Standing, Guy (2005) *Promoting income security as a right: Europe and North America*, London: Anthem Press

Standing, Guy (2008) 'How cash transfers promote the case for Basic Income', *Basic Income Studies*, 3(1): 1–30

Standing, Guy (2009) *Work after globalization: Building occupational citizenship*, Cheltenham: Edward Elgar

Standing, Guy (2011a) 'Behavioural conditionality: Why the nudges must be stopped – an opinion piece', *Journal of Poverty and Social Justice*, 19(1): 27–37

Standing, Guy (2011b) *The Precariat: The new dangerous class*, London: Bloomsbury

Standing, Guy (2012a) 'Social insurance is not for the Indian open economy of the 21st century', *Citizen's Income Newsletter*, issue 1 for 2012: 5–7

Standing, Guy (2012b) *Cash transfers: A review of the issues in India*, New Delhi: UNICEF India

Standing, Guy (2013) 'Can Basic Income cash transfers transform India?' *Citizen's Income Newsletter*, issue 2 for 2013, pp 3–5

Standing, Guy (2014) *A Precariat Charter: From denizens to citizens*, London: Bloomsbury

Standing, Guy (2015) 'Why Basic Income's emancipatory value exceeds its monetary value', *Basic Income Studies*, 10(2): 193–223

Standing, Guy (2016) *The corruption of Capitalism: Why rentiers thrive and work does not pay*, London: Biteback

Standing, Guy (2017) *Basic Income: And how we can make it happen*, London: Penguin Random House.

Standing, Guy, with Michael Samson (2003) *A Basic Income Grant for South Africa*, Cape Town: University of Cape Town Press

Stapenhurst, Chris (2014) 'Experiments in Euromod', *Citizen's Income Newsletter*, issue 3 for 2014: 11–17

Steiner, Ivan (1972) *Group process and productivity*, New York: Academic Press

Stirton, Lindsay and Jurgen De Wispelaere (2009) 'Promoting Citizen's Income without bashing bureaucracy? (Yes, we can)', *Citizen's Income Newsletter*, issue 2 for 2009: 5–6

Story, Michael (2015) *Free market welfare: The case for a Negative Income Tax*, London: Adam Smith Institute, www.adamsmith.org/research/free-market-welfare-the-case-for-a-negative-income-tax

Stouffer, Samuel A., Edward A. Suchman, Leland C. DeVinney, Shirley A. Star and Robin M. Williams, Jr. (1949) *Studies in social psychology in World War II, vol I, The American soldier: Adjustment during army life,* Princeton, NJ: Princeton University Press

Sullivan, Dan and Dave Wetzel (2007) 'Let's use natural wealth to pay for a Citizen's Income', *Citizen's Income Newsletter,* issue 2 for 2007: 16

Suplicy, Eduardo Matarazzo (1995) 'Guaranteed Minimum Income in Brazil?' *Citizen's Income Bulletin,* no 19, February 1995: 4–6

Suplicy, Eduardo Matarazzo (2012) 'The best income transfer program for modern economies', in Richard Caputo (ed.) *Basic Income Guarantee and politics: International experiences and perspectives on the viability of Income Guarantee,* New York: Palgrave Macmillan, pp 41–53

Svendsen, Gunnar Lind Haase and Gert Tinggaard Svendsen (2016) *Trust, social capital and the Scandinavian welfare state: Explaining the flight of the bumblebee,* Cheltenham: Edward Elgar

Swift, Jamie, Brice Balmer and Mira Dineen (2010) *Persistent poverty: Voices from the margins,* Toronto: Between the Lines

Tabatabai, Hamid (2011a) 'Iran's economic reforms usher in a de facto Citizen's Income', *Citizen's Income Newsletter,* issue 1 for 2011: 1–2

Tabatabai, Hamid (2011b) 'The Basic Income road to reforming Iran's price subsidies', *Basic Income Studies,* 6(1): 1–24

Tabatabai, Hamid (2012a) 'Iran: A bumpy road toward Basic Income', in Richard Caputo (ed.) *Basic Income Guarantee and politics: International experiences and perspectives on the viability of Income Guarantee,* New York: Palgrave Macmillan, pp 285–300

Tabatabai, Hamid (2012b) 'Iran's Citizen's Income scheme and its lessons', *Citizen's Income Newsletter,* issue 2 for 2012: 2–4

Tawney, R.H. (1964) *Equality,* 5th edition, London: George Allen and Unwin (first published 1931)

Taylor, Phil and Peter Bain (1999) 'An assembly line in the head: Work and employee relations in the call centre', *Industrial Relations Journal,* 30(2): 101–17

Taylor-Gooby, Peter (2009) *Reframing social citizenship,* Oxford: Oxford University Press

Thaler, Richard H. (2015) *Misbehaving: How economics became behavioural,* London: Allen Lane

Thane, Pat (1996) *Foundations of the Welfare State,* 2nd edition, London: Longman

Thane, Pat (2011) 'The making of National Insurance, 1911', *Journal of Poverty and Social and Justice,* 19(3): 211–19

Thompson, Spencer (2013) *To tackle in-work poverty, start with second earners*, London: Institute for Public Policy Research, www.ippr.org/articles/56/11507/to-tackle-in-work-poverty-start-with-second-earners

Thurley, Djuna and Richard Keen (2017) *State pension increases for women born in the 1950s*, briefing paper no. CBP-07405, London: House of Commons Library, http://researchbriefings.files.parliament.uk/documents/CBP-7405/CBP-7405.pdf

Tideman, Nicolaus and Kwok Ping Tsang (2010) 'Seigniorage as a source for a Basic Income Guarantee', *Basic Income Studies*, 5(2): 1–6

Titmuss, Richard (1962) *Income distribution and social change*, London: Allen and Unwin

Titmuss, Richard (1968) *Commitment to welfare*, London: George Allen and Unwin

Tobin, James (1966) 'The case for an Income Guarantee', *Public Interest*, 4 (Summer): 31–41, reprinted in Karl Widerquist, José A. Noguera, Yannick Vanderborght and Jürgen De Wispelaere (eds) (2013) *Basic Income: An anthology of contemporary research*, Chichester: Wiley Blackwell, pp 195–204

Tobin, James (1978) 'A proposal for international monetary reform', *Eastern Economic Journal*, 4(3–4): 153–59

Tonkens, Evelien, Ellen Grootegoed and Jan Willem Duyvendak (2013) 'Introduction: Welfare state reform, recognition, and emotional labour', *Social Policy and Society*, 12(3): 407–13

Torry, Malcolm (1992) 'The two Williams', *BIRG Bulletin*, no 14, February 1992: 15–17

Torry, Malcolm (1996) 'The labour market, the family, and social security reform: A dissertation for the Master of Science degree in Social Policy and Planning at the London School of Economics', unpublished dissertation

Torry, Malcolm (2002) 'A contribution to debate: The reform of Housing Benefit', *Citizen's Income Newsletter*, issue no 1 for 2002: 10–11

Torry, Malcolm (2008) 'Research note: The utility – or otherwise – of being employed for a few hours a week', *Citizen's Income Newsletter*, issue 1 for 2008: 14–16

Torry, Malcolm (2009) 'Can Unconditional Cash Transfers work? They can', a report of a seminar, *Citizen's Income Newsletter*, issue 2 for 2009: 1–3

Torry, Malcolm (2010) 'Review article: Richard Wilkinson and Kate Pickett, *The Spirit Level*', *Citizen's Income Newsletter*, issue 1 for 2010: 4–7

Torry, Malcolm (2012a) 'The United Kingdom: Only for children?' in Richard Caputo (ed.) *Basic Income Guarantee and politics: International experiences and perspectives on the viability of Income Guarantee*, New York: Palgrave Macmillan, pp 235–63

Torry, Malcolm (2012b) 'Research Note: A Citizen's Income scheme's winners and losers', *Citizen's Income Newsletter*, issue 3 for 2012: 2–4

Torry, Malcolm (2013) *Money for everyone: Why we need a Citizen's Income*, Bristol: Policy Press

Torry, Malcolm (2014a) *Research note: A feasible way to implement a Citizen's Income*, Institute for Social and Economic Research Working Paper EM17/14, Institute for Social and Economic Research, University of Essex, Colchester, www.iser.essex.ac.uk/research/publications/working-papers/euromod/em17-14

Torry, Malcolm (2014b) 'A new policy world for the benefits system', *Policy World*, Spring 2014, London: Social Policy Association, pp 12–13, www.social-policy.org.uk/wordpress/wp-content/uploads/2014/06/Policy-World-2014.pdf

Torry, Malcolm (2015a) *Two feasible ways to implement a revenue neutral Citizen's Income scheme*, Institute for Social and Economic Research Working Paper EM6/15, Institute for Social and Economic Research, University of Essex, Colchester, www.iser.essex.ac.uk/research/publications/working-papers/euromod/em6-15

Torry, Malcolm (2015b) *101 reasons for a Citizen's Income: Arguments for giving everyone some money*, Bristol: Policy Press

Torry, Malcolm (2016a) *The feasibility of Citizen's Income*, New York: Palgrave Macmillan

Torry, Malcolm (2016b) *Citizen's Basic Income: A Christian social policy*, London: Darton, Longman and Todd

Torry, Malcolm (2016c) *An evaluation of a strictly revenue neutral Citizen's Income scheme*, Institute for Social and Economic Research, Colchester, Euromod Working Paper EM 5/16, www.iser.essex.ac.uk/research/publications/working-papers/euromod/em5-16

Torry, Malcolm (2016d) *Citizen's Income schemes: An amendment, and a pilot project*, Institute for Social and Economic Research, Colchester, Euromod Working Paper EM 5/16a, www.iser.essex.ac.uk/research/publications/working-papers/euromod/em5-16a

Torry, Malcolm (2016e) *How might we implement a Citizen's Income*, London: Institute for Chartered Accountants of England and Wales, www.icaew.com/-/media/corporate/files/technical/sustainability/outside-insights/citizens-income-web---final.ashx?la=en

Torry, Malcolm (2016f) 'Citizen's Basic Income – Is it feasible?' in Brigid Reynolds and Sean Healy (eds) *Basic Income: Radical utopia or practical solution?* Dublin: Social Justice Ireland, pp 31–47

Torry, Malcolm (2016g) 'An attempt to study the intra-household transfers generated by a Citizen's Income scheme', *Citizen's Income Newsletter*, issue 2 for 2016: 8–9

Torry, Malcolm (2017a) '"Unconditional" and "universal": Definitions and applications', a paper prepared for the Foundation for International Studies on Social Security at Sigtuna, June 2017

Torry, Malcolm (2017b) 'What's a definition? And how should we define 'Basic Income', a paper prepared for the Basic Income Earth Network (BIEN) congress in Lisbon, September 2017

Torry, Malcolm (2017c) *A variety of indicators evaluated for two implementation methods for a Citizen's Basic Income*, Institute for Social and Economic Research, Colchester, Euromod Working Paper EM 12/17, www.iser.essex.ac.uk/research/publications/working-papers/euromod/em12-17

Torry, Malcolm (2018) 'Primary care, the basic necessity: Part I: explorations in economics', in John Spicer (ed.) *Handbook of Primary Care Ethics*: Oxford: Radcliffe

Townsend, Peter (1972) *The scope and limitations of means-tested social services in Britain*, Manchester: Manchester Statistical Society

Townsend, Peter (1979) *Poverty in the United Kingdom*, Harmondsworth: Penguin

Twine, Fred (1994) *Citizenship and social rights: The interdependence of self and society*, Beverly Hills, CA: Sage

Twine, Fred (1996) 'What kinds of people do we wish to be?' *Citizen's Income Bulletin*, no 22, July 1996: 16–17

Tymoigne, Eric (2013) 'Job guarantee and its critiques', *International Journal of Political Economy*, 42(2): 63–87

University and College Union (2016) *Precarious work in Higher Education: A snapshot of insecure contracts and institutional attitudes*, London: University and College Union, www.ucu.org.uk/media/7995/Precarious-work-in-higher-education-a-snapshot-of-insecure-contracts-and-institutional-attitudes-Apr-16/pdf/ucu_precariouscontract_hereport_apr16.pdf

Vanderborght, Yannick and Toru Yamamori (2014) *Basic Income in Japan: Prospects for a radical idea in a transforming welfare state*, New York: Palgrave Macmillan

Van der Veen, Robert J. (1997) 'Basic Income in the Netherlands?' *Citizen's Income Bulletin*, no 23, February 1997: 11–13 van der Wel, Kjetil A. and Knut Halvorsen (2015) 'The bigger the worse? A comparative study of the Welfare State and employment commitment', *Work, employment and society*, 29(1): 99–118

Van Parijs, Philippe (1990a) 'Getting paid for doing nothing: Plain justice or ignominy? The ethical foundations of a Basic Income', translated by Hermione Parker, *BIRG Bulletin*, no 11, July 1990: 15–19

Van Parijs, Philippe (1990b) 'The second marriage of justice and efficiency', *Journal of Social Policy*, 19(1): 1–25

Van Parijs, Philippe (1995) *Real freedom for all: What (if anything) can justify capitalism?* Oxford: Clarendon Press

Van Parijs, Philippe (1996) 'Basic Income and the two dilemmas of the welfare state', *The Political Quarterly*, 67(1): 63–6

Van Parijs, Philippe (2001), 'A Basic Income for all', in Joshua Cohen and Joel Rogers (eds) *What's wrong with a free lunch?* Boston, MA: Beacon Press, pp 3–26

Van Parijs, Philippe and Yannick Vanderborght (2017) *Basic Income: A radical proposal for a free society and a sane economy*, Cambridge, MA: Harvard University Press

Van Trier, Walter (1995) *Every one a king*, Leuven: Departement Sociologie, Katholieke Universiteit Leuven

Vince, Philip (1983) *Tax Credit – the Liberal plan for tax and social security*, London: Women's Liberal Federation

Vince, Philip (1986) 'Basic Incomes: Some practical considerations', *BIRG Bulletin*, Spring 1986: 5–8

Vince, Philip (2004) 'Second thoughts on the report *Citizenship and Citizen's Income*', *Citizen's Income Newsletter*, issue 1 for 2004: 2–3

Virjo, Ilkka (2006) 'A piece of the puzzle: A comment on the Basic Income experiment debate', *Basic Income Studies*, 1(2): 1–5

Vollenweider, Camila (2013) 'Domestic service and gender equality: An unavoidable problem for the feminist debate on Basic Income', *Basic Income Studies*, 8(1): 19–41

Wadsworth, Mark (2016) 'Childcare costs', *Citizen's Income Newsletter*, issue 2 for 2016: 4–8

Wagner, Richard E. (2007) *Fiscal sociology and the theory of public finance: An exploratory essay*, Cheltenham: Edward Elgar

Walker, Alan, Adrian Sinfield and Carol Walker (eds) (2011) *Fighting poverty, inequality and injustice: A manifesto inspired by Peter Townsend*, Cambridge: Polity Press

Walker, Carol (2011) 'For universalism and against the means test', in Alan Walker, Adrian Sinfield and Carol Walker (eds) *Fighting poverty, inequality and injustice: A manifesto inspired by Peter Townsend*, Cambridge: Polity Press, pp 133–52

Walker, Robert (2016) *Free money for all: A Basic Income Guarantee solution for the twenty-first century*, New York: Palgrave Macmillan

Walker, Robert et al (2013) 'Poverty in global perspective: Is shame a common denominator?' *Journal of Social Policy*, 42(2): 215–33

Walker, Robert and Elaine Chase (2014) 'Separating the sheep from the goats: Tackling poverty in Britain for over four centuries', in Erika K. Gubrium, Sony Pellissery and Ivar Lødemel (eds) *The shame of it: Global perspectives on anti-poverty policies*, Bristol: Policy Press, pp 133–56

Walley, John (1986) 'Public support for families with children: A study of British politics', *BIRG Bulletin*, no 5, Spring 1986: 8–11

Walsh, Alison and Ruth Lister (1985) *Mother's Life-Line: A survey of how mothers use and value Child Benefit*, London: Child Poverty Action Group

Walter, Tony (1988) 'What are Basic Incomes?' *BIRG Bulletin*, no 8, Autumn 1988: 3–5

Walter, Tony (1989) *Basic Income: Freedom from poverty, freedom to work*, London: Marion Boyars

Welfare Reform Team, Oxford City Council (2016) *Evaluation of European Social Fund Pilot Project 2014–2015*, Oxford: Oxford City Council, www.oxford.gov.uk/downloads/file/2119/welfare_reform_european_social_fund_project_evaluation_report

Werner, Götz W. and Adrienne Goehler (2010) *1.000 Euro für jeden*, Berlin: Econ, Ullstein Buchverlage

West, Anne and Rita Nicolai (2013) 'Welfare regimes and education regimes: Equality of opportunity and expenditure in the EU (and US)', *Journal of Social Policy*, 46(3): 469–93

White, Mark (2014) *The illusion of well-being: Economic policymaking based on respect and responsiveness*, New York: Palgrave Macmillan

White, Stuart (2003) *The Civic Minimum: On the rights and obligations of economic citizenship*, Oxford: Oxford University Press

White, Stuart (2006) 'Reconsidering the exploitation objection to Basic Income', *Basic Income Studies*, 1(2): 1–24

White, Stuart (2007a) 'The Republican case for Basic Income: A plea for difficulty', *Basic Income Studies*, 2(2): 1–7

White, Stuart (2007b) *Equality*, Cambridge: Polity Press

Whiteford, Peter, Michael Mendelson and Jane Millar (2003) *Timing it right? Tax credits and how to respond to income changes*, York: Joseph Rowntree Foundation

Widerquist, Karl (2005) 'A failure to communicate: What (if anything) can we learn from the negative income tax experiments', *The Journal of Socioeconomics*, 34(1): 49–81

Widerquist, Karl (2006) 'The bottom line in a Basic Income experiment', *Basic Income Studies*, 1(2): 1–5

Widerquist, Karl (2010) 'Lessons of the Alaska Dividend', *Citizen's Income Newsletter*, issue 3 for 2010: 13–15

Widerquist, Karl (2013) *Independence, propertylessness, and Basic Income: A theory of freedom as the power to say no*, New York: Palgrave Macmillan

Widerquist, Karl and Michael Howard (2012a) 'Conclusion: Lessons from the Alaska model', in Karl Widerquist and Michael W. Howard (eds) *Alaska's Permanent Fund Dividend*, New York: Palgrave Macmillan, pp 121–7

Widerquist, Karl and Michael W. Howard (eds) (2012b) *Exporting the Alaska model: Adapting the Permanent Fund Dividend for reform around the world*, New York: Palgrave Macmillan

Widerquist, Karl, and Allan Sheahan (2012), 'The United States: The Basic Income Guarantee – Past experience, current proposals', in Matthew C. Murray and Carole Pateman (eds) *Basic Income worldwide: Horizons of Reform*, New York: Palgrave Macmillan, pp 11–32

Widerquist, Karl, Michael Anthony Lewis and Steven Pressman (2005) *The ethics and economics of the Basic Income Guarantee*, Aldershot: Ashgate

Widerquist, Karl, José A. Noguera, Yannick Vanderborght and Jürgen De Wispelaere (eds) (2013) *Basic Income: An anthology of contemporary research*, Chichester: Wiley Blackwell

Wilkinson, Richard and Kate Pickett (2009) *The spirit level: Why more equal societies almost always do better*, London: Allen Lane/Penguin Books. Second edition published in 2010

Wind-Cowie, Max (2013) *Control shift*, London: Demos, www.demos.co.uk/files/Control_Shift.pdf

Wong, Wilson (2012) 'The new deal for Britain?' in Andrew Adonis (ed.) *New forms of work*, London: Fabian Society, pp 10–11

Wright, Sharon and Alasdair B.R. Stewart (2016) *First wave findings: Jobseekers*, Welfare Conditionality first wave findings, York: University of York, www.welfareconditionality.ac.uk/wp-content/uploads/2016/05/WelCond-findings-jobseekers-May16.pdf

Yamamori, Toru (2014) 'Feminist way to Unconditional Basic Income: Claimants unions and women's liberation movements in 1970s Britain', *Basic Income Studies*, 9(1/2): 1–24

Young, Iris Marion (1989) 'Polity and group differences: A critique of the ideal of universal citizenship', *Ethics*, 99(2): 251

Zelleke, Almaz (2005) 'Distributive justice and the argument for an Unconditional Basic Income', *The Journal of Socioeconomics*, 34(1): 3–15

Zelleke, Almaz (2008) 'Institutionalizing the universal caretaker through a Basic Income?' *Basic Income Studies*, 3(3): 1–9

Zelleke, Almaz (2011) 'Feminist political theory and the argument for an unconditional basic income', *Policy and Politics*, 39(1): 27–42

Zelleke, Almaz (2012) 'Basic Income and the Alaska model: Limits of the resource dividend model for the implementation of an Unconditional Basic Income', in Karl Widerquist and Michael W. Howard (eds) *Alaska's Permanent Fund Dividend*, New York: Palgrave Macmillan, pp 141–68

Names index

Subject index

L

labour
  civic 147
  returns to 35, 84, 164, 166, *see also*
    capital, returns to
  wage elasticity of 43, 162
  work for 39
labour market
  active labour market policies, *see* active
    labour market policies
  bifurcation of 38, 85
  changing 6, 8, 15, 30, 37–49, 56–7, 69,
    141, 164
  choices/decisions 19, 24, 43, 44, 70, 77,
    85, 157, 158, 167, 207, *see also* choice
  coercion in, *see* coercion
  disincentives xi, 2, 4, 15–17, 22, 42–4,
    47, 55, 60, 63, 74, 86, 95, 114, 115,
    122, 151–8, 169, 184, 198–9, 206, *see
    also* labour market – incentives
  diversity of 15, 38, 41
  efficiency of viii, xx, xxi, 16, 19, 24, 36,
    46–7, 153, 156–7, 164, 172, 190–1
  flexibility of xxi, 36, 38–9, 40–41, 54,
    62, 72, 121, 122, 133, 153
  free or classical 152–3, 158, 164
  global xix, 39, *see also* economy – global;
    globalisation
  incentives xi, 5, 9–10, 15, 18, 21, 23,
    24, 43, 45–7, 55, 63, 79, 84, 89, 95,
    100, 103, 114, 118, 121, 145, 149,
    151–8, 170, 174, 184, 193, 198,
    206, 209, *see also* labour market –
    disincentives
  security/insecurity, *see* security/
    insecurity
  status, *see* employment – status
  transitions 41, 43, 72
  withdrawal from 155, 184
  women in 38, 57, 153
  see also employment; job
Labour Party 18, 22, 28, 29, 103, 189
Land Value Tax 22, 128, 162, 165, 171
Latin America 130, 135–6, 141
legal residence, *see* residence requirement
leisure 158
Liberal(ism) 22, 23, 102), *see also*
  Neoliberal(ism)
liberty 87, 88, 122, *see also* freedom
London School of Economics (LSE) xv,
  xxii, 16, 29, 65, 192
lone parent 54, 56, *see also* trap – lone
  parent
losses, *see* gains and losses

M

marginal deduction rate xi–xii, xix, 4,
  44, 74, 79, 82, 86, 89, 100, 123, 146,
  153, 161, 169, 198, *see also* Citizen's
  Basic Income – effect on marginal
  deduction rate
Marginal Effective Tax rate, *see* marginal
  deduction rate
marriage 54, 55–7, 62, 96–8, 183
  financial dependence within 55–7
means test x, xix, 2, 10, 13–15, 20, 22–3,
  25, 59–60, 95, 97, 105, 129, 130, 218
means-tested benefits xi, xiii, 1, 6, 9–10,
  17–20, 24–6, 36, 40, 55–7, 59–64, 81,
  83–6, 88, 90, 94–5, 97–8, 100, 113–
  19, 121–2, 145–6, 148–54, 156–8,
  166–70, 174–5, 185, 188–90, 193
  administrative burden/costs of 5, 41–2,
    70–75, 78–9
  definition of xii, 10
  escape from 1, 29, 42, 44, 60, 90, 94,
    100, 121, 169, 207, 218
  history of 13–16, 21
  retained alongside Citizen's Basic
    Income 5, 9, 27, 29, 42–4, 70, 100,
    114–18, 139–40, 160–61, 174,
    197–203, 209, 211, 214
  see also Education and Support
    Allowance; employment disincentives;
    Family Credit; Family Income
    Supplement; Guarantee Credit,
    Income Support; Jobseeker's
    Allowance; National Assistance;
    Pension Credit; relationships; stigma;
    'Tax Credits'; 'Universal Credit'
Megabyte Tax, *see* tax, Megabyte
migrants 145, 148–51
Minimum Income Guarantee x
Minimum Income Standards 160
money creation 164–5
motivation, *see* employment – motivation/
  demotivation

N

Namibia 127, 130–33, 135, 137–41, 159,
  184
National Assistance 14, 17, 22, 25
National Audit Office 72, 73, 76
National Health Service (NHS) 2, 27–8,
  33, 37, 40, 51, 82, 84, 127, 139
National Insurance Act 23
National Insurance Benefits 14, 15, 22,
  25, 33, 69, 124, 139, 189–90, 200, *see
  also* contributory benefits